Elementary School Guidance

ELEMENTARY SCHOOL GUIDANCE

**James C. Hansen and
Richard R. Stevic**

State University of New York at Buffalo

THE MACMILLAN COMPANY

COLLIER-MACMILLAN LIMITED
London

The Macmillan Company
Collier-Macmillan Canada, Ltd., Toronto, Ontario

Printed in the United States of America

To Carolyn and Pauline

Preface

Guidance has long been an informal and incidental role of the elementary school teacher. Formal guidance services are replacing these random activities in the elementary school. Trained personnel are now providing guidance services to pupils, teachers, and parents at this level. The guidance specialist is an integral part of the pupil personnel service team, bringing special competencies in counseling, consulting, curriculum involvement, testing and measurement, and child development to provide meaningful services for the pupil.

This book is designed for use in an introductory course of elementary guidance. It provides an introduction to the concept of elementary school guidance, the function of various pupil personnel specialists, and the services provided within a guidance program. The primary purpose is to stimulate teachers to examine the area of elementary guidance and perhaps choose to become counselors. Persons desiring to become counselors will explore each of the areas more thoroughly through formalized educational activities. A further purpose is to help the elementary school staff to provide more effective educational experiences for elementary children. Teachers and principals may better understand the general guidance process so all services can be strategically integrated.

The basic approach to guidance in this book is the application of social learning or behavioral theory. It seems appropriate for persons working in a school setting to believe in and practice the principles of learning theory in changing behavior. The guidance specialists and all school personnel are interested in the pupil's behaviors. Further, they are interested in those processes and procedures which bring about behavioral patterns or change necessary for the pupil to move in meaningful directions. In the guidance process the child learns about his environment, himself, and those behaviors which help him meet school, social, and personal tasks. The book includes the theoretical and practical aspects of guiding elementary school youth. At times the reader will find suggestions concerning various tasks or roles of the counselor. These suggestions flow from basic theoretical positions appearing to be most valuable for work with the elementary pupil.

We would like to express appreciation to George Appleton, Thomas Niland, and Gary Margolis for assistance in preparing the manuscript, to Thomas Caulfield and Edward Panther for editorial assistance, and to Mrs. Ruth Bryant and Mrs. Barbara Kauffman for secretarial assistance. A special acknowledgment should be given to Mrs. Gloria Dotterbock for her dedication and commitment in preparation of the final manuscript. We are grateful to Stanley Cramer for the preparation of sociogram materials.

J. C. H.
R. R. S.

Contents

1 CONCEPT OF ELEMENTARY SCHOOL GUIDANCE   **1**

Aims of Education / Foundations of Elementary Guidance / Goals of Elementary Guidance / Approaches to Guidance in the Elementary School / The Teacher and Guidance / Differences Between Secondary and Elementary School Guidance / A Frame of Reference for Elementary Guidance

2 ORGANIZING A GUIDANCE PROGRAM   **25**

Principles of Organization / Planning the Guidance Program / Determining the Guidance Function / Staffing the Guidance Program / Organizing the Guidance Program / Summary

3 DEFINITIONS OF ROLES AND FUNCTIONS 45

Pupil Services / The Administrator's Role in Elementary Guidance / Guidance Role of Elementary Teachers / Summary

4 INDIVIDUAL COUNSELING WITH CHILDREN 73

Learning and Behavior / Learning and Counseling / Behavior Modification / Techniques of Counseling / Summary

5 THE COUNSELOR AS A CONSULTANT 101

Consulting with Parents / Guidelines for Parent Consultation / Methods of Consultation with Parents / Conferences / Other Methods of Communication / Consultation with Teachers / Consulting Services / Methods of Consultation / Summary

6 GUIDANCE AND THE CURRICULUM 129

Concept of Curriculum / Factors Affecting the Curriculum / The Emerging Grouping Plans / The Counselor's Role in Implementing the Curriculum Goals / Summary

7 GROUP PROCESS IN ELEMENTARY GUIDANCE 153

Purposes of Group Guidance / Principles of Group Guidance / Initiating and Continuing Groups / Role of the Counselor / Teacher Involvement / What Outcomes Might Be Reasonably Expected / Summary

8 VOCATIONAL DEVELOPMENT IN THE ELEMENTARY SCHOOL **175**

Vocational Development Theories / Relevant Research Findings / Vocational Information / Counselor Competencies in Vocational Guidance / Summary

9 GUIDANCE INSTRUMENTS AND TECHNIQUES **207**

Purposes of Testing / Some Statistical Concepts / Measures of Comparison / Guidance Instruments / Standardized Tests / Organization of the Testing Program / Summary

10 APPRAISAL IN GUIDANCE **235**

Principles of Appraisal / Rationale for Appraisal / Types of Appraisal / Interpretation of Data / Idiographic Vs. Nomothetic Assessment / Summary

11 EVALUATION IN THE ELEMENTARY SCHOOL GUIDANCE PROGRAM **255**

The Importance of Evaluation / Purposes of Evaluation / Limitations in Evaluation / Approaches to Evaluation / Objectives in Evaluation / Steps in Conducting an Evaluation Study / Summary

INDEX **285**

CONCEPT
OF ELEMENTARY SCHOOL
GUIDANCE

Guidance activities have always been an important part of the efforts of school staffs. Whenever a teacher shows an interest in and concern for full development of the pupil's potential, guidance is given expression. In the elementary school, this expression has been the province of the teacher who contacted the same pupils over an extended period of time. Such arrangements as self-contained classroom or core curricular programs emphasize the relationship of the teacher to the guidance and counseling needs of pupils. Assistance offered the elementary teacher is outside the classroom guidance philosophy and is directed toward special needs or specific problems. Social workers, reading specialists, and school psychologists are common staff adjuncts in the elementary school. Under this arrangement guidance is afforded a secondary position in the school. The teachers emphasize academic achievement; pupil psychological needs are assigned lesser priority.

Guidance activities are incidental, varying widely from school to school and classroom to classroom. Some children receive considerable guidance assistance, whereas others receive little or none. The luxury of this type of guidance in the elementary school can no longer be afforded. The needs of the pupils and the demands of an increasingly complex society are met most adequately in schools having guidance and pupil personnel specialists integrated with the instructional team; the pupil personnel team complements and supplements the instructional program.

Aims of Education

The elementary school is the child's first major exposure to society. At a time when the child is establishing his own personality, he is expected to integrate certain cultural and social learnings into a behavioral pattern. Changes in statements of general, school aims occur as a result of the attempt to enhance this integration. For example, the Commission on the Reorganization of Secondary Education suggested in the early part of the present century that the youth's education is concerned with health, fundamental processes, worthy home membership, vocation, citizenship, worthy use of leisure time and ethical character.[1] During the 1930s, this was restated and amplified by the Educational Policies Commission to reflect the problems of the

---

[1] Commission on the Reorganization of Secondary Education, "Cardinal Principles of Secondary Education," U.S. Office of Education Bulletin 1918 No. 35 (Washington, D.C.: Government Printing Office, 1918).

depression, including self-realization, human relationship, economic efficiency, and civic responsibility.[2] Redirecting the focus of the educational process toward enabling the individual and society to move out of depression conditions to a more normal pattern of life was necessary. In 1961, the Commission suggested that the central purpose of education was to develop critical thinking abilities.[3] Though not negating the other needs, this statement defined more adequately and completely, the needs of contemporary society.

Other agencies have been involved in the development of aims for the schools. The most potent of these is the Federal government, which, through legislation and guidelines, have given increased support and direction to the nation's schools. The White House Conference of 1955 published a list of aims which the members felt should be part of the school's objectives. These were:

1. The fundamental skills of communication—reading, writing, and spelling, as well as other elements of effective oral and written expression; the arithmetical and mathematical skills, including problem solving. Although schools are doing the best job in their history in teaching these skills, continuous improvement is desirable and necessary.
2. Appreciation for our democratic heritage.
3. Civil rights and responsible knowledge of American institutions.
4. Respect and appreciation for human values and for the beliefs of others.
5. Ability to think and evaluate constructively and creatively.
6. Effective work habits and self-discipline.

[2] Educational Policies Commission, "The Purposes of Education in American Democracy" (Washington, D.C.: National Education Association, 1938).
[3] Educational Policies Commission, *The Central Purpose of American Education* (Washington, D.C.: National Education Association, 1961), p. 12.

7. Social competency as a contributing member of his family and community.
8. Ethical behavior based on a sense of moral and spiritual values.
9. Intellectual curiosity and eagerness for life-long learning.
10. Aesthetic appreciation and self-expression in the arts.
11. Physical and mental health.
12. Wise use of time, including constructive leisure pursuits.
13. Understanding of the physical world and man's relation to it as represented through basic knowledge of the sciences.
14. An awareness of relationship with the world community.[4]

In 1960 another Conference convened to examine important problems of youth. As part of the preparatory materials, Tyler identified five primary purposes for education. For each person, education is to provide the opportunity to realize his potential and to become a constructive and happy person in the station of life which he would occupy because of his birth and ability; secondly, for the nation, the education of each child was essential to provide a literate citizenry. Three more aims have been added. These are social mobility, preparation of young people for the world of work, and developing in students understanding and appreciation of the wide range of experiences, services, and goals which can contribute much to their health and satisfaction.[5]

The final report of the Conference included a number of specific recommendations. Closely following the passage of the National Defense Education Act of 1958, these recommendations added increased strength to the need for school guidance services. In several cases the recommendations pointed out the need to

[4] *The Reports of the White House Conference on Education* (Washington, D.C.: U.S. Government Printing Office, 1955), pp. 1, 2.
[5] Ralph W. Tyler, "Educational Objectives of American Democracy," in Eli Ginzberg, *The Nation's Children*, Vol. 2, *Development and Education*, White House Conference on Children and Youth (New York: Columbia University Press, 1960), p. 70.

include elementary schools in the guidance effort. The following list is abstracted from these recommendations and specifically relates to the elementary school.

1. Guidance and counseling programs should be strengthened, expanded, and coordinated at all levels.
2. Guidance and counseling should begin in the elementary school with educational and vocational planning based upon early, continuous, and expanded testing and diagnostic appraisal of each child.
3. The ratio of students to elementary counselor should be 600 to 1.
4. The training of guidance and counseling personnel should be intensified and improved to meet the demands of the schools and students within the school.[6]

Each elementary school reflects an unique interpretation of these aims. In the development of programs and policy these aims are included to a greater or lesser extent depending upon the population being served, the support of the school by the public, and the quality of leadership and teaching associated with the school. The aims of education are important in meaningful guidance programs. Without an understanding of where the school is going, it is difficult to promote meaningful educational or service programs.

Foundation of Elementary Guidance

Several social and educational developments have fostered increased guidance involvement at the elementary level. These

[6] *Ibid.*

developments are a solid foundation upon which to build guidance efforts.

The passage of various Federal education acts have had great impact upon the total guidance movement. Although the National Defense Education Act of 1958 was directed toward improving and increasing secondary programs of guidance, the impetus stimulated attention to other educational levels. The success of NDEA prompted the passage of new and amended laws, supporting special services for the elementary school. The two acts considerably important to the elementary school are the amendment of National Defense Education Act of 1958, which included the training of elementary counselors in guidance institutes and the passage of the Elementary and Secondary Education Act, which supplies monies for many new services, including guidance at the elementary level.

Implications arising from developmental psychology suggest that any process involving humans is a slow, developmental act; if attention is given over a period of time, the pupil has a better chance for achieving his potential, of making reasonably adequate choices, or of fulfilling the prerequisites of various educational and vocational positions. An excellent example of this developmental aspect is in the area of reading. Without an adequate foundation and reasonable achievement throughout the first few years of school, the pupil begins to experience extreme difficulty at the junior and senior high school levels. The difficulty does not only affect his reading or his academic efforts, but it becomes a causal agent of personal problems.

Forerunners of the drop-out problem, juvenile delinquency, and other social problems occur in the elementary school.[7,8] If the school offers the most meaningful preparation program for its

[7] Sheldon Glueck and Eleanor Glueck, *Predicting Delinquency and Crime* (Cambridge: Harvard University Press, 1959).

[8] Seymour L. Wolfbein, "The Transition from School to Work," *The Personnel and Guidance Journal 38*, October, 1959.

pupils, it should also assist the pupil in these areas. The elementary school is charged with providing an adequate academic, psychological, and personal foundation for each pupil. This means that planned involvement of various personnel in the lives of all pupils is essential.

The teacher is faced with an increasingly complex body of knowledge. She no longer satisfies all pupil psychological or academic needs. Once labeled "progressive education," it is now highly accepted that the education of the whole child is necessary. The classroom in the elementary school, once a haven for a self sufficient teacher, is giving way to a new concept; the most competent teacher has available to her special personnel, consulting and giving individual assistance, helping the teacher meet the needs of individual pupils, and creating new learning experiences for all children.

Education is a community project. Although never having been allowed to be isolated from the community, cooperation is becoming more important. The community supports the school. Integration, bussing, new methods of teaching, and the technical revolution all create a need to communicate more effectively with the community. Parents are better educated and have fairly definite ideas about their children's education. The successful school involves the public and the counselor provides specialized assistance in establishing a cooperative relationship.

The foundational developments listed above preclude the possibility of leaving complete responsibility in the hands of one classroom teacher. She simply cannot give all the assistance necessary. A growing body of information suggests that there are specific skills required for guidance and counseling activities. The elementary teacher is prepared to perform classroom activities of a wide variety, however, there are unique skills for the guidance and counseling relationship. The specifics of these skills are discussed throughout the remainder of this book. Guidance and counseling competence is gained in exactly the same way that any set of skills are obtained, namely, through exposure to and assimilation of a body of knowledge and through study, research, practice, and supervision in the understanding and application of these skills.

Goals of Elementary Guidance

It is difficult to specify an inclusive set of goals or objectives applicable to the myriad of situations within the elementary school. Each program fits the needs of the school. However, certain general objectives point to goals for school guidance.

Mathewson lists the following key practices generally applied to guidance programs:

1. Pupil-parent involvement in self-situational appraisals in the key areas of academic progress, personal-social relations, and educational vocational orientation.
2. Orientation of pupils and parents as to expectations of the school regarding pupil progress and attainments in the three key areas.
3. Self-integrative movement of the individual pupil in maturational and developmental progress in the three areas.
4. Teacher participation in the growth of the pupils in self-situational awareness, adjustment, orientation, and development.
5. Information supplied to pupils at common points of group need, and on special occasions of individual need, as these arise.
6. Interpretation and evaluation of self-situational patterns for individual pupils and their parents by counselors at critical problem- and decision-points.
7. Evaluation of pupil progress in self-situational development

and maturation at key check-points by teachers and counselors.

8. Consultative assistance to administration on pupil classifications and individual evaluations used for group, placement, and recommendation.[9]

The unique elementary school level demands statements of objectives relative to young individuals. The following list contains some guidance objectives evolving from the examination of the elementary school and the personnel and pupils at that level.

1. The guidance program, through the professional personnel, enhances and makes more functional the staff's understanding of children and themselves.
2. The guidance program, in connection with the school program, provides opportunities for children to develop socially.
3. The guidance program helps pupils with their goal-seeking, choice making, and life planning activities.
4. The guidance program provides specialized assistance to staff and pupils in understanding the societal, psychological, and environmental forces which act upon them.

Peters, Shertzer, and Van Hoose illustrate guidance objectives by suggesting nine tasks for guidance personnel:

1. The early identification of each pupil's learning capacities.
2. The design of each pupil's achievement pattern in terms of learning capacities.
3. The analysis of the child's responses to others.
4. The assembly of data on the child's concept of himself.
5. A portrait of the child's habits of study and living in school.
6. Interpretation of the child in his home and cultural setting.

[9] Robert Hendry Mathewson, *Guidance Policy and Practice*, 3rd Ed. (New York: Harper and Row, Publishers, 1962).

7. Interpretation of the child in his developmental progress against child development norms.
8. Follow-up of pupils in later school years—the junior and senior high schools.
9. The use of guidance functions in the other phases of the school program.[10]

Program objectives are established prior to the beginning of the program. The philosophical foundation upon which the program rests is established when the objectives are delineated. In many cases the elementary counselor is called upon to organize the guidance program. This is an unique opportunity for the counselor to establish relevant objectives for the program and to institute those activities which enhance the possibility of attaining the objectives. Unless these preliminary efforts are completed, the program grows without meaningful direction and falls far short of elementary guidance's potential.

Approaches to Guidance in the Elementary School

Although elementary guidance is traced back as far as secondary guidance, it has gained impetus during the latter part of the 1960s. There are many programs operating, some of which are in the initial stage. The focus of these programs is quite diverse and represents a search for directions best meeting the needs of elementary school pupils. The types of programs most often distinguished are:

THE SECONDARY APPROACH. Elementary guidance is a downward extension of services provided at the secondary level. The counselor performs the traditional activities of gather-

---

[10] Herman J. Peters, Bruce Shertzer, and William Van Hoose, *Guidance in Elementary Schools* (Chicago: Rand McNally, 1965), p. 231.

ing information on individuals, providing information to individuals, giving educational and vocational assistance, researching the effectiveness of various programs, and counseling individuals.

THE EFFECTIVE TEACHING EQUALS GUIDANCE APPROACH. This concept purports that the effective teacher in his classroom activities provides all the guidance necessary for the pupil in terms of academic, social, and personal growth. If effective teaching is occurring, there is no need for specialized guidance personnel or activities.

THE MENTAL HEALTH APPROACH. The teacher develops a healthy school climate in which the pupil is assisted toward maturity. The guidance worker, as a specialized staff member, contributes to the climate by identifying pupil-oriented or school-oriented concerns detracting from the climate. Pupil to pupil and pupil to teacher interpersonal relationships are considerably important.

THE SPECIALIST APPROACH. The guidance worker is concerned with problems with which he is specifically trained to deal. The worker can be a psychologist, a social worker, or a medical technician. The counselor becomes a specialist in the area of adjusting learning difficulties. He is concerned with child learning problems. In cooperation with the teacher, appraisals are made to determine why the pupil is not learning efficiently. Alternatives are developed which the classroom or special teacher implement. The counselor can become a curriculum specialist, studying children's needs and preparing a curriculum most beneficial to each individual. He is as much concerned with the curriculum as with the pupil's existential life.

THE CHILD STUDY APPROACH. The counselor consults with the teaching staff in developing their competencies to observe and understand children. By studying and working with one pupil intensively over a long period of time, the necessary skills for understanding other children are enhanced. The teacher generalizes this technique and assists other children.

THE COORDINATED APPROACH. Aspects are combined from several approaches into a complete guidance program. The counselor counsels, creates a climate, consults and coordinates. Within each school the counselor fills various, distinct roles; between schools more variation is noted.

Although these are the most widely published approaches, there are other possibilities. For example, the counselor can become a child development specialist emphasizing understanding developmental patterns and completing developmental tasks. Regardless of the approach or approaches which the counselor adopts, he establishes the goals and type of program from the beginning. Hopefully, the specialist devises a role compatible with his training and the pupil's needs. He avoids some of the pitfalls troubling the secondary counselor, including clerical and administrative duties which can overshadow guidance and counseling activities.

The Teacher and Guidance

Elementary school guidance is concerned with the teacher's role in its program. The elementary teacher is in a most advantageous position to guide pupils. This is continually true in the elementary school, regardless of the inclusion of new staff members. The sensitive teacher is intensely concerned with the individual pupil. However, the teacher is also aware that she has other obligations having greater priority than guidance activities at certain times. The transmission of knowledge, though often maligned, is still important and the *raison d'être* for teachers. The teacher is obliged to teach pupils; in general this deals more with academic subject matter than the subject matter of guidance, e.g., self-understanding and decision making ability.

The following limitations seem pertinent to the inclusion of guidance specialists to assist teachers: First, the teacher is probably not prepared to work in the one-to-one counseling relationship which is a vital part of the specialist's role. To assume that the opportunity and desire to provide guidance are sufficient prerequisites indicates a lack of knowledge concerning the goals and activities of guidance. There is a body of knowledge, a set of skills, and a professional attitude necessary for becoming a guidance worker, and these are gained through study, research, practice, and supervisory activities prior to intensive involvement in guidance by any school staff member.

Second, the roles of a teacher and a guidance specialist are considerably different, and the pupil may not be able to sort out teacher activities from guidance activities. The teacher evaluates the pupil and makes judgments concerning the skill of the pupil in learning the materials and completing the tasks of a particular developmental unit. The guidance specialist assists the pupil in examining himself and in promoting the pupil's ability to make relevant judgments and movement toward a more realistic appraisal of himself, whether this fits into the value system of the specialist or not. Although the specialist does not permit self-destructive activities on the part of the pupil, he encourages those activities which are of value to the pupil, regardless of how they relate to others in the class or to a predetermined standard of action or behavior. Thus, whereas the teacher is concerned with the progress of the pupil toward mastery of subject matter or skill areas, the guidance specialist is concerned with the progress of the pupil toward understanding himself, regardless of how fast or slow this occurs.

Third, although the teacher recognizes certain needs within a classroom there is often a question as to whether there is time to fulfill all the roles she is called upon to fill as a teacher. The teacher establishes priorities and decides how much time and effort can be diverted from the teaching role and devoted to other roles. The teacher often cannot include guidance and counseling activities, in addition to all the other tasks she handles. Specialists support the program in specific areas, e.g., reading. The needs of the elementary pupil are sufficiently important that a guidance specialist provides valuable assistance to the teacher. The dignity, worth, and integrity of each person is basic to our society. Fostering these ideals is essential, so that the pupil reaches his fullest potential and contributes meaningfully to society.

Differences Between Secondary and Elementary School Guidance

The development of guidance often follows a pattern of imposing a currently designed program upon a new situation. An approach listed earlier implies that this is the case with some elementary programs. Although some elements of guidance at the secondary level are relevant, it is important to delineate the unique needs of the elementary school. The foundation for the introduction of specific preparation, the accumulation of a body of research and knowledge relative to the elementary school, and the development of a guidance program falls into two categories, i.e., differences in population and specialist activity.

Differences in Population

The elementary pupil depends more upon his parents. Parents know more about their children during the first years of life. They are interested in the child's school activity; their attendance at various school functions is predominant. The physical limitations of elementary age children are greater. They are usually not allowed to cover a large geographical area, and, until they are in junior high school, they are given little personal responsibility. Parents take them places and pick them up. Parents decide when piano lessons, bowling, or dancing are necessary. The child in the elementary school has a life which is closely tied to the life style of the parents. Any change is affected by this dependency relationship.

Differences in psychological development are noted between pupils at various school levels. For example, in Erikson's stages, the elementary pupil cuts across three stages crucial to his total development and forms the foundation for later stages. First, the pupil moves out of the imitative stage in which he has learned methods of undertaking, planning, and attacking new tasks, and during which he has made his first acts of defiance. He moves through the industry stage, becoming a member of a productive situation or society. He learns to apply himself to tasks and to follow these through to some product conclusion. Finally, he enters the identity stage, finding out who he really is. This stage is filled with many problem-creating times for the pupil as he attempts to work out a role for himself in society and to insure that he retains his individuality. The world becomes difficult, because he needs to be similar to his peers but still retain his uniqueness. Many times this manifests itself in the fads of youth, seemingly diametrically opposed to the adult society but really designed to promote individual identity.[11] The various tasks and behaviors flowing from the place of the individual within each level suggests that pupils need different types of assistance. There are obviously other systems describing psychological development. The point made here is that the elementary child has unique needs as a result of his physical and psychological development which are the major foci of the guidance specialist's work at the elementary level.

Another difference is in the area of communication. The elementary child has had less opportunity to learn methods of

[11] Erik H. Erikson, *Childhood and Society,* 2nd Ed. (New York: Norton Press, 1963) p. 273.

communicating his ideas, concerns, and feelings to others. He has many methods at his command, and he uses these, at times, to his advantage. For example, it is not unusual for a child to learn that crying or creating a disturbance in the school or class-room helps him escape from something for which he does not care. This type of behavior can get the child into further diffi-culty. The pupil may be unaware of the reasons for his behavior, but he does communicate in his way. He is not able to communi-cate what he does know about himself. The specialist at the elementary level is skilled in and able to promote communication in order to assist pupils in meeting the appropriate tasks.

An important difference existing between elementary pupils and others is in the child's concept of time. The elementary pupil finds it difficult to conceive of the time factor, either past or future, and tends to view himself in the present. Undesirable be-havior may not need change from the pupil's point of view, and, although the child's developmental nature is still important, the pupil does not always see the relevance of this concept. The counselor deals in different ways with the pupil at the elementary level.

Slavson describes the different nature of the elementary pupil as opposed to his junior and senior high contemporaries.

> The most outstanding characteristics of a child are his comparatively weak ego organization and his limited ability to deal with inner impulses and external de-mands. The second difference, which is a direct out-growth of the first, is the basically narcissistic quality of the child's libido organization, his lack of ego control, hence impulsiveness, his still narcissistic character, hence self-indulgence and feelings of omnipotence. The third distinction is the surface nature of his unconscious. One is impressed with the readiness and almost com-plete unself-consciousness with which young children

act out and speak about matters that are embarrassing to an older person. This can be attributed to the incomplete superego development, the lack of repressive forces (ego), and undeveloped sublimation channels. Finally, the child's identifications are in a fluid state.[12]

Differential Activities

The second area of differentiation lies in the activities of the guidance counselor. At the elementary level his involvement provides supplemental and complementary assistance to teachers. Although he is still expected to provide many traditional activities, such as individual assistance to pupils in a counseling relationship, he is required to provide greater input in such activities as curriculum development and consultation with teachers and parents than his counterparts in junior and senior high.

The particular concept or pattern under which the school's curriculum develops determines the type and amount of guidance specialist involvement in curriculum. He supplies information concerning the psychological factors of the child and their relation to acceleration, grouping, and modified classes. He provides input for teachers and curriculum specialists in altering present curricular offerings. He uses the information gained through interviews, observation and interpretation of data to assist in the individualization of the school's effort in providing meaningful experiences for the elementary pupil.

The elementary counselor has greater involvement as a consultant to others in assisting this interaction with children. The teacher's role as a central figure in education cannot be abrogated. She continues to be a major functionary in guidance activities. However, the guidance specialist assists the teacher in understanding certain pupils and in determining strategies for

[12] S. R. Slavson, *Child Psychotherapy* (New York: Columbia University Press, 1952).

working effectively with the individual. The counselor gives information and assistance to parents by interpreting the psychological and evaluational data to them. The parent seeks assistance to better promote the development of the child, and the counselor serves as a liaison between the school and parent.

A Frame of Reference for Elementary Guidance

Several strategies are identified for guidance programs and practices. Three described by Stewart and Warnath[13] are the remedial, the preventive, and the promotional. Each is based upon a concept of what types of pupil concerns are most relevant. In the remedial strategy the concerns are current with the pupil and need immediate adjustment. In the preventive strategy the assistance is provided to the pupil to ward off certain difficulties related to his developmental progress. The promotional approach stresses those attitudes and habits leading to the best possible pupil behavior. There are parts of each in most guidance programs, but the major direction of any program is determined by the primary strategy espoused by the school and guidance staff. Although the counselor is concerned with changing existing problem behaviors, the guidance program emphasizes the promotion of pupil behavior and a school environment conducive to the attainment of guidance goals.

This book proposes a behavioral approach to guidance as having the greatest value for the elementary guidance program. The concern of the guidance specialist is learned behaviors. The counselor assists the child in learning about his environment, about himself, and behaviors to meet school and social tasks.

---

[13] Lawrence H. Stewart and Charles F. Warnath, *The Counselor and Society: A Cultural Approach* (Boston: Houghton Mifflin Company, 1965), pp. 35–43.

Implicit in this definition is the aim that guidance and counseling assist all pupils in their normal, social, and educational development. Although counseling is not always problem- or crisis-oriented, the counselor works with pupils who have difficulties. If a child has not learned behaviors to meet certain developmental tasks or has learned inappropriate behaviors, the counselor assists him in changing. Through the process of individual counseling or group guidance, pupils express difficulties and find assistance in solving them. Success in these types of problems leads to solution of larger present and future problems.

The counselor is an active participant in the counseling process with elementary pupils. He identifies the present problem behaviors of the individual. He assists the pupil in determining his goals, objectives, and concerns. The counselor then assists the pupil toward learning the necessary behaviors to accomplish the desired change. In short, the counselor's strategy is one of assisting the pupil to identify goals, objectives, undesirable behaviors and desirable behaviors. He creates an environment in which the pupil learns behavioral patterns appropriate to the attainment of goals.

The child's environment is recognized as a significant factor in how the child behaves and what he learns. Modifying his environment, then, helps him change behaviors. Parents and teachers are particularly influential by changing the way they behave with the child. The counselor consults with parents and teachers and helps them understand the child, by working out techniques to help him.

It is important for the counselor to be able to consult with parents and secure their cooperation. The counselor helps parents have more meaningful relationships with the pupil. As his experience with parents increases, the counselor's insights become keener and his efforts more effective with the pupil.

The counselor assists the teacher by gathering, organizing, synthesizing, and interpreting information about pupils, so that solutions can be found. He communicates with teachers, providing information about his efforts with pupils referred from the classroom. The counselor provides in-service assistance to teachers in such areas as learning, child development, and the guidance program. He helps the teacher offer more appropriate guidance in the classroom.

The counselor aids the school staff in gathering and using various kinds of data through techniques of assessment and appraisal. For example, data from cumulative records, psychological information about pupils, and standardized test scores are utilized by the counselor for interpretative work with pupils and teachers. This aids the teacher in providing greater individualized assistance to pupils. The pupil gains information about himself which can be used in a meaningful fashion in the decision-making process or change of behavior.

The counselor assists staff and pupils in the educational-vocational area. Elementary school youths are interested in vocational exploration. Opportunities for the teacher and counselor in the area of education-vocational information vary from grade level to grade level and even within grades, but this does not lessen its value in the elementary school. The goals include developing positive attitudes toward work, increasing the pupil's awareness of the rapidly changing characteristics of work, and indicating the need to be better prepared for future employment opportunities. These and other possibilities exist within the elementary school, and the guidance worker enhances and expands the child's exposure to the world of work.

The counselor provides specialized assistance in the area of curriculum development. He has data concerning the pupils, community expectations for the pupils, and continuing educational and vocational opportunities. If the pupil is to move toward optimum functioning, it is necessary to adjust the curriculum to more individual and meaningful levels. The teacher, the administrator, and curriculum specialists, as well as the counselor, are deeply involved in this activity. The specific involvement of the counselor is determined, in part, by the situation in the school and the available facilities. The elementary counselor needs to explore curriculum development, formally and experientially, as part of his preparation program.

The counselor understands and works with those pupils who need assistance beyond that which the school can offer. He knows the various community agencies and the services they provide. The counselor is not the only person involved in referral. However, his unique position in the school implies that he is able to effectively identify, refer, and follow-up pupils. The counselor interprets the exceptional pupil to school personnel. Information gained from interaction with other pupil personnel specialists is beneficial to the teacher as he works with the exceptional child, regardless of the type of pupil identified under this rubric.

Evaluation of guidance services determines if the goals of guidance are being attained. The counselor evaluates his guidance practices through casual observation; however, he establishes a more formal program of evaluation. Through such a program the counselor learns how effectively various aspects of the guidance process are meeting the pupil's needs.

The counselor has a multifaceted role; generalized subroles overlap. This book supports the point of view that the counselor is a specialist in assisting the child to better understand himself and his environment. The primary responsibility of the school is instructional, so the counselor is concerned with those aspects of physical development, peer relations, self-understanding, and parental relationships which affect the person's ability to learn. He works with teachers, parents, groups of pupils, and individual pupils in consulting and counseling relationships. A social learning or behavioral approach to counselor tasks is most meaningful and productive. The elementary counselor needs competency in a wide variety of areas, including counseling, consulting, administration, testing, measurement, and curriculum.

This book is intended for the beginning course in the sequence of elementary guidance preparation. The potential elementary counselor is expected to continue the total preparation sequence and to obtain further in-depth understanding of the areas. However, as the reader is involved at an initial level, there is an opportunity to begin the process of establishing a role. Commitment must be toward meaningful involvement in the lives of elementary pupils. When it is necessary, parents, teachers, other specialists, and administrators are also involved. The beginner clearly delineates the tasks of the guidance worker. In this way the entire spectrum of necessary activities are established.

There is much to learn from counselors at other levels. There is a need to understand the role most beneficial to the school and articulate a role from the beginning of one's involvement. Too many secondary people are not able to commit themselves to meaningful guidance activities because inaccurate roles were established, and they are difficult, if not impossible, to change. The guidance specialist has the opportunity to avoid these problems at the elementary level.

Summary

Guidance services have been part of the elementary school for many years. The current trend is away from providing incidental services and toward establishing formal guidance programs. The involvement of a wide variety of specialists is designed to help the teacher provide more meaningful assistance to pupils. An elementary counselor adds new dimensions to the administrative and instructional aspects of the elementary school program. The approach in this book illustrates the need for an elementary guidance specialist to apply social learning principles in assisting and meeting the needs of pupils, as well as parents, teachers, and other personnel charged with providing learning and developmental experiences for all pupils.

SELECTED REFERENCES

Robert Hendry Mathewson, *Guidance Policy and Practice,* 3rd Ed. (New York: Harper & Row, Publishers, 1962).

Leslie E. Moser & Ruth Small Moser, *Counseling and Guidance: An Exploration* (Englewood Cliffs, N.J.: Prentice-Hall, Inc., 1963).

Herman J. Peters, Bruce Shertzer and William Van Hoose, *Guidance in Elementary Schools* (Chicago: Rand McNally & Company, 1965).

ORGANIZING
A GUIDANCE PROGRAM

Elementary schools can provide a number of guidance services without an organized program. However, experts in administration agree that effectiveness increases as a result of coordinated guidance activities. An organized guidance program reduces duplication, thus making it possible to extend services to more children. Also, an organized program makes it possible to anticipate the most critical needs. The organizational pattern which is implemented may be the key to effective guidance.

As each elementary school is unique, it is not realistic to establish a model guidance program with expectations for universal effectiveness. The guidance program should be organized to meet the needs of a particular school and its personnel. The following organizational guidelines are appropriate for development or modification of a program in all schools.

Principles of Organization

Humphreys, Traxler, and North[1] list principles that should be observed in organizing a guidance services program. Each principle is presented as a suggested course of action.

1. Prepare a clear-cut statement of the objectives of the program of guidance services. These objectives should take into account the characteristics and needs of the student body. They should be consistent with the objectives of the educational institution as a whole.
2. Determine precisely the functions of the guidance services program—that is, what the program should do for the students.
3. Assign specific duties to those who are to participate in the program. Allocate tasks to individuals on the basis of their qualifications for the work and give them definite responsibilities for performing these tasks.
4. Give each person assigned to a task in guidance services authority commensurate with his responsibility.
5. Define clearly the working relationships: (a) among those people who are directly responsible for guidance services, and (b) between those members of the guidance staff and other personnel in the school or college who participate in the program of guidance services directly or indirectly. Recognize

[1] Anthony Humphreys, Arthur Traxler, and Robert North, *Guidance Services* (Chicago: Science Research Associates, Inc. 1960), pp. 361, 362.

that some of the personnel of the institution will work directly and full time in the field of guidance services; others will work directly and part-time, and still others will work indirectly and during a small share of their total work time.

6. Set up the form of organization that is best adapted to the institution's purposes, personnel, size, financial resources, and other characteristics.

7. Keep the plan of organization and its operations as simple as possible.

Segmented into four processes, these principles are: planning the guidance program, determining the guidance function, staffing, and organizing the guidance program. Although the process can be segmented for analysis, they are not independent. Each one depends upon the other and is strategically relevant and related to the over-all educational function.

Planning the Guidance Program

The planning process involves the preparation that takes place prior to initiation or revision of the program. Such preparation includes establishing the objectives of the program and determining the procedures to achieve those objectives. Development of objectives and procedures may take the following form: First, there must be cooperative planning. If a readiness for and acceptance of a guidance program are to be anticipated, then all pertinent individuals should participate in the planning, with the counselor outlining the purposes, functions, and responsibilities. It may be advantageous to form a committee composed of administrators, teachers, and staff specialists to participate in the planning.

A second factor necessary for guidance program initiation or expansion is the determination of guidance needs. Plans and action must be based upon known pupil needs and problems. Peters, Shertzer, and Van Hoose[2] state that guidance should be focused on the developmental needs of the pupils. The developmental task concept indicates that maturing pupils face a series of learnings to be mastered. By anticipating the developmental tasks confronting pupils, a more appropriate action program can be planned. Information about personnel resources and areas for improvement also warrant consideration. Identification of these anxiety sources may be obtained through anecdotal records, pupil checklists, sociograms, teacher checklists of pupil problems and needs, and parent-teacher conferences. Similar methods will yield concerns of teachers and parents.

Another step in organizing a guidance program is to appraise the existing guidance services. In each elementary school some guidance services are provided, with or without organization. Even so, they are the foundations for developing a guidance program.

One of the first steps in surveying the present program is to examine what role teachers are playing in guidance. Teachers contribute to the guidance function by individualizing instruction, helping pupils use the decision-making process, providing vocational information, analyzing individual differences, and making contributions to pupil anecdotal records.

The counselor should also review other parts of the program. He can examine the cumulative record system to determine the type of information that is filed. More important, he should investigate how the data are being used by various school personnel. In the same manner, he may examine the testing program to

---

[2] Herman Peters, Bruce Shertzer, and William Van Hoose, *Guidance Services in Elementary Schools* (Chicago: Rand McNally and Company), pp. 10–17.

learn the type of information it yields, uses for the test data, and the actual facilitation of the results by school authorities. Equally important is the appraisal of the educational and vocational information available in the school. This includes appropriate library books, as well as general vocational literature. Additional educational and vocational services can be provided by field trips, e.g., to museums, art galleries, and various industries. Community resources and agencies may be available to the elementary school counselor.

Individual school guidance programs should reflect the wider image of the school system. Although each elementary school may manifest unique aspects, the pupil will enter junior high and senior high schools so that some consistent information may be necessary. Evaluation should include how students are guided in making the transition from home to school and between the elementary and junior high school.

Change in the program can be made at any time. As new information identifies new needs, changes can be made. Change in the guidance program may parallel other school changes.

A new or modified program is best inaugurated in stages, beginning with one specific phase and expanding to include the entire program. Future success of the entire program may depend upon the acceptance of the first phase. Beginning with a phase of the program that is likely to receive a positive response and yield measurable results is important. Such results can be used to evaluate this area and project the next phase of the program.

The establishment of a program is extended over a period of time in which many activities are implemented. Sound program organization depends upon a long range development of guidance services. The initiation or revision of the program will require several steps which probably involves more than one year's work. Pupils, staff, and parents need to understand the long range as well as the immediate goals. They can then see how each phase of the program fits into the over-all program and where they presently are on a model guidance program continuum.

Determining the Guidance Function

After studying existing services and learning the needs of the pupils, the counselor can decide what provisions an organized program should make for the pupils. The inauguration or revision of a program must be developed by the counselor and guidance committee on the basis of clearly defined purposes that are both intra- and inter-school consistent.

The constellation of guidance services is designed to help the school do a better job of meeting individual pupil needs. These services also help the pupil better meet the demands of the school, his peer groups, members of his family, and other adult groups. Hatch and Stefflre[3] suggest two objectives in the selection of titles and scope of the guidance program services. Titles should reflect the specific activities of the service, and the scope should be sufficiently discrete to permit implementation, administration, and evaluation of the service.

Guidance programs concern themselves with three broad functions: providing services for the pupils, providing information to the school, and assisting others in their work with pupils. Specific services of counseling, consultation, testing, appraisal, information, and evaluation contribute to one or more of the broad guidance functions. Each of these services will be discussed in detail later.

---

[3] Raymond Hatch and Buford Stefflre, *Administration of Guidance Services,* 2nd Ed. (Englewood Cliffs, N.J.: Prentice-Hall, Inc., 1965), p. 21.

Staffing the Guidance Program

Functional leadership and staff involvement are imperative for development and improvement of a guidance program. Staffing a school system is a major aspect of school administration. In selecting and assigning a counselor, the administrator seeks an individual who can provide leadership in the guidance area and stimulate staff involvement.

As the elementary school counselor is the primary person in developing the program, he must assume a leadership role. Most school personnel will develop limits of responsibility and play the proper decision-making roles connected with their own duties.

The Counselor as a Person

The success of a counselor is greatly affected by his interpersonal skills and his education. A counselor education program provides him with knowledge of the counselor's role and an opportunity to develop his skills. However, the counselor's personal characteristics determine his behavior.

Standardized personality instruments have been used to identify counselor characteristics. Research studies indicate that counselors have a greater need for intraception, exhibition, and affiliation, whereas school administrators show higher in achievement and aggression needs and need to manipulate others. After reviewing the research in this area, Shertzer and Stone[4] suggest that counselors are understanding, sensitive, friendly; they value others and have a tolerance for ambiguity in interpersonal relationships.

Numerous lists of counselor personality traits have been sug-

[4] Bruce Shertzer and Shelley Stone, *Foundations of Guidance* (Boston: Houghton Mifflin Company, 1966), pp. 102–109.

gested. Such lists usually include friendliness, good sense of humor, stability, openmindedness, objectivity, sincerity, good interpersonal skills, acceptance of others, and self actualizing. It is nearly impossible for any one person to possess all these attributes. Fullmer and Bernard[5] point out that two of the attributes, becoming a self-actualizing person and learning to accept others are particularly important. The process of self-actualization calls for the counselor to be a growing person, to understand himself, to be open to himself and others, and to have confidence in himself rather than depend on authority. In order to accept others, the counselor must overcome his own prejudices. These two aspects of counselor development suggest the counselor may need to seek greater self understanding and possibly change his behavior. Involvement in the process of counselor education helps the counselor achieve these ends.

The Counselor as a Leader

Leadership has been defined as the process of influencing the activities of an organized group in the efforts toward goal setting and goal achievement.[6] This definition of leadership seems appropriate for the role of an elementary school counselor. The counselor is not a leader chosen by the staff members, but is appointed by his superiors. He is then the self-appointed leader of the guidance movement within his school and needs to function as a leader among the other staff members. In order to enlist the assistance of the administration and teachers in developing and managing a guidance program, the counselor must understand the dynamics of a group behavior and the roles and functions of leadership.

Leadership is a role which a person occupies at a given time

[5] Daniel Fullmer and Harold Bernard, *Counseling: Content and Process* (Chicago: Science Research Associates, Inc., 1964), pp. 161–181.
[6] Ralph Stogdill, "Leadership, Membership, and Organization," *Psychological Bulletin,* **47**, 1–14 (1950).

in a group. The principal is the leader of the entire school and furthers the guidance program by supporting and participating with the staff in policy making. The counselor leads in development and management of the guidance program. Each teacher leads in his classroom by teaching and providing many guidance activities.

The leader's ability to influence group members in pursuing certain activities is affected by role boundaries, role repertoire, and role consonance.[7] Role boundary refers to the limit of acts that the members will accept for the counselor. The faculty validates particular acts as appropriate or inappropriate for the counselor. Expectations evolve from their needs, reading, and observation. These may develop into stereotypical assumptions about their role boundaries and those of the counselor. Such boundaries can impose restrictions upon the role of a counselor.

Role repertoire refers to the variety and adequacy of the counselors' behavior. Some may focus on only a few roles, trying to perform them well, rather than widening their range. Others show little consistency in their roles and become influenced more by the situation. Gibb found evidence that role repertoire was a function of three factors: (a) understanding of the situation or environment, (b) the adequacy of hypotheses formulated about the necessary role of a high influence entry into the situation, and (c) the adequacy of role skill. The counselor with the greatest range and general potency of behaviors will tend to show more leadership in a variety of situations.

Role consonance is the harmony of his behavior with the ideas and overall goals of the staff. Role consonance tends to meet three levels of need in a staff: (a) the need to accomplish the task that they agree upon, (b) the need to relate to each other, and (c) the need to satisfy their own personal needs.

---

[7] Jack Gibb, "Defense Level and Influence Potentials in Small Groups," In *Leadership and Interpersonal Behavior,* Luigi Petrullo and Bernard Bass, editors (New York: Holt, Rinehart & Winston, Inc., 1961), pp. 68–75.

This implies that a counselor's influence will be greatest when his behavior is within acceptable boundaries, somewhat diverse, and in agreement with the general goals of the school faculty.

The counselor leads the activities of his staff through different means. Three main leadership styles dealt with by Lewin, Lippitt, and White[8] are authoritarian, democratic, and laissez-faire; Bonner[9] adds bureaucratic and charismatic.

In authoritarian style all policy is determined by the leader and is most effectively used where firm control is necessary. Democratic style policies are a matter of group discussion and decision. Laissez-faire offers complete freedom for group or individual decisions. This can be effective when there is complete agreement on the goals. Charismatic leadership is based on "supernatural" or spiritual qualities that emotionally attract followers. Bureaucratic leadership refers generally to impersonal leadership exhibited by individuals occupying an office of position.

A counselor does occupy a position in the school; however, he should not operate as a bureaucrat. In his position the counselor typically uses a combination of the first three leadership styles, emphasizing democratic qualities. The counselor thinks through situation alternatives and then makes a decision. In this process he considers the others' interests and shows them how their interest and goals could be advanced by the decision. At other times the counselor may make a tentative decision and ask for reactions before finalizing the decision. This gives the staff members more freedom and allows participation. He could present a problem to the staff and ask for their suggestions, reserving the right to join with the staff in making a decision.

[8] Kurt Lewin, Ronald Lippitt, and Ralph White, "Patterns of Aggressive Behavior in Experimentally Created 'social climates'," *Journal of Social Psychology*, **10**, 271–299 (1939). See also A. White and R. Lippitt, "Leadership Behavior and Members Reaction in Three 'social climates'," in *Group Dynamics*, Dorwin Cartwright and Alvin Zander, editors (Evanston: Row, Peterson and Company, 1962), pp. 527–553.

[9] Hubert Bonner, Group Dynamics (New York: The Ronald Press Company, 1959), pp. 185–190.

Schmidt[10] has described the effective leader as one who is flexible, rather than rigid in his range of leader behavior; is aware of the forces in himself, the group, and the situation; keeps in mind both the immediate problem and long-range effectiveness of the program; does not try to avoid responsibility by the simple expedient of involving others in decision-making; and makes certain decisions.

Staff Involvement

Counselors provide many, but not all, guidance services for pupils. Therefore, they must have active assistance and cooperation from the staff members, who include administrators, teachers, and other pupil personnel specialists. If the guidance program is to operate effectively, the working relationships among various personnel must be defined. Individuals will work most effectively when they know their roles and responsibilities. It is important that they not only know their guidance role but that they also have the authority to fulfill the concomitant responsibilities. It is essential that the working relationships between involved personnel be understood and confusion minimized. The roles of the various personnel working in a guidance program will be discussed in Chapter 3.

Two formal devices are used in a school system to establish the necessary involvement for meaningful guidance. First, there may be a system-wide representative staff council to assist in the leadership of guidance and pupil personnel services. Second, there may be a school committee that is concerned with the pupil personnel services of their building.[11]

The system-wide council includes staff from various grade levels and buildings. Teachers, counselors, and other pupil per-

---

[10] Warren Schmidt, "Executive Leadership," *The National Elementary Principal,* **41,** 35–39 (1962).
[11] George Hill, *Management and Improvement of Guidance* (New York: Appleton-Century-Croft, 1965), pp. 88–91.

sonnel workers should be appointed or elected to the council, yet it should remain small enough to function well. The council would investigate and advise, working with the director of guidance or pupil personnel services. It might study possible policy or functional program change, the public relations program, plans for program evaluation, staff proposals or complaints, and budget and facilities.

It may prove useful to establish a building committee which studies and advises the guidance program within that school. The functions of this committee are similar to the system-wide council, except they are concerned with one school. The committee is an important agency both for improved guidance and for in-service education.

Although councils and committees are important, the informal relationships with staff members are most significant in building understanding and involvement. When counselors and teachers share their problems and concerns they can understand and work cooperatively with each other. Actually, working individually with a teacher toward a solution of a specific concern will probably elicit the greatest involvement in the guidance function.

Organizing the Guidance Program

Tight organizational structure is a means of achieving the program's goals. This primarily involves grouping and assigning activities, and establishing inter-personal working relationships. Organization type is based upon the personnel involved in the program and their skills in particular activities. Administrators, teachers, and pupil personnel specialists participate jointly in program development and revision. They inadvertently define various roles for one another.

Organizational Plan

Effective program development does not occur automatically. It results from many factors, but particularly the cooperative working relationships of the personnel. A clear organization plan of the school system, individual schools, and integration of various programs help develop cooperative relationships. A chart can show the responsibilities of each department and relationships among the personnel in departments. Such a plan specifies, coordinates, and integrates the guidance services.

In organizing a program, a counselor needs to understand the role of line and staff positions in the administrative structure. A person in a line position is responsible for supervising activities of specific groups. He has authority to instruct the staff under his supervision. He is responsible to the executive immediately above him in the structure. In a line organization the direction and control of guidance services flow in a straight vertical line from the chief administrator down to his assistants and from them to their subordinates. In this type of organization, the administrator maintains a high degree of centralized authority. He assigns responsibilities and checks on their fulfillment.

In a staff organization the chief administrator classifies activities according to function and assigns these functions to department heads. The ultimate control still rests in his hands, but he delegates definite responsibilities to department heads or staff specialists. Because each specialist serves as a staff officer to the chief administrator, he has an important role in the development of policies and procedures for the organization. He serves in capacities that assist the line officer in performing his assigned responsibilities.

For an organization to function effectively, line and staff positions and services must be made clear. Line personnel issue instruction along the line of their operating responsibilities. Staff personnel gain identification to the extent they influence all executives through their effectiveness. Problems arise when role assignment is vague.

The elementary school counselor needs to clarify his line of responsibility. It includes responsibility to the principal of his school; the principal in turn has a line of authority to the superintendent. The counselor could have a line of responsibility to the director of guidance, who is responsible to the director of pupil personnel services, who has a line of authority to the superintendent. It is not sound administration to have the counselor equally responsible to two individuals. It is obvious that there needs to be an integration of the policies of the special services and the instruction branches. However, the counselor will need to clearly understand which is his line of authority.

The counselor, teachers and other pupil personnel specialists must function as a team. Staff interrelationships must be utilized to provide a meaningful guidance program. The staff will be responsible for carrying out the general school system policies. In many instances they will be involved in establishing policies. Information which flows from the team operation often will indicate new needs and directions for the school guidance program. From this identification new policies, roles and positions can emerge. The administrator must be alert to the needs of the staff, and the guidance personnel must be aware of pressures facing the administrator.

Organizational charts are to be found in most textbooks prepared for the administration of guidance or pupil personnel services. A counselor may examine the significant features of these charts in studying organizational patterns for guidance programs. A most productive task would be to analyze the pattern of his own school system and develop a chart of that organization.

Organizational plan is important. However, the use of sound principles of human relations is the best way to avoid problems. If it is remembered that the school system is a structure of line responsibility and that activities must be appropriately allocated; the staff will develop the cooperative working relationships necessary to provide a sound guidance program.

Organizational Climate

Whether organizing, administering, or revising a guidance program, the counselor must be aware of the organizational climate of the school. The behavior of the principal usually has the primary impact on the organizational climate. However, teachers also influence the behavior of the principal and each other.

Halpin[12] constructed the Organizational Climate Description Questionnaire (OCDQ), which portrays the organizational climate of elementary schools. Based upon national research, he describes six organizational climates. Each description includes the distinctive features of a school climate. It is apparent that different climates exist and that the climate affects grouping of activities and working relationships involved in a guidance program.

In interpreting the profiles, the behavior of the principal upon the climate of the school is emphasized. Although there is interaction among all staff members affecting the organizational climate, the principal sets the tone of the organizational climate and influences others' behavior. Teachers can control the organizational climate, particularly when a new principal comes into a building and proposes to make changes. He may meet a great deal of resistance.

A counselor initiating or revising a guidance program may face the same situation. Suppose a new counselor, with good experience and training, is assigned to an elementary school and tries to exert leadership and stimulate change in organizing a program. He may meet resistance; both he and the guidance program

[12] Andrew Halpin, *Theory and Research in Administration* (New York: The Macmillan Company, 1966), pp. 352–385.

could be rejected. He must recognize the possibility that if he enters certain climates, he could be a threat to the principal or some faction of the faculty.

Besides the principal and teachers, organizational climate may be affected by the social matrix of the school system. School systems vary in respect to control exerted by the superintendent and the central office. The principal of each elementary school may be permitted only a limited range of discretion in administering his school, whereas in other systems principals are given autonomy. The organizational climate of the school may be related to such factors as whether it is a new or old school; whether it is located in a wealthy suburb or in a deteriorating slum; whether it is in an urban center, a village, or a rural area.

Organizational climate affects the initation of a guidance program in the elementary school. The counselor must be cognizant of the climate before he makes any attempts to organize a program. The organizational climate may also affect the type of guidance program that can function in a particular school.

The organizational structure should be designed to fit the local school system. The needs of the school determine the goals and philosophy of the guidance program. This will serve as a guide for the type of organization to be developed. The organizational structure should facilitate better guidance activities. When revising an organizational structure, the new plan should complement the old and provide continuity to the program.

Budget and Facilities

Budget and facilities are involved in organizing a guidance program. Adequate facilities and a satisfactory budget permit a competent staff to maintain an effective program.

Space requirements should be determined according to the current program needs, but it is important to consider long-range goals. A U.S. Office of Education report on physical facilities suggests guidelines for space allocation. There should be an attractive and comfortable reception area with materials appropriate for profitable use of waiting time. Each counselor needs a private counseling office. A conference room should be available for case conferences, individual testing, and use by other pupil personnel specialists. A larger multipurpose room adjacent to the counseling offices can be used for group testing, group work, and in-service activities.[13]

Location of guidance facilities should be easily accessible to pupils, teachers, pupil personnel specialists, administrators, and parents. The offices might be located near but separate from the administrative offices. It would be advantageous to locate the counseling offices adjacent to the offices of the pupil personnel program. Therefore, all pupil personnel specialists could use a common reception room, the cumulative records would be available to all personnel, and the close proximity would encourage good working relationships. Both Hatch and Stefflre[14] and Zeran and Riccio[15] suggest floor plans worthy of consideration.

Equipment for the guidance offices is chosen to fit the allocated space. Each office needs a desk, chairs, filing cabinets, and bookshelves. The reception area requires secretarial equipment, filing cabinets, lounge chairs, storage cabinets, bulletin board, magazine and book racks. Additional tables, chairs, and files are needed in the conference rooms.

The budget is a significant factor in establishing or maintaining a program. When a program is being initiated a special budget expenditure may be needed to finance additional salaries, office space, furniture, and materials. Once the program is established, the budget will include professional salaries, clerical

---

[13] *Physical Facilities for Guidance Services,* Office of Education Report OE-25013 (Washington, D. C.: U. S. Department of Health, Education, and Welfare).

[14] Raymond Hatch and Buford Stefflre, *op. cit.,* pp. 236–247.

[15] Franklin Zeran and Anthony Riccio, *Organization and Administration of Guidance Services* (Chicago: Rand McNally & Company, 1962), pp. 278–295.

salaries, and the materials needed to provide guidance services. Opinions of experts vary regarding the cost of an adequate guidance program. However, 4 or 5 per cent of the total school budget appears to be a general guideline for guidance program budgets.[16] An adequate budget is an important variable in determining the potential activities. Only activities which are supported can be performed by the guidance staff. The effectiveness of a program is impaired by inadequate finances.

The director of pupil personnel usually has responsibility for the budget of the entire program. The elementary school counselor may be called upon to prepare a budget for his school or simply to submit an inventory of needed materials and services. A counselor may wish to review chapters on budget in the suggested references.

Summary

The counselor needs to be knowledgeable about theory and practice of administration so his contributions to program development are objective and appropriate. The guidance program must be compatible with the total administrative process and led by the same general principles.

The process outlined in this chapter has direct implications for guidance program organization. The steps for determining the functioning, planning, staffing, and organizing of a guidance program have been described independently. However, they are interrelated and are carried out simultaneously. Each school organization is unique and each guidance program will be unique. By following general principles of developing a functional organization, progress in initiating or revising a program is insured.

[16] Raymond Hatch and Buford Stefflre, *op. cit.*, pp. 248–257.

SELECTED REFERENCES

Raymond Hatch and Buford Stefflre, *Administration of Guidance Services* (Englewood Cliffs: Prentice-Hall, 1965).

Joseph Hollis and Lucile Hollis, *Organizing For Effective Guidance* (Chicago: Science Research Associates, Inc., 1965).

Herman Peters and Bruce Shertzer, *Guidance: Program Development and Management* (Columbus: Charles E. Merrill Books, Inc., 1963).

DEFINITIONS
OF ROLES AND FUNCTIONS

It is important that various school personnel understand the role which the elementary guidance counselor can play. In addition there is a need to clearly delineate guidance tasks which are to be performed by the teacher and other specialists in the school. It is helpful to have a job description for each person. Of course even carefully established job descriptions cannot always cover the multitude of services which may be part of the actual role of the individual functionary. Further there is a need to coordinate the program minimizing overlap in services.

There are many persons who are called upon to perform guidance activities within the elementary school. In addition, those who provide the support of the school through financial means are involved and need to be included in any formal guidance program and counselor role discussion. Thus teachers, parents, specialists, those who have no children in schools, local and state leaders may be contacted to provide information for the type of guidance which is most meaningful within a specific school. There are certain basic factors which provide the foundation for elementary guidance. First, elementary guidance is provided in an attempt to prevent the development of long-range difficulties. This means longitudinal involvement. Second, the causes of academic, personal, and social concerns are complex. Efforts to prevent or solve these concerns must also be complex. Third, many people can provide assistance and must be utilized in any program. Teachers, parents, administrators, and specialists can contribute to the positive growth of the child and should be included in the guidance process.

It is necessary to highlight areas of responsibility for various school staff personnel. The eventual job description will be based upon these generalities and upon the continuing experience of the specialist. Roles will be examined *vis-a-vis* the three primary positions in the school, i.e., pupil services, instruction, and administration. Under each heading there can be many tasks and several functionaries. Delineating every task and assigning it to a particular person would be impossible and impractical. However, major areas of responsibility will be discussed.

Pupil Services

In pupil services there are several types of personnel. In general the title of these persons describes their major responsibility. Thus the school nurse teacher's role would highlight involvement in the health needs of pupils. However, tradition and job demands might dictate a differing role than would be described in a textbook or by state guidelines. It is valuable within the context of the school to examine the major specialists in the pupil personnel area to arrive at a generalized role for each and to interrelate these roles. This process will provide comprehensive pupil personnel services founded upon the needs of the pupil and the availability of pupil personnel workers.

The Elementary Counselor

With each new publication the list of references concerning elementary guidance increases. Many of these include a tentative list of duties. For example, the U.S. Office of Education published the results of a research by Smith and Eckerson[1] in which the following tasks were suggested.

The guidance consultant:

1. Tests and observes children who have learning difficulties, who are underachievers, who show signs of emotional disturbances, who need curricular advice or placement in special classes, and who are being considered for referral to other specialists.
2. Counsels children with minor personal troubles that interfere with school life.
3. Helps needy children obtain glasses, hearing aids, clothes, food, and other essentials.
4. Consults with teachers, principal, and parents to help them understand normal children as well as children with problems.
5. Refers children needing intensive diagnosis and treatment to pupil personnel specialists and community agencies, and in-

[1] Hyrum M. Smith and Louise Omwake Eckerson *Guidance for Children in Elementary Schools,* U.S. Department of Health, Education, and Welfare (Washington, D. C.: U.S. Government Printing Office, 1965), pp. 5–6.

terprets their findings and recommendations to teachers and parents.

6. Provides in-service education for teachers. Through scheduled meetings and informal conferences relating to normal development and behavior in children, the guidance consultant aids teachers in meeting difficult classroom situations with understanding and composure. Other subjects included in in-service training are mental health, administration and interpretation of tests, maintenance and use of cumulative records, and techniques of interviewing.

7. Develops group guidance programs in common personal problems, study habits, occupational orientation, and preparation for the secondary school.

8. Interprets the guidance program to parent and community organizations.

9. Conducts research and evaluative studies relative to the effectiveness of the guidance program.

Peters, Shertzer, and Van Hoose[2] state the guidance function in succinct fashion, namely "sustaining and developing the pupil's self—intellectually and affectively. It is to assist children in growing and developing within a wide framework of normalcy."

From these and similar statements a role for the elementary counselor emerges. It is important that this role be one which meets the needs of the child and school within the framework of the uniqueness of guidance. Thus, undertaking many tasks with many pupils is no more appropriate than transposing the role and function of the secondary counselor to the elementary area. This may be a major problem of elementary counselors. With greater numbers of pupils with guidance needs, there is neither time, energy, nor finances to evaluate and realign the

[2] Herman J. Peters, Bruce Shertzer, and William Van Hoose, *Guidance in Elementary Schools* (Chicago: Rand McNally & Company, 1965), p. 21.

tasks which are properly counseling oriented. In fact guidance or counseling often are inappropriate terms for the work that is being done. Frequently in these cases the 'counselor' performs various clerical, administrative, or accounting tasks and labels himself a counselor retaining the status accrued to this title. We hope this is avoided by new personnel as they assume counseling roles in elementary schools.

The elementary counselor is faced with several variables which will dictate specific kinds of guidance activities. First, he is working with an age range which precludes immediate meaningful counseling interaction. This does not mean that counseling cannot take place. It does suggest that the pupil may need to learn what occurs in counseling, i.e., what counseling is all about, before gaining value from this activity. The counselor's skill in establishing the relationship is essential.

Second, elementary school pupils have established a relationship with one teacher extending over a relatively long period of time. This should not be overlooked. In many cases the pupil will turn to the teacher for assistance rather than to an elementary counselor. The counselor, in these cases, should assist the teacher in providing aid to the pupil. Thus, the counselor becomes a consultant for the teaching staff. Debating which person most adequately serves the child avoids the basic concern, namely, how can the child best be helped?

Counselor and teacher must also be knowledgeable in child development. There is a continuing need to differentiate normal developmental deviations from those which may be pathological in nature. As the counselor is concerned primarily with a wide range of normalcy, the identification of the "normal" is an important part of the counselor's role.

What then can be expected of the elementary counselor? First, the counselor must be prepared to work in a counseling relationship with individual pupils and groups of pupils. The counseling process is designed to allow the pupil freedom to develop a healthy self-concept. It is a time when the pupil can explore his personal life with another individual. The counseling session is not restricted to educational concerns or vocational decision-making. The pupil uses the session as he pleases, discussing any topic he sees as appropriate and meaningful. The counselor helps clarify the pupil's thinking and aids him in interpreting the consequences of his activities in the society in which he lives. Counseling, under this definition, is time-consuming and does not occur with every individual who comes to the counselor's office; however the opportunity must still be present.

The counselor also consults with teachers. In this capacity, the counselor works closely with the teaching staff in identifying learning difficulties and interpersonal problems. He may also suggest methods for helping the teacher alleviate personal concerns about pupils. Typical problems would be underachievement, poor reading, personal-social interactions, and low motivation. However, the counselor must also assist the teacher to understand all pupils, not simply "problem" children. One method by which this can occur is illustrated in Figures 1 and 2.

The teacher is encouraged to complete these sheets for his class. The information called for on the sheets will help the teacher gain awareness of the pupils with whom he is working. On the basis of this information strengths of the pupils can be ascertained and additional assistance provided for all children. Health factors are also identified and provide information which can lead to individual attention. The aim is to provide the best learning-living climate for all children.

The counselor must collect and distribute information within the school. This includes record-keeping, testing and test interpretation, and cumulative folders. However, the focus is upon the collection and dissemination of data rather than its storage. Use of information is essential and the effort of the counselor must be toward this end rather than the clerical details of the process.

An unique part of the counselor's role at the elementary level

Figure 1.
Pupil Data Summary[a]

Pupil's name _____

Address _____ Age _____

Telephone _____ Birthday _____

Factors	Information	Source	Date
Home Background			
Father's occupation			
Mother's occupation			
Siblings (ages)			
I.Q. Test			
M.A.			
C.A.			
I.Q.			
Achievement			
Reading			
Arithmetic			
Health			
Vision			
Hearing			
Vigor			
General			
Social-Emotional			
Cooperation			
Friendly with children			
Liked by other children			
Best friend			
Interests			
Favorite subject			
Individual interests			
Group interests			
Outside interests			

[a] G. R. Sherrie, *Pupil Data Summary* (State University College at Buffalo: Evaluation Service Center, 1963).

Figure 2.
Teacher's Class Data Summary[a]
(Purpose: To see composition of class as a whole)

Name Last, First	Sex	(Sept.) Age In Years, Months	Date of Birth	M.A.	I.Q.	Reading Grade	Arith. Grade	Physical Problem (Use Code Below)[b]	Special Interest or Aptitude (Write In)	Stability and Maturity (Use Code Below)[c]
1										
2										
3										
4										
5										
6										
30										

[b] CODE: Physical Problem
S—Sight
H—Hearing
SP—Speech
C—Cardiac
O—Orthopedic
V—Very large or small for age
L—Lacks vigor

[c] CODE: Stability, Maturity
(5—Excellent, 4—Very good, 3—Average, 2—Fair, 1—Needs special guidance)
Accepts responsibility? Shows self confidence? Has friends? Considers others? Controls temper? Shows dependability? Accepts criticism? Likes other children? Likes school? Gives attention to task?

N.B.: List boys alphabetically, followed by girls alphabetically.

[a] Division of Exceptional Children Education, *Teacher's Class Data Summary* (State University College at Buffalo: Evaluation and Instructional Research Center).

will be his concern with curriculum. He is not a curriculum specialist. However, he is in a favorable position to recognize curriculum needs and to make positive suggestions toward more meaningful curriculum. He should have information on individual learning levels and the effect of various materials on learning ability. The special curricular decision of grouping should be made in consultation with several school personnel including teachers and counselors.

Working with parents and other community organizations reflects an important facet of the counselor's responsibility. The counselor assists the child by utilizing knowledge about his home experience and how this affects his classroom activity. Parents often are not completely aware of the child's in-school behavior pattern and thus are sometimes surprised at low grades, disciplinary problems, or other educational and administrative observations. It is also true that parents lack adequate information as to how the child can be assisted toward more effective performance either in or out of school. In some cases, the counselor works with parents to help toward better understanding and consistent treatment of their children. In other cases the counselor may assist them in gaining professional assistance with the hope that the home climate will become more conducive to healthy child growth and maturation.

The counselor's relationship to the home suggests he have a general image of the community and individual neighborhoods. The knowledge he possesses concerning ethnic background and community attitudes will assist him in diagnosing pupil concerns. A note of caution should be injected here regarding possible generalization. Child consideration includes his individuality and background information gathered by the counselor must be interpreted in light of the child's present experience. The counselor should never make such statements as "he is a first-generation American" and assume that the meaning will be immediately understood. Further, he must guard against such ethnic-related statements as "he is a Negro" and against then generalizing anything concerning Negroes.

The counselor must also consider the number of pupils for whom he is to provide assistance. He is concerned with the general administrative arrangement of the school and the organization of the pupil personnel program. He determines whether there is administrative and staff support for the program. Briefly, he needs to obtain answers to a number of questions and to utilize this information in clearly defining his role in the school. A major factor to be considered is the pupil as he is functioning in the school. Unless his activities are clearly related to the learning potential of children, there is a need to question the activity.

A final word for prospective counselors is in order. It is necessary that counselors in training have some clear ideas concerning the position and its appropriately related preparatory activities. These, together with the school situation, will dictate the counselor's role. There will be a need to establish priorities in most cases, as it is doubtful that many completely ideal counselor positions exist. Establishing these priorities will be a most crucial aspect of beginning counseling activities at the elementary level. Consideration given early in the year may well prove to be the most valuable part of the counselor's activity.

In summary, the elementary school counselor, like all school personnel, must be concerned with the learning situation and pupil potentials. The counselor brings to the examination of learning certain specialized abilities. These include the ability to work closely with individuals: pupils, teachers, and others, in a one-to-one counseling relationship. In this relationship he focuses upon the identification of counselee strengths and weaknesses and the counselee's understanding of himself. Second, he consults with various persons. The counselor's training should assist him to provide new insights into the pupil's situation, in or out of school and he should help the individual identify and move in more satisfying directions. This is related to many situations ranging from retention to acceleration, from grouping to individualization of instruction, from motivating reluctant learners to widening the horizons of strong pupils. The counselor must also be involved in the curricular function of the school. His role is one of consultation rather than direct involvement in development or change. However, his knowledge of the pupil population will be valuable for curriculum committees as they attempt to provide the most meaningful subject matter for pupils. Finally, the counselor coordinates diverse groups which have the potential to provide assistance to pupils.

The School Psychologist

The school psychologist in role and preparation may closely resemble an elementary school counselor. However, the psychologist is concerned with several specific noncounselor tasks which are essential in the elementary school and which are best handled by the trained clinician. In general, his activities include individual and group testing. Emphasis is given here to individual testing which consumes time and requires special training and skills. The psychologist also consults with other school personnel and parents on child problems, more remedial or therapeutic in nature. Ideally, the psychologist should provide therapy for certain children whose problems are more critical and require longer treatment periods. In some cases, the psychologist diagnoses and then refers children to other agencies or individuals for specialized treatment. Finally, the psychologist is involved in remedial and special education programs within the school. He brings his knowledge of human growth and learning to the classroom, so that the child is better able to function, academically and personally.

In some cases he supervises special classes for exceptional children. His training and experience prepares him for working most effectively with exceptional groups, e.g., gifted and retarded.

He often is called upon to work with individual pupils who are outside the normal range in such areas as intelligence or emotional difficulty.

It is difficult to describe specifically the total role and involvement of the psychologist. Many factors will be involved in establishing the role of the psychologist including the number of pupils for whom he is to provide psychological assistance, the type and number of other pupil personnel specialists, interrelationships with other pupil personnel specialists, with the teaching staff and the administrative personnel of the school. As with other specialists there are certain tasks which form a foundation for the school psychologist's role. The following list includes some of these specific areas.

1. Cooperate in the development, organization, and administration of a basic group testing program for the school system.
2. Conduct detailed individual analyses of particular children in order to furnish deeper insights into their educational problems.
3. Furnish clinical and diagnostic information concerning the particular emotional and psychological problems which interfere with a child's effective learning.
4. Suggest and recommend programs designed to remedy these psychological problems.
5. Assist in interpreting to teachers and parents psychological data concerning individual children.
6. Consult with teachers in the development of curricular adaptations and classroom practices for pupils with special needs.
7. Consult in the development and operation of the total school program for exceptional children.
8. Work in a team approach with other school personnel toward the solving of educational problems of pupils.
9. Assist in developing efficient referral procedures for cases requiring the diagnostic or therapeutic services of specialists.

10. Orient staff members to be alert to the symptoms of psychological disorders in children and to refer any children displaying such symptoms.
11. Cooperate with other staff members in the development and use of psychological data.
12. Interpret to school, parent, and community groups the purpose and program of the school psychological services.[3]

The reader will note that the psychologist is called upon to develop programs for diagnosing and analyzing child problems. He then must be able to communicate these data to various persons in order to provide assistance leading to resolution. The school psychologist must be skilled in interpersonal relationships. If he does not communicate with others in the school or system any results which occur will be incidental.

The school psychologist has an obligation to assist pupils in better understanding themselves and functioning more effectively in their life and learning activities. He is charged with working with pupils who are psychologically, socially, or mentally unfit for the competitive situations in which they find themselves. These individuals need assistance from many sources; the psychologist provides direct and coordinating assistance toward integrating the activities of the pupil.

The School Social Worker

The school social worker provides additional specialized assistance for the elementary school pupil. The social worker assists pupils with social-emotional problems which interfere with normal school progress. His training and experience prepare him to make significant contributions toward the maturation of pupils.

He is skilled in the use of social case work methods and utilizes

---

[3] Council of Chief State School Officers, *Responsibilities of State Departments of Education for Pupil Personnel Service* (Washington, D. C.: Council of Chief State Officers, 1960), pp. 16, 17.

these in working with several significant specialists to provide assistance to the pupil. He has extensive knowledge of various community and social institutions and agencies. His relationship to these institutions facilitates the referral of cases for more extensive study. He contributes to the study and adjustment of pupil problems through the use of school and community resources, through an understanding of human growth and behavior, and an ability to share his competencies with others.

The pupil personnel team should include a social worker in order to be fully functioning. At the elementary level pupils' adjustments may result from working closely with the parents. At times this means assisting the parents to create a more desirable home atmosphere for the child, while at other times it means facilitating parent-teacher-pupil communication.

The social worker coordinates the social service agencies in the community with the school. For children who need to be treated or are being treated at various social agencies the social worker acts as a communication liaison.

Specific lists of activities have been prepared for social work personnel for various types of situations. Most states provide general guidelines for every pupil personnel specialist although not all states use the same titles for these people. Perhaps the most comprehensive list has been prepared by Johnson, Stefflre, and Edelfelt.[4] They offer the following description of social worker task areas.

1. The school social worker provides casework service to families in helping them to work toward solutions for problems which the child encounters in making use of school experiences.

[4] Walter F. Johnson, Buford Stefflre, and Roy A. Edelfelt, *Pupil Personnel and Guidance Services* (New York: McGraw-Hill Book Company, Inc., 1961), pp. 167, 168.

2. The school social worker collaborates with the teacher and other school personnel when direct casework service is being given to a child and to his parents.

3. The school social worker consults with teachers and other school personnel regarding certain children who are not referred for direct casework service.

4. The school social worker consults with teachers and other school personnel regarding school and community problems affecting the total welfare of the children in the school.

5. The school social worker helps children and parents to use other services or agencies outside the school when problems are of such a nature that the school cannot offer appropriate help.

6. The school social worker participates with other staff members in developing the curriculum of the school and in helping to formulate policies and procedures which facilitate more effective use of the school by children and their parents.

7. The social worker participates in in-service education of teachers and other school personnel in child study and in other parent education groups.

8. The school social worker participates in the coordination of school and community services for the welfare of the child.

9. The school social worker participates in interpreting the school to the community and the community to the school.

10. The school social worker participates in identifying and planning what needs to be done for the unmet needs of the children in the school and community.

11. The school social worker has duties in the area of planning, organizing, and administrating responsibilities necessary for effective school social work services.

12. The school social worker maintains records for his own and the use of other school personnel.

13. The school social worker participates in research in areas re-

lated to the total educational program and those specifically
related to the area of school social work.

14. The school social worker may supervise social workers and
students in training in schools of social work.

In essence the social worker provides liaison activities between
the school and home. In those cases where the adjustment of the
child and thus his learning potential is impaired by the home or
community, the social worker assists in alleviating the problem
so that the pupil can function more effectively.

Other Pupil Personnel Services

Several other specialists are often included in the pupil personnel area, e.g. the school nurse teacher, the attendance officer,
and, in some cases, the speech and hearing therapist. The school
nurse teacher provides information concerning the physical condition of the child. She verifies information for teachers when
the teacher notes a change in the pupil or suspects that a
physical problem may be causing ineffectiveness in the pupil's
academic and social performance. The nurse should be included
in any case conference since she may have considerable insight
concerning the pupil's physical and health status.[5]

The attendance officer is no longer the hooky cop with all
the misperception attached to the position. Although he is still
charged with the responsibility of checking on pupils whose
absences, whether excessive or not, are unexplained, the more
modern concept is that the positive aspects of school attendance
must be emphasized. Thus the attendance officer investigates
absences to determine if there is a home or family problem which
is affecting the pupil attendance. The attendance officer is often
in charge of census taking in the school district. In this role he is

---

[5] Council of Chief State School Officers, op. cit., pp. 14–16.

able to observe home and neighborhood situations.[6] This information is of considerable importance to other school personnel when any action is anticipated with any pupil. The attendance officer contributes to the pupil personnel team by providing information of a personal nature concerning the home environment of the pupil.

The speech and hearing therapist has, as a major focus, diagnosis and treatment of problems in learning created by disorders of communication. In addition to his relationship to communication disorders he promotes the development of language skills with all pupils. The speech and hearing specialist provides information for case conferences on those pupils he knows. This specialist is essential in the elementary school since it is at this level that identification and amelioration of communication and language difficulties can be most easily handled.

Depending upon the school system there may be other specialists directly related to the pupil personnel services program. However, many schools are without the services of one or more of the above specialists or they may be given different titles even though similar in function. In any case, it is necessary that task areas be delineated for the available personnel and that overlap be kept at a minimum. There is a need to identify a hierarchy or priority of services which will be provided. If possible, however, the entire range of pupil personnel specialists involvement is invaluable to the success of a modern school system.

Interrelationships of Pupil Personnel Specialists

Cooperation between pupil personnel specialists is essential. The various specialists are responsible for communicating effectively with the publics they serve and with the other members of the team. An administrator should be designated to coordinate the personnel involved. The key factor is that the individual

[6] Ibid, pp. 10–12.

specialist assumes responsibility for coordinated action to effectively meet the needs of students.

The Administrator's Role in Elementary Guidance

Presently, there are many administrative arrangements in elementary schools. For example, the building principal may be designated as the leader in establishing and maintaining various programs, including pupil personnel programs. In other systems this responsibility is given to a director of special services, i.e., health, guidance personnel, and attendance. The administrative designee provides leadership in the development, maintenance and coordination of programs at various levels in several buildings. The specialist may be given responsibility for organizing and directing his and similar functionary's activities within the school. Regardless of the pattern followed there is a need for support and involvement of administrators in the success of any program.

Mathewson[7] suggests the following directions for administrative activity and involvement. The administrator and supervisor of guidance:

1. Coordinates over-all program activities and directs development of the program on all levels.
2. Provides leadership in direction, planning, and evaluation of the program.
3. Supplies professional supervision of technical phases.
4. With the school administrator, determines policies and fixes responsibilities.
5. Interviews and recommends personnel for employment.

[7] Robert Mathewson, *Guidance Policy and Practice,* 3rd Ed. (New York: Harper and Row, Publishers, 1962), p. 212.

6. Confers and consults with pupils, teachers, parents and counselors on request, concerning special needs and problems.

Roeber, Smith and Erickson[8] list the following administrative tasks:

1. He provides active, informed leadership through self-study of the values, purposes, and organization of the guidance program.
2. He recommends to the superintendent the employing of a competent counselor.
3. He assigns school personnel to any responsibility regarding the development of the program, such as individuals responsible for the occupational information file or the testing plan.
4. He arranges for the facilities, and the nonteaching duties of the counselor so that adequate space time and acceptance are provided for the counselor.

It is apparent that the administrator cannot go it alone in establishing a program and insuring its implementation. As the designated leader, the principal in the school develops relationships and programs which foster pupil centered activity. The uniqueness of the elementary school provides some guidelines for the administrator.

First, a realistic guidance program is necessary. Teachers have traditionally provided most of the guidance for their pupils. With the initiation of formal guidance services, the administrator must be the educational leader and work out the functional arrangements for each individual, teacher or pupil personnel specialist. This means in-service work for teachers emphasizing the improvement of learning and personal adjustment. As with any school

---

[8] Edward C. Roeber, Glenn F. Smith, and Clifford E. Erickson, *Organization and Administration of Guidance Services* (New York: McGraw-Hill Book Company, Inc., 1955), p. 30.

program, the principal must be convinced that guidance and counseling is desirable and necessary at the elementary level or success will be minimal. His leadership role in guidance is most important.

Second, the principal must be involved in selecting and recommending qualified personnel for the program. This suggests that the principal has clear ideas concerning counselor potential and attributes in the elementary school. Guidance is not a reward for successful teaching or a place to put a teacher who can no longer function in the classroom. The success of the program depends upon the quality of activity by the counselor.

Third, the administrator involves himself in the guidance program. He contributes to case study discussion offering his unique professional perspective. Disciplinary measures are handled by the principal. The teacher or counselor may be involved in working with the pupil, but eventually any decision of a disciplinary nature resides with the principal.

Finally, the principal provides adequate financial support for the program. Although budget problems are handled at various levels, the principal voices his opinions when either insufficient personnel, financial support, or facilities lessen the quality of the program. It is impossible to develop a successful program unless the counselor has reasonable time, location, and support. Attempting to work with large numbers of pupils in insufficient facilities will do more harm than good. The principal assumes leadership to insure the physical and monetary support necessary to positive guidance operation.

Guidance Role of Elementary Teachers

Teachers have and will continue to play a key role in elementary guidance activities. Increasing social complexity dictates that the teacher provides more assistance to each pupil. Although the teacher is primarily concerned with teaching pupils there are certain important aspects of the learning climate which must be considered.

The teacher must believe that he teaches children. Subject matter is important but classroom experience must go beyond acquisition of subject matter. The child must learn to apply subject matter to the solution of his problems, to decision-making, and to choosing between alternatives. Learning is closely related to the learner's condition, e.g., psychological, physical, or social. Past and present experiences and environment will affect learning. The teacher must understand these factors in order to meet the learning needs of his pupils. Learning varies in rate of acquisition and style. Understanding and utilizing these facts of pupil readiness, ability, aptitude, and motivation are important factors in affecting learning, a form of behavior change.

The successful teacher must understand the background, needs, and concerns of his pupils. Any factor which inhibits or improves the pupil's ability to function adequately in the classroom must be identified and necessary assistance provided. Interwoven with other activities composing the teacher's role is the activity described throughout this book as guidance.

The school and the teacher are responsible for preparing youth for active leadership and social participation. To this end, the following guidance activities are the teachers in cooperation with other members of the pupil personnel team:

1. Adequate identification of the intellectual and emotional needs of pupils, including the aptitudes, capabilities, interests and aspirations of each pupil is essential.
2. There must be an established method or procedure for utilizing the information for school and out-of-school assistance to all children.

3. Continuous evaluation of the process is necessary so that optimum development of each pupil is fostered.

There is a need to differentiate guidance activities and counseling activities so that the available school specialists can be efficiently utilized. Detjen and Detjen,[9] express one point of view when they state:

> The key person in the guidance program is the *classroom teacher*. Because of his close daily contact with the children, he has an excellent opportunity to know each one well and to find ways of meeting individual needs. He is in a strategic position to observe children closely, and being familiar with their usual appearance and knowing their normal reactions and responses in various situations, he is able to recognize any deviation from the normal. He can thus watch all indications of growth or failure to grow both mentally and physically.

The teacher must be aware of his limitations in guidance involvement. First, there is the problem of time. An elementary teacher has increased opportunity to observe children and to know them individually but the teachers primary responsibility is related to the teaching-learning dyad. By this we mean that the pupils in the classroom are there to learn particular basic and advanced mathematical, scientific, and grammatical concepts which "society" has determined as necessary for individual enhancement and societal perpetuation. Neglecting this important aspect results in incomplete educational experience. The teacher is forced to establish priorities within the classroom. Is the fact that Johnny does not function well in the playground

[9] Erwin Winfred Detjen and Mary Ford Detjen, *Elementary School Guidance*, 2nd Ed. (New York: McGraw-Hill Book Company, Inc., 1963), p. 13.

period of a sufficient degree of concern to warrant one, two, or three hours of effort on the teacher's part? How many Johnnies are in each classroom? And what, if anything, can a teacher do with children with problems?

This leads to another factor which will limit the ability of the teacher to be all things to all people, namely, preparation in the areas of counseling or individual interviewing. There are those who maintain that this is not necessary, that all teachers can and do provide this service naturally. However counselors who complete the practicum course during the preparation generally report that the demands of counseling are considerably different than they envisioned prior to the course.

The general arrangement of the elementary classroom dictates that the teacher must be a primary functionary in any child activity. First, the teacher is an observer of children. This observation helps the teacher learn more about each child. It also enables him to learn the normal behavior patterns; deviations can then be judged more accurately. On the basis of pupil observation the teacher can hypothesize about the concerns of the pupils.

Observation is only the first step. The teacher must begin to make tentative plans about what might be the best course of action to take with the twenty-five to thirty-five individuals who make up the classroom. The teacher then translates these observations into actions with and for the pupils. Individualization of instruction begins.

The classroom teacher uses assistance in interpreting certain data which are gathered. Various specialists are called to provide the aid. The counselor is called in most of these cases. On the basis of these informal or formal case conferences, decisions about individual assistance can be made. These then are the first two tasks of the teacher: observation of pupils and consequent decision-making concerning what might be done.

The teacher then works with pupils who have been identified

as needing extra guidance. Conferences are initiated with the pupils over a period of time. The conference primarily allows the pupil to examine his own attitudes, motivations, and interests. The conference is not designed to fulfill the needs of the teacher nor is it simply to gather more data for the cumulative record system. Conferences are not intended to fulfill the requirements of the school system. Unless the welfare of the pupil is foremost, the conference will be less than effective.

The conference helps the teacher and child develop guide-lines for future activity. One outcome might be that the pupil realizes someone is interested in him as a person. He learns per-haps for the first time what is his potential. He also begins to see meaning in school activities. The teacher gains additional insights into pupil behavior and valuable experience in interpersonal relationships.

Guidance with Individuals

In order for the teacher to provide guidance for the children in the classroom, there is a need for understanding pupil needs. One well-known classification system is Havighurst's. Under this sys-tem certain general tasks are identified for each period of one's growth. The individual is expected to accomplish most of the tasks within the given age period. If he does not he has difficulty in later task areas. Typical tasks for middle childhood include:

1. Learning physical skills necessary for ordinary games.
2. Building wholesome attitudes toward oneself as a growing organism.
3. Learning to get along with age-mates.
4. Learning an appropriate sex role.
5. Developing fundamental skills in reading, writing and cal-culating.
6. Developing concepts necessary for everyday life.
7. Developing conscience, morality, and a scale of values.

8. Developing responsible attitudes toward social groups and institutions.[10]

The teacher's guidance activities include pupil observation indicating deviations from normal growth patterns. Careful assessment of those individuals should verify whether or not their behaviors are out of the normal range. The teacher must assist all pupils, but is careful to avoid the idea that one incident of nonnormal behavior is sufficient evidence of the need for individual counseling. The goal of the teacher should be to foster uniqueness rather than conformity, and pressure on children to fit a given mold must be avoided.

Perhaps, the most important part of the teacher's guidance role is to assist the pupil to move as rapidly as he wishes in his personal and social development. The teacher understands growth patterns and psychological development of children. Kagan and Moss[11] state that there has always been an explicit and rather dogmatic conviction that selected adult motives, attitudes, and behaviors begin their growth during the first ten years of life. Once established during childhood years, these responses are likely to remain permanent aspects of the individual's behavior repertoire. This concept, derived from the biological critical period notion that future development is dependent upon the time and stages of previous development, means that certain periods of growth are extremely important for future development. The work of Glueck and Glueck[12] supports this notion; juvenile delinquency can be predicted from the events of certain periods of the child's life. It would appear crucial

[10] Robert Havighurst, *Human Development and Education* (New York: Longmans, Green, 1952), pp. 15–28.
[11] Jerome Kagan and Howard A. Moss, *Birth to Maturity* (New York: John Wiley and Sons, Inc., 1962), p. 1.
[12] Sheldon Glueck and Eleanor Glueck, *Predicting Delinquency and Crime* (Cambridge: Harvard University Press, 1959).

that the teacher be involved in careful guidance of the elementary age pupil.

Thus, the teacher's role in guidance stems from the demands of the school, the classroom, and individuals and is tempered by the range of his training and experiential background. The teacher's primary responsibility is promoting learning. In this regard, the teacher must understand the pupil's ability, aptitudes, and needs and utilize this knowledge to assist each individual toward optimum growth. The teacher, limited by time and sometimes training in providing all guidance functions, should use others in the school for specialized assistance in counseling and assessing pupils.

In summary, the teacher's continuing responsibilities in the guidance program are essential. He is called upon to provide meaningful assistance to the pupil through observation of behavior, through accurate interpretation of this behavior, and in many cases, through individualization of the classroom interaction with the pupil. The teacher may need assistance in this portion of his guidance role and should be able to utilize various specialists, e.g., the counselor or the psychologist.

Summary

The need to formalize guidance activities at the elementary level dictates that the role of various functionaries be established and the assignment of tasks be clearly outlined. The teacher remains a key guidance person but should be able to call upon various guidance and pupil personnel specialists to assist in meeting the psychological, social, and intellectual needs of pupils. A team approach to the provision of guidance services will result in more meaningful assistance to pupils, the ultimate goal of any guidance program. Support from the administration is necessary and the principal is called upon to provide leadership in program development and management. The cooperation of all school personnel appears to be the *sine qua non* of any effective guidance program, and this depends, to a great extent, upon the professional attitudes and behaviors of the personnel in the school.

SELECTED REFERENCES

Dean L. Hummel and S. J. Bonham, Jr., *Pupil Personnel Services in Schools* (Chicago: Rand McNally and Company, 1968).

Leslie E. Moser and Ruth Small Moser, *Counseling and Guidance: An Exploration* (Englewood Cliffs: Prentice-Hall, Inc., 1963).

Herman J. Peters, Bruce Shertzer and William Van Hoose, *Guidance in Elementary Schools* (Chicago: Rand McNally, 1965).

INDIVIDUAL COUNSELING WITH CHILDREN

The elementary school child is in the process of development: intellectually, physically, socially and emotionally. His powers of self-acceptance, understanding and evaluation mature with a growing recognition of his assets and liabilities. He is developing patterns of social relationships through belonging to groups and identifying with others. A child is learning to be independent, to accept responsibility, to make choices, and to assume responsibility for these choices. He learns to make plans and carry them through. He is learning the role of work as it first appears in educational achievement and then in the environment, as related to jobs and employment. The child is learning to realistically appraise his capacities, interests, and attitudes as they relate to work tasks.

The counselor must be aware of normal change and wide individual difference in patterns of development. Developmental differences create adjustment problems for children in responding to the tasks of school and social situations. Although children will experience problems in their development, counseling is not always problem- or crisis-oriented. Counseling is individualized learning. Counseling assists the child in learning about his environment, learning about himself, learning methods of using his capacities, and learning behaviors for handling those roles and relationships that will be necessary for succeeding through his stages of development. A manifestation of change in behavior should occur as a result of counseling. For example, a child may wish to improve his marks or reduce his anxiety in a specific situation. In either case he wishes to learn a new, more acceptable behavior. Beginning with the premise that behavior is learned, the child can change his behavior by learning a new one. The child must determine what he wants so that he and the counselor can translate his wishes into feasible behaviors. Wishes having been clarified, it is then the responsibility of the counselor to determine what learning must take place in order to implement the agreed upon behavior changes.

There are two main methods of changing behavior. The situational events that operate to elicit particular behaviors in the child can be altered. Much of this will be done through consultation with other persons who have more control over the child's environment than the counselor. These procedures will be described in the chapter on consulting. The second method of changing a child's behavior repertoire is through learning new behaviors in the counseling interview. Not all change, though, will be the result of within-counseling events. Determinants other than the counseling interview continuously operate to change the behavior, thus the counselor must assume the role of consultant as well as role of counselor.

Counseling with elementary school children is one of the major roles of the counselor. A study of elementary school counselors in California indicated that 50 per cent of their working time was spent with the pupils.[1] According to their responses, principals and counselors were in agreement that counseling was the most important function of the counselor. In the Elementary School Guidance Pilot Projects in New York State, the counselors reported that the largest segment of their time, 34 per cent, was spent in counseling individual pupils.[2]

Goals in Counseling

A counselor cannot help a child to resolve his difficulties, or change his problematic behaviors, unless he has some idea of what is wrong. An explanatory theory is required to account for the manner in which maladaptive behaviors are acquired and persist, in spite of the fact they are unwanted, ineffective, and inappropriate. This knowledge will help determine the counseling procedures in changing the behavior.

Simply, change implies that new behavior will replace old behavior. It is necessary to identify both the behavior that is to be eliminated and that which is to be acquired. This is one primary goal of counseling. If a counselor is to work effectively, he must be able to accurately predict the outcomes he both desires and expects. Specific and precise procedures are more likely to arise from specific outcome statements. In counseling as in other problem-solving tasks, a knowledge of the objective helps define the ways it can be accomplished. Who should select the goals? This question relates to the question of which behaviors are

[1] William McCreary and Gerald Miller, "Elementary School Counselors in California," *Personnel and Guidance Journal*, 44, 494–498 (1966).
[2] *Status of Elementary School Guidance Pilot Projects in New York State* (Albany: The State Department Bureau of Guidance, 1966), pp. 1–14.

problematic and should be changed. A teacher or parent may wish the child to change his behavior. However, these changes may not coincide with those the child desires. Certainly before any real change can be expected, the child and the counselor must agree on what behaviors are to be changed and what outcomes are desired.

Formulation of goals is necessary for the counselor to ascertain the progress of the child and to determine the effectiveness of his approach. Formulating goals becomes a partnership between the pupil and counselor, the latter attempting to clarify the desired outcome. The most important statement of goals comes from the pupil and should be applicable to his life situation. The goals of the counseling interviews are also influenced by the counselor's professional value system and his conception of human development in terms of process and outcome.

Counseling and Theory

As the purpose of counseling is to change relative behavior, it seems necessary to study the conditions under which specific behavior can be changed in the direction desired by both client and counselor. Counseling must be rooted in the general behavioral sciences. The counselor must understand fundamental aspects of human behavior, such as motivation, emotion, perception, thinking, learning, and the developmental process.

The job of the counselor is the application of behavioral knowledge. It is clear that counseling is an applied field. A counselor's primary purpose is to apply established principles of behavior to achieve behavioral change. Understanding theory is needed to account for the manner in which undesirable behaviors develop and for the procedures that can change them. Without a systematic viewpoint, counselors may be inefficient and, occasionally, haphazard in assisting their pupils toward behavior change. Theory is functional. Every counselor behavior is made on the grounds of some expectations, in terms of some frame of reference. Counselors need an adequate set of propositions on which to base their efforts for change. Since many of the behaviors they seek to change may not be directly observable during the counseling interview, the propositions of the counselor must rest on theories developed from study of much wider ranges of behavior.[3]

Ford and Urban propose a hierarchy of theory that is represented in Figure 3.[4] The base for the practice of counseling must ultimately depend on general theories of behavior, i.e., personality theory, perception, motivation, emotion, and learning. More specifically, counseling practice depends on theories of behavioral change, such as learning, of which counseling theory is a particular case. An increasing degree of specificity includes the

Figure 3.
Representation of Relationships Among Theories

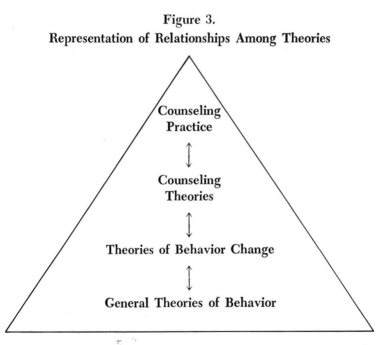

Counseling
Practice

↕

Counseling
Theories

↕

Theories of Behavior Change

↕

General Theories of Behavior

---

[3] Donald Ford and Hugh Urban, *Systems of Psychotherapy* (New York: John Wiley and Sons, Inc., ©1963), pp.1–13.
[4] *Ibid.,* p. 10.

theory of counseling which leads to the application of techniques of counseling. Counseling technique then is dependent upon the counseling approach derived from the theory of behavioral change, which is based on the broad general theories of behavior.

The general theories of behavior will be learned through child development and educational psychology courses. A theory of behavior change as well as theories and techniques of counseling should be covered in the process of counselor education. There are several counseling theories; however, this text emphasizes a behavioral or learning theory approach. Most counselors state that counseling is a learning process. Learning and counseling are both concerned with changes in behavior.[5] It would seem appropriate for persons working in a school setting to believe in and be willing to practice principles of learning theory in order to change client behavior. The remainder of this chapter will cover how children learn behaviors, some general principles of learning, behavior modification, and counseling techniques leading to behavior modification.

Learning and Behavior

Most behavior is learned. It is learned by the individual through his interaction with his environment. Each person interacts or reacts to an environment that is meaningful to him. The environment is meaningful as it relates to the person, and it is differentiated from the rest of the world. A person's meaningful environment enlarges as he grows older. At first only the mother is important, later the number of significant others enlarges. Behavior changes with experiences.

[5] Julian Rotter, *Social Learning and Clinical Psychology* (Englewood Cliffs, N.J.: Prentice-Hall, Inc., 1954), p. 335.

Individual environmental experiences will influence one another. A new behavior is partially a function of previous learning. However, old learning is changed by new experiences. We cannot expect to state the cause of behavior by knowing a past experience. We must take into account the previous experience and the present conditions. We should talk about describing the relevant variables at the time a behavior occurs as well as the previous behavior. In order to understand a child's behavior, we must take into account the learned habits, present stimuli, and the reinforcements of the behavior by the significant others. We need to look for a chain, rather than single events.

Behavior is goal-directed. The direction of the behavior is inferred from the effect of rewarding conditions. The motivational principle seems to be that of need satisfaction. A reward or reinforcement is any action or condition that affects behavior toward a goal. Positive reinforcements would facilitate behavior directed toward a goal that a negative reinforcement would inhibit. A child responds with those behaviors that he has learned will lead to the greatest satisfaction in a given situation.

Most needs of a person are learned. Early goals or need satisfactions arise through association with the reinforcement of physiological movements. Later goals or needs arise as a means of satisfying earlier learned goals. Behavior is goal directed and new goals derive importance from their association with earlier goals. Gradually a set of differentiated needs develops in each child, varying from specific to general. The more specific the category of the need, the greater the possibility for predicting and understanding behavior. This behavior is called need potential, meaning its potential strength—the likelihood that the behavior will be used in given situations.

Early acquired goals appear as a result of satisfaction or frustration, generally controlled by other people. Thus, the development of a child's behavior pattern is primarily concerned with his relationship to other people. Hence, the concept of social learning.[6]

Bandura,[7] Krumboltz[8] and Krasner[9] maintain that the process of learning is shortened because a large part of behavior is learned through imitation. This requires the introduction of models for imitation as a vital aspect of social learning. According to this concept behavior is learned because a model, having the power to mediate rewards for the individual, exhibits behavior which then becomes paired with positive reinforcement. Such behavior is learned through imitation.

Although behavior is directed toward certain goals, the individual has some controls. He is not a robot. A person frequently behaves in accordance with anticipated future rewards. Besides the goals or reinforcements, behavior is determined by a person's expectations that reinforcement will occur.[10] The expectation results from previous experience. The child behaves because he expects that unique behavior to lead to satisfaction or a goal which he values. He may know other behaviors that have led to his goal, i.e., getting attention, but at the present time he may have little expectation that they would lead to satisfaction. For example, crying will gain attention and care for an infant, but a child in school using the same technique may find himself rejected by his peers.

Another general component of understanding behavior is the value (need value) attached to the goal, e.g., the degree to

<hr/>

[6] *Ibid.*, pp. 82–101.

[7] Albert Bandura and Richard Walters, *Social Learning and Personality Development* (New York: Holt, Rinehart, and Winston, Inc., 1963), pp. 47–108.

[8] John Krumboltz, editor *Revolution in Counseling* (Boston: Houghton Mifflin Company, 1966), pp. 14, 15.

[9] Leonard Krasner, "The Therapist as a Social Reinforcement Machine," in Hans Strupp and Lester Luborsky, editors *Research in Psychotherapy* (Washington, D. C.: American Psychological Association, Inc., 1962), pp. 61–94.

[10] Rotter, *op. cit.*, p. 107.

which the child prefers one satisfaction to another.[11] Given an opportunity to obtain two satisfactions, a child might prefer or value doing something for which others will like him (affection need) while another child might prefer doing something that will control the action of others (dominance need).

Learning Maladaptive Behaviors

A child may place high value on a goal, such as achievement in school, but at the same time have low expectations of reaching that goal. He may have learned to anticipate failure or punishment, when attempting to achieve his desires. When this occurs, the child frequently learns pain-avoiding behavior. Occasionally he tries to obtain satisfaction by daydreaming or other behaviors which represent to him, though no one else, a way of obtaining satisfaction. Thus, avoidance methods are learned maladaptive behaviors. Maladaptive behavior is not a disease or disorder but an attempt to avoid certain punishments.

With reinforcement, a behavior pattern may occur repeatedly, even if it is maladaptive. Maladaptive behaviors, for example, may be understood through the application of learning principles. Such behaviors may be seen as the result of inappropriate generalization of responses to stimulus situations, perhaps caused by inattention to appropriate aspects of the situation. In some cases the behaviors may be understood in terms of the limitations of an individual's behavior potentialities. In either case, inappropriate responses result. For example, a maladaptive response resulting from attention to the wrong cues, occurs when habits, previously adaptive, are maintained after the conditions no longer warrant the response. Thus, the child coming from a family in which sibling rivalry is encouraged by the parents (albeit unwittingly) may not find it difficult to generalize these behaviors to the school situation where he is among his peers. Maladaptive

---

[11] *Ibid.*, pp. 107–108.

responses resulting from the limitation of behavior potentialities occur when alternative responses are prevented. This introversion and attention to a social or antisocial behavior may result from the aversive treatment of a child who possesses socially unacceptable characteristics. The rejection of small or late maturing boys by members of the opposite sex may result in behavior which is characterized by aggressiveness or withdrawal. It is important to note that a learned pattern of behavior may be maladaptive, although it still does have direction. The purpose of counseling is to help the child replace the maladaptive behavior with a new learned behavior.

Learning and Counseling

A behavior that has been learned can be changed by replacing that behavior with a new learned behavior. This is different from forgetting. A pupil may learn a mathematics theorem incorrectly. His teacher can point out that he has mislearned, then help the student relearn correctly. If asked to recite the incorrect theorem, he can still do it. Forgetting has not taken place, new learning has replaced it.

In counseling, a pupil should: (a) learn to evaluate himself and his opportunities, (b) learn to make realistic choices, (c) learn to accept responsibility for his choices, and (d) learn to initiate action in accordance with his decisions. This implies that the pupil must replace old behavior or knowledge and skills with new behavior.

It appears that most learning theories agree that there are four basic elements involved in the process: drive, stimulus or cue, response, and reinforcement or reward.[12] Let us examine each

[12] John Dollard and Neal Miller, *Personality and Psychotherapy* (New York: McGraw-Hill Book Company, Inc., 1950), pp. 25–47.

of these in terms of their meaning for the learning process and the counseling relationship.

Drive

A drive is a strong stimuli that impels a person to act. It is both motivation and energy. It urges him to respond. Some drives such as hunger or thirst are primary or innate drives. For this discussion, secondary or learned drives are more critical. "These learned drives are acquired on the basis of the primary drives, represent elaborations of them, and serve as a facade behind which the functions of the underlying innate drives are hidden."[13] Many extremely important drives, such as desire for things, fear, or anxiety are learned.

It is the desire to learn which motivates a child in the classroom. It is the desire to change a behavior, feeling, or situation that may bring a child to the counselor.

Cue

The second factor in learning is the stimulus or cue. When the child is impelled by the drive, "cues determine when he will respond, where he will respond, and which response he will make."[14]

The stimulus may vary in two respects, one in strength and the other in kind. Variations in strength of a stimulus can serve to elicit different responses. For example, the use of words can have different strength. You can say "no?" meaning "Is that so?" or "no" meaning "that's not correct," or "no!" to mean absolutely not. It is the same cue, but it varies in strength, perhaps in quality, too. The point is that quick analysis of a cue might lead one to believe that the same stimuli had been given, but more careful examination shows a variation in the cue. Stimulus vari-

---

[13] *Ibid.*, pp. 31, 32.
[14] *Ibid.*, p. 33.

ation in kind is self-revealing. A cue of "yes" is certainly anti-thetical to a cue of "no."

It is important to recognize that a cue must be discernible to the child, before he can respond to it. Pupils who fail to discern a cue can be classified by two behavior patterns: (a) those who act as though they had not received the cue, and (b) those who apparently received the cue but whose response is not acceptable to themselves or to others.

In the first situation, a pupil may say, "I thought I was doing all right. The teacher never said anything to me. And then all of a sudden I got an 'F.'" Some pupils are able to sense when their work is satisfactory or not and others apparently are not able to judge the teacher's reactions. All of them have approximately the same kind of cues available to them to which they could respond. The needs of some pupils help in learning to see cues of apparent dissatisfaction on the part of the teachers with their present behavior.

In the second situation, a pupil may perceive the cues, but his response is not acceptable to himself or to others. For example, the cue "examination" might elicit the response of great anxiety leading to random studying. The pupil needs to learn a new way of behavior. He needs to associate the cue "examination" with less anxiety and with systematic study habits.

Response

Cues lead to responses. One must keep in mind that a child can respond only in ways which are in his repertoire of responses. Hence, his developmental level will in part determine what responses he can make. Reward or reinforcement can only occur after the pupil has made a response. Then the counselor must arrange the situation so that the pupil can make the first correct response, thus being rewarded. What ways do people have for acquiring the first correct response?

There are various ways in which a child can acquire the first correct response to a cue.[15] One way of making the correct response is through trial and error. A drive elicits a response. If one response is not rewarded, it will be extinguished and another response will appear. If this happens to be a desired response, it can be rewarded and the possibility for habit formation is established. Trial and error unfortunately has the connotation of being purely random activity. It gives the impression that one tries everything under the sun until something clicks. Ordinarily, one does not respond randomly. Instead, the responses we try are influenced partially by our developmental level and partially by our previous experience. One expects the first response to be rewarded.

A person can learn to eliminate unnecessary trial response by learning to respond to verbal cues. A child learns the meaning of "hot" when he comes into contact with a hot object; because he has been burned, he does not touch that object. Once he learns that the word "hot" means an unpleasant feeling, it is possible to teach him that other objects are hot without having him touch them. With a more mature child, a counselor can open new response patterns to verbal cues. This will save the pupil trials and lead to more efficient learning.

Another way a child learns a first response to a cue is through imitation. Much learning is imitation. It is a good teaching device, and counselors can make strategic use of it. By using tape recordings, films, or directed reading and observation, the counselor can assist pupils in seeing others making effective responses in situations similar to their own. Thus, they may learn to respond in a self-satisfying manner.

Conditioning is another way in which the child learns to make the first correct response to a cue. The basic principle of conditioning is that a response that is not itself reinforced must be associated with one that is, if it is to be rewarded. Counselors

---

[15] *Ibid.,* pp. 37–39.

can use conditioning in the counseling relationship. When a student comes into the interview, he may be reticent to talk about himself, but responds to the stimulus of the interview situation by chatting socially. The counselor conditions him to engage in such an activity by rewarding talking, even though it is not about himself. As he makes comments about himself, the counselor ceases to reward peripheral chatting in areas where the client feels safe. The fact that he is in a counseling relationship would cue the alternate response of exploring his feelings and attitudes.

A final way in which a student can learn to make the first correct response is through insight or reasoning. All persons are able to take certain facts, think about them, and come to a conclusion. Although little is known about the process, reasoning will produce responses, and if these are reinforced, they are maintained. Counselors have placed great confidence in the process of insight or reasoning. Most counselors are convinced that if the pupil has all the facts, through the process of reasoning, he can learn to make a response which will be rewarded.

Reinforcement

A fourth factor in the learning process is reinforcement or reward. Whenever a drive has been reduced by a response, the response is said to be reinforced. A reinforcement is any event that strengthens the tendency for a response to be repeated. Mere repetition does not always strengthen the tendency for a response to occur. To be reinforcing, a response must reduce the drive. Pupils can be subjected to a large number of experiences, and, because they are not drive-reducing, they apparently have little effect on the pupil. That may be one reason pupils can sit in class day after day and not learn the presented material.

There are learned reinforcements, e.g., money, as well as innate reinforcements. Learned rewards function the same as innate reinforcements: that is by reducing a specific drive. It is seeking the secondary reward that probably brings a pupil to the counselor's office. He must receive some satisfaction if he is to continue to return for guidance. People do not keep making the same response unless it is drive-reducing and they are rewarded.

Reinforcement may operate in an awareness situation, such as getting a drink of water when thirsty. Reinforcement may also operate directly without the person's awareness. Numerous studies have shown that client use of certain words, i.e., self-referent or plural nouns could be increased by reinforcing those words with positive words, such as "mmm hmm." The effective counselor will be aware of the reinforcements he gives to his clients, rather than simply reinforcing indiscriminately. The counselor must use these principles of learning if he is to help pupils effect behavior modification.

Behavior Modification

Of primary importance in counseling is the definition of the problem or problems with which the child is concerned, as well as the recognition of the behavior which must be changed or implemented for the solution of the problem. Our concern with changing behavior and the methods of their implementation should not obscure the importance of the initial definition of the problem in the counseling process. At this point, the counselor must use his skills in helping the child to understand the implications of his behavior and decide which behaviors must be changed. Without this understanding and agreement between child and counselor, the solution of the child's problem will be long and difficult at best, or, more than likely, impossible. The child must then be aware of the need for behavioral change and be willing to work at trying to effect such change. Furthermore, he must have confidence that he is able to change and that his counselor can help him do so.

When the modification of behavior through the application of learning principles is attempted, a variety of methods may be used. The objectives of such methods generally are: (a) to inhibit responses already acquired, (b) to arouse responses which are incompatible with anxiety-producing or fear-reactions, and (c) to substitute more adequate responses for maladaptive behavior. It has been pointed out that maladaptive behavior is maintained by the individual because of its reinforcing properties. Not only may the child have utilized the behavior to avoid some previously expected punishment, but also to obtain satisfaction. Furthermore, the behavior may have some secondary reinforcing values for the child, such as increased attention or sympathy. Consequently, the behavior may have a history of reinforcement.

Although a counselor emphasizes the development of adequate responses, it is at times necessary to concentrate on the extinction of certain behaviors. In some cases, extinction may be accomplished by the withdrawal of the reinforcer. In turn this lowers the child's expectancy that the behavior will lead to gratification. Thus in a counseling session, the consequences of the behavior in question may be emphasized in the discussion. The counselor may show the child how a behavior, rather than maximizing his satisfaction, has prevented the optimal development of all his behavior potentials. In effect the counselor has changed the reinforcement value of the behavior. Another direct way of extinguishing maladaptive behavior may be found in the withdrawal of the anticipated reward. For example, failure on the part of the counselor to reward a child with sympathy, support, or attention reduces the secondary reinforcing properties of the behavior. Thus the expectancies for reward are diminished. This may also be accomplished through methods of verbal analysis, whereby the inappropriateness of maladaptive behavior is brought out by the counselor.

The counselor's attempt to elicit anti-fear or anxiety responses from a child is known as counterconditioning. An anticipated sense of gratification resulting from previously avoided behavior may be imparted to the child by discussion with the counselor. At such times the counselor may point out why the behavior was formerly reinforced negatively and that such reinforcement will probably not occur in the future. The counselor is interested in helping the child to abstract from his experience and also to develop his understanding of the relationships between behaviors. Reinforcement of such behaviors results in the child's increasing ability to solve his own problems. For example, the youngster who cannot exert himself in class because he is prevented from doing so at home by brothers and sisters may be encouraged to express himself before the class.

The counselor has many opportunities to make use of direct reinforcement leading to an increase in client behavior potentials. A counselor encourages problem-solving behavior by verbally rewarding the child's attempts to deal frankly with his problems. Often, however, specific adaptive behaviors do not occur during the counseling situation, and the child may not be able to discover the behaviors for himself. In such cases, the counselor may directly suggest some alternate behaviors. This will increase the child's expectation that the adoption of the alternative will yield gratification. New responses may be introduced into an individual's behavioral repertoire in a relatively short period of time through the concurrent use of models with positive verbal reinforcement. After listening to taped interviews, observing, or conversing with models there is a likelihood that the constructive behaviors under discussion will increase. Evidence indicates that the child's level of attention to the model's responses must be considered as a factor affecting the amount and role of learning that takes place. The level of emotional arousal appears to be another factor. Presumably, in most cases, the child observing the model is highly motivated and emotionally involved, as a result of the degree of commitment developed in the initial stages of counseling.

Inasmuch as the social learning theorist believes that the behavior of the child is determined by the reinforcement he receives, it is important to the counselor that the child's adaptive behavior be reinforced in his environment. It is paramount, therefore, that guidance extend beyond the counseling session. The counselor would like to insure the reward of the desirable behavior. To promote the occurrence of such behavior, changes in curriculum may have to be considered. Alerting the child's teachers to the situation and enlisting their help in reinforcing specific behaviors is essential. In addition, it may be necessary for the counselor to contact the child's family and alert them to the significance of certain adaptive and maladaptive behaviors which occur in parental relationships. Thus the child's total environment may be manipulated to provide more opportunities for the occurrence of adaptive behavior with its ensuing rewards. The important point is that the counselor has a responsibility which extends beyond the counseling session itself. In addition to helping the child to understand himself and his problems, the counselor must implement the social learning process.

Techniques of Counseling

Previous sections of this chapter have presented a theoretical overview of how children learn behaviors, some principles of learning, and behavior modification. An understanding of these principles will be the basis for the development of a counselor's techniques. Some general methods in counseling which are derived from these principles will be discussed. However, a counselor will need additional coursework on counseling theory and process, as well as a supervised practicum to develop his own counseling skills.

Conditions for Producing Behavior Change

Although not necessarily a technique of counseling, many writers in the field believe the counseling relationship is the most important aspect of the process of behavior change. Those factors which facilitate the development and maintenance of an effective relationship include the counselor's attitudes, values, and his behavior with each pupil.

Rogers is specific in describing the necessary conditions for behavior change.[16] He states specific attitudes which he believes are essential for the development of a counseling relationship. Although these conditions are most closely identified with client-centered theory, they are prevalent in all counseling, and Truax[17] has illustrated their use and effectiveness in the learning theory position. Three specific conditions which are imperative in developing a counseling relationship are, the counselor's positive regard, empathy, and genuineness.

POSITIVE REGARD. A counselor must experience a warm, positive, acceptant attitude toward the pupil. This means the counselor praises the pupil in a non-possessive way, as a person capable of changing. These are neither paternalistic, sentimental, nor superficial feelings. He respects the child as a separate person. This acceptance leads to a relationship of warmth and safety, the feeling of acceptance seemingly being an important condition in a "helping" relationship.

EMPATHY. A second important condition is the counselor's empathic understanding of the pupil. The relationship is signifi-

[16] Carl Rogers, "The Interpersonal Relationship: The Core of Guidance," *Harvard Educational Review,* 32, 416–429 (1962).
[17] Charles Truax, "Some Implications of Behavior Therapy for Psychotherapy," *Journal of Counseling Psychology,* 13, 160–170 (1966).

cant to the extent the counselor feels a continuing desire to understand the pupil's feelings and communications. The acceptance is not significant until it involves understanding. It is imperative that the counselor communicates these attitudes to the pupil.

GENUINENESS.   A counselor needs to be genuine or congruent in the counseling relationship. This means the counselor does not put on a role, a facade, or a pretense. It is necessary for a counselor to be aware of his feelings, rather than presenting an outward facade of one attitude while actually holding another. Being genuine also involves the willingness to express, in words and behavior, the various feelings and attitudes which exist in him.

Truax[18] has pointed out that research derived from the molar approach of conversation, psychotherapy, and counseling has accumulated overwhelming evidence suggesting that counselors who provide relatively high levels of accurate empathic, understanding, nonpossessive warmth, and genuineness causally induce greater self-exploration during the counseling process and also produce constructive behavioral and personality change in people. Further evidence suggests that these same conditions lead to similar consequences in studies of parental effects upon children, as well as teacher effects upon learning and personality development in pupils.

There is a possibility that counselors who offer high conditions are more effective ". . . because they are more potent positive reinforcers, and because they elicit a high degree of positive affect in the client (which increases the level of the client's positive self-reinforcement, decreases anxiety, and increases the level of positive affect and positive reinforcement from others)."[19]

Although we talk about high conditions, these do not remain

[18] *Ibid.*
[19] *Ibid.*

constant. However, some counselors would average higher than others. A counselor may respond differentially to various pupil behaviors, i.e., more accepting and empathic to some behaviors and less to others. Hence, these conditions are reinforcing, rewarding, or somehow encouraging. The pupil behaviors, hopefully the more adaptive ones, that are followed by high levels of these conditions will increase during the course of counseling. This in fact is borne out even in Rogers' counseling.[20]

It has been proposed that these conditions have direct and indirect effects upon pupil change in four ways: They reinforce positive aspects of the pupil's self-concept, thus modifying his existing self-concept and leading to changes in his own self-reinforcement. Second, they reinforce self-exploratory behavior, which elicits self-concepts and anxiety laden material which can then be potentially modified. Third, these conditions serve to extinguish anxiety responses associated with specific cues, including those elicited by the pupil, counselor, and the situation. The fourth effect these conditions serve is to reinforce human relating and extinguish avoidance learning associated with human interaction.

Structuring

Structuring is a discussion of the purposes and goals of counseling, as well as the roles and responsibilities of the counselor and child. The purpose of structuring is to give the pupil a clear picture of what is to take place, rather than having him in an ambiguous situation which is to say learning by chance. The counselor points out that in many cases the pupil must discuss his attitudes and feelings, if he is to understand his problem and find alternate behavior.

The pupil should also be made aware of the limitations of

---

[20] Charles Truax, "Reinforcement and Nonreinforcement in Rogerian Psychotherapy," *Journal of Abnormal Psychotherapy,* **71,** 1–9 (1966).

counseling. The objective is not psychotherapy, but rather helping him learn to handle present and future problems.

With children, early structuring will be reassuring and provide cues as to appropriate behavior. However, structuring will need to be a continuing part of counseling, in order to keep the pupil aware of why he is doing what he is doing and what the ultimate purpose of counseling is.

Verbal Reinforcement

Although there are many behaviors available to the counselor, the techniques he uses are primarily verbal. Regardless of their orientation, all counselors use verbal reinforcement techniques. Even Rogers uses differential reinforcement to alter the behavior of his clients.[21] Although the counselor attempts to alter the pupil's behavior, he does not usually tell a pupil what he should do.

The content of the conversation is controlled through the use of words designed to elicit pupil comments, to reward their comments, or to withdraw reinforcement. Such techniques are influenced by the types of reinforcement (positive or negative), and the schedules of reinforcement.

The cues afforded by the counselor range from head nodding with the voicing of "mmm-hmm" or "good," to verbal encouragement, agreement, reassurance, and approval (positive reinforcement), or looking away, ignoring the comments, or other negative reinforcements. The withdrawal of reinforcement is characterized by techniques such as the maintenance of silences; however this technique is useful only when there is a pupil need for such reinforcement. The effectiveness of stimuli as reinforcers depends to a great extent on the subjective meaning of the stimulus to the pupil. This, in turn, depends upon the pupil's past experience, the relationship between the counselor and pupil and other

[21] *Ibid.*

situational variables, such as the atmosphere in which the influence process occurs, the sensory deprivation of the counselee, and the set and ambiguity of the situation.

If particular behaviors are to be perpetuated by the pupil, it is necessary that he have the ability to recognize behaviors as appropriate or inappropriate, and that the behaviors themselves be recognized as positively or negatively reinforcing. The counselor acts as positive and/or negative reinforcer and, therefore, affects the results of counseling. He is in a position to help the pupil increase or decrease the level of positive self-reinforcement or act as an aversive reinforcer with the result that the pupil's level of negative self-reinforcement is increased. The importance of the relationship variables, therefore, must not be overlooked.

A pupil may come to the counselor because he is having difficulty in school. By talking with the child, this vague problem may become clearly stated as a study skill problem. For example, the most recent event of failing a spelling test could be what brought the pupil to the counselor.

A counselor should listen carefully for pupil responses which would indicate plans to study. A counselor would verbally reinforce indications that the pupil had or was planning some change in his study habits, such as "I'm going to study my spelling words." Although the comment cannot be termed reinforcing until it actually strengthens the frequency of the behavior, from past experience it can be assumed that such counselor comments as, "excellent idea" or "yes, that's good" would be positively reinforcing. Nonverbal communication such as smiling and head nodding are also used. When the pupil makes irrelevant comments or brings in an irrelevant topic, the counselor should ignore it and make a statement which will lead them back on the subject.

The counselor may use cue questions such as "How do you plan to study your spelling?" to increase planning responses. The counselor may encourage the pupil to carry out a study plan which has built-in reinforcers. He may suggest that the pupil study the spelling words for ten minutes and then take a break to do something he enjoys, like listening to a record—then study for another ten minutes before another break.

At the conclusion of the interview the counselor may ask the pupil to summarize the specific steps he is going to take in learning study skills. Each summary statement would be verbally reinforced, and the counselor would also add steps omitted by the pupil. The counselor and pupil could make a subcontract or agreement that the student would put the procedure into practice during the week. The next session would start with a report of what had been done.

Model-Reinforcement

Model reinforcement counseling involves the presentation of a social model who demonstrates the desired behavior. Previous research has shown the effectiveness of models in promoting certain types of learning.[22] The rate, magnitude, and subsequent performance of learned responses from the models is influenced by reinforcement. If a model is being used to increase the probability that certain types of behavior will occur, it is important that the pupil be able to identify with the model. However, oral or visual models are as useful as physical models. Through modeling, the pupil can increase the congruency existing between the reinforcement provided by the counselor and reinforcement provided by himself.

Much of the counseling interview would be similar to a verbal interview. The pupil and counselor would discuss the situation and identify the behaviors the pupil desires. If, as in the previous example, he has had difficulty with study skills, the counselor

---

[22] John Krumboltz and Carl Thoresen, "The Effect of Behavioral Counseling in Group and Individual Settings on Information-Seeking Behavior," *Journal of Counseling Psychology,* **11,** 324–333 (1964); see also Albert Bandura and Richard Walters, *op. cit.,* pp. 47–108.

may introduce a tape recording of another pupil with the same problem. In that interview the model pupil would talk about possible ways of improving his study skills. The model counselor would reinforce such comments and suggest additional study techniques. After listening to the tape, the counselor may inquire about the pupil's ideas for improving his study skills. Frequently the pupil will discuss plans he has heard from the model and apply them to himself. The counselor would reinforce any comment concerning change in study behavior. At the termination of the interview the pupil should summarize the steps he plans to carry out until the next interview.

In the next meeting he should discuss what he has done. The counselor again would reinforce the study behavior. The counselor may or may not play additional tapes to illustrate other aspects of study skills.

Play Media

An opportunity for expression is necessary for the young child and may be used advantageously with older children. Instead of feeling uncomfortable in a situation, a child can communicate through play. Many times just having something to manipulate or handle while talking with the counselor will make the child more comfortable.

Play media is useful because of the difficulty a child may have in competently expressing himself verbally. Play aids the child in developing more elaborate and effective techniques for controlling his environment and seems to present him with the opportunity to interact with an adult who takes a different attitude toward him.[23]

By manipulating toys a child can more adequately express how he feels about himself, significant people, and crucial events

[23] Lawrence Brammer and Everett Shostrom, *Therapeutic Psychology* (Englewood Cliffs, N.J.: Prentice-Hall, Inc., 1960), pp. 336–340.

in his life. Although adults are able to ventilate feelings through verbalization, play can provide similar values for many children. An adult may "talk through" a problem of coping with a situation that confronts him; similarly, the child may use toys to gain insight into ways of coping with aspects of his environment.[24]

The purpose of play media, then, provides an opportunity where the child plays or acts out certain situations and behaviors to help himself, his teachers, and counselor to more readily understand the child's situation, his attitudes, emotions, and behaviors.

A P P R O A C H E S. There are two rather distinct approaches to using play media.[25] Both of these approaches are based on the fact that play is a child's natural medium of self expression. These approaches allow the child to act or play out his feelings or problems just as an adult might describe his problems with words. Both approaches can be an integral part of the educational program.

In one approach, free or nondirective, the counselor or teacher would leave the responsibility and direction of the action to the child. In elementary school, considerable time needs to be scheduled for free play. This is time when the children are allowed to use toys or play with their friends and take on any role they wish to. This provides an excellent opportunity for the teacher and counselor to observe the pupil in a relatively unrestricted environment. One can observe the children acting out their whole concept of family relationships and interactions. The children readily begin to see the differing roles of the father and the mother in families. One is able to see, by the children's actions, those who are leaders, who are shy, who are aggressive, and who seemingly are completely withdrawn; this does not exclude the socially well-adjusted child.

---

[24] Richard Nelson, "Physical Facilities for Elementary School Counseling," *Personnel and Guidance Journal,* **45,** 552–556 (1967).
[25] Lawrence Brammer and Everett Shostrom, *op. cit.,* pp. 336–340.

There is time devoted to imitating and portraying desirable behavior, with or without subsequent discussion. Literature is used as a background, and pupils role play the different story book characters they have read about. Through careful observations of these personality traits the counselor and teacher can plan a program of play and decide how to approach desirable behavior development with the pupils.

In the second approach, controlled or directive, the counselor or teacher may assume complete authority and responsibility for guiding and interpreting the action. Children can be taught to look at human relations through such procedures as role-playing, unfinished stories, simplified interviews, observation techniques, and group projects.

Role playing is one example of play media. It may be used to teach social behavior. Role playing affords an opportunity for developing understanding of interpersonal relationships in every day contacts. It can develop spontaneity, encourage self-expression, and promote empathy. During role playing, the teacher or counselor should stay in the background, thus permitting the drama to be centered on the feelings and attitudes of the children. The feeling of the children should be discussed after the acting is over. This reflective thinking enhances understanding of the feelings of others. After a discussion, the gleaned understanding that was demonstrated is reinforced by acting out the situation again.

At times a child may be called upon to play a role, even though he has not volunteered. Certain shy, inhibited children may not volunteer, because they do not feel they could do the role well. They need praise and encouragement from the teacher and counselor to help them gain a better self-concept. The effectiveness of role playing is directly related to participation whether this is actively portraying a role or discussing the behavior presented.

It takes a skillful counselor with special training to conduct play therapy. Most counselor education programs do not have special training to develop these skills. However, play media may be used for observation and understanding of children.

Summary

Counseling with elementary school children is one of the major roles of the counselor. He will help the pupil learn about himself and his environment. The pupil can then learn appropriate behaviors for handling the roles and relationships that are required at later stages of his development.

The counselor's techniques will be developed from a counseling theory that is derived from a theory of behavior change, all of which is based upon general theories of behavior. This chapter has briefly covered how children learn behaviors, some principles of learning, behavior modification, and counseling techniques to modify behavior. A counselor will want to supplement this introduction with additional reading and courses in counseling theory and process.

SELECTED REFERENCES

Albert Bandura and Richard Walters, *Social Learning and Personality Development* (New York: Holt, Rinehart and Winston, Inc., 1963).

John Krumboltz (Ed.), *Revolution in Counseling: Implications of Behavioral Science* (Boston: Houghton Mifflin Company, 1966).

Julian Rotter, *Social Learning and Clinical Psychology* (Englewood Cliffs, N.J.: Prentice-Hall, Inc., 1954).

THE COUNSELOR
AS A CONSULTANT

It has been noted that parent or teacher attitude or behavior change may be considerably more effective in changing a child's behavior than individual counseling. Rotter[1] explains that any realistic discussion of counseling must be concerned, not only with the technique of the face-to-face situation, but also with the practical aspects of manipulating, changing, or controlling the child's environment.

It is not always necessary for the counselor to weaken or ex-

[1] Julian Rotter, *Social Learning and Clinical Psychology* (Englewood Cliffs, N.J.: Prentice-Hall, Inc., 1954), pp. 401–433.

tinguish the child's inappropriate responses to the environment. These behavioral repertoires need to be replaced with more adequate responses, which is to say providing reinforcement in a meaningful environment. The counselor helps change the environment. Environmental change can be induced through consultation with parents and teachers of elementary school children.

Consultation is based on the concept that the child's behavior is determined by reinforcement and, therefore, that a change in his social environment, i.e., people who are reinforcing his behavior, leads to change in the child's behavior. Receiving satisfaction directly from his behavior is sufficient to build up well-adjusted behavior potentials for the child without the counselor having to weaken his earlier learned behavior by verbal explanations or other one-to-one experiences.

As problems of elementary school children frequently originate within the family or the school, the counselor's understanding of the environmental press upon the pupil is important. Individual counseling may only be partially effective unless teacher or parent attitude or behavior change is effected. The counselor goes beyond individual counseling, by trying to improve the child's interaction with his significant others. It is also necessary to provide this assistance for all children rather than just those experiencing problems. Because of his dependency, a child will be restricted from changing his environment. His behavior is limited by the restrictions placed upon him by adults. The counselor works intensively with parents and teachers to change the child's environment. Contact with significant adults is aimed at changing their behavior and thus the child's.[2]

Evidence attesting to the necessity of consultation as a major function of the elementary school counselor is to be found in professional journals, convention speeches, and IRCOPPS re-

---

[2] Don Dinkmeyer, "Developmental Counseling in the Elementary School," *Personnel and Guidance Journal,* **45,** 262–266 (1966).

ports. A study of elementary school counselors in California showed that 17 per cent of their time was spent with teachers, 10 per cent with administrators, and 12 per cent with parents. Both counselors and their administrators ranked teacher consultation and parent consultation second and third behind counseling, as the most important functions of the counselor.[3] In New York State the elementary school counselors reported 27 per cent of their time spent in consultation with teachers and 18 per cent with parents. Ninety per cent of the counselors in the study held conferences with staff members, and 86 per cent held conferences with parents.[4]

Learning is a process involving the child with many helping persons who sometimes facilitate, sometimes inhibit, but who rarely have no influence on the child's behavior. Hence, we must recognize the impact of different persons. Many people share responsibility for child guidance. The counselor keeps others aware of their contributions and serves as a consultant to them in implementing their roles.

Consulting with Parents

Why Work Together?

The counselor believes that it is his duty to help create a better understanding between the school and the home. This can be done by interpreting the school's program, philosophy, and services to the parents. The counselor assumes the role of school interpreter—explaining how the school views the child, his ad-

[3] William McCreary and Gerald Miller, "Elementary School Counselors in California," *Personnel and Guidance Journal*, 44, 494–498 (1966).
[4] *Status of Elementary School Guidance Pilot Projects in New York State* (Albany: The State Education Department Bureau of Guidance, 1966) pp. 4–14.

justment and progress. In this way, the counselor learns how parents have already interpreted the school's program.

The parents sustain an intense and concerted interest for the child. Because the child belongs to the parents, they will be interested and want the best for their child. While a teacher divides her attention, parents center their whole being on the child's development.[5]

In consultation, parents share their ideas and knowledge with the school. They contribute data regarding the child, helping the school to work with him by providing information bearing on the child's development. The parents and counselor explore together the various events in the child's behavioral past and present, while the counselor identifies significant data in helping parents to understand their child more objectively. Information from the parents and the school is pieced into a meaningful pattern, resulting in more meaningful assistance for the child.

The counselor learns a great deal about a child's problems by understanding his home history, background, and environment. The home is the major criterion in determining a child's socio-economic status, temperament, habits, interests, physical and social development, and parents' attitudes. How the child is treated by his parents gives the counselor and teacher an understanding of the way in which a child expresses his needs in school.

Sometimes it is necessary for counselors to reeducate parents in recognizing and accepting the responsibilities of helping their child. It may be necessary to assist parents in modifying attitudes and goals and helping the children accept more reasonable goals. The counselor may serve as a mediator in the process of direct parent-child or parent-school encounters.

A parent usually is very interested in his child's progress and development in school. The picture the child brings home and

---

[5] Marion Heisey, "A Differential Approach to Elementary Guidance," *Elementary School Guidance and Counseling,* **1,** 18–21 (1966).

the picture the school presents are often quite different. Parents want to know, and they have a right to know, what the school is doing for their children. Parents want to know ways children are being taught, their subjects, and they also want to see some of their children's work. Educational change between the generations of parents and child may arouse a curiosity that is enough to bring some parents to the schoolroom. Methods of reporting pupil progress on a report card are not always enough. Parents want to know not only a grade for a particular subject, but they may desire information concerning their child's social progress. They want to know if their child is working up to his ability or if he is underachieving.

Some parents faced with extreme problems with their children turn to the school for professional help and advice. Often the teacher or counselor cannot solve the problem, but he could suggest an agency or person who might be able to work with the problem.

Parents are the greatest agent of change in the child's environment. However, they may feel and be inadequate in implementing behavior change. Because parents are in the best position of effecting necessary changes in the child's behavior, they could use preventive techniques if they had a capable and reliable resource to assist them.

Parents' Contributions

Grams[6] describes four areas in which parents ready the child for learning and which support, encourage, and sustain him during the process. He believes parents have a major responsibility for supplying a sound emotional base, providing adequate social skills, stimulating special abilities and talents, and transmitting values to the child.

[6] Armin Grams, *Facilitating Learning and Individual Development* (St. Paul: Minnesota Department of Education, 1966), pp. 49–78.

Emotional maladjustment is an important component in the problem of learning disabilities as well as in personal development. Fear, anxiety, anger, jealousy, and even excessive excitability can interfere with the child's situational effectiveness. The parents supply the emotional base for the child through acceptance and security. Without acceptance or security, the child may have a separation anxiety when he goes to school. If there are problems in the home, the child may not be able to concentrate when he is in school. He may not be lazy or disrespectful, but he simply has more important things on his mind than paying attention in school. The child is more likely to behave effectively when his parents communicate their affection to him and help him develop self-sufficiency and independence.

The child's social adjustment is closely related to his emotional adjustment. Social skills of the child are related to those of his parents. Social competence leads to acceptance by others as well as feelings of personal worth and adequacy. The sense of interpersonal competence is learned through experiences of acceptability and accomplishment. The parent's role is paramount, for they are the first persons who accept the child as a person. The manner in which they respond to his attempts to do things independently influence his social competence.

Certainly, social skills are important for success in school. The child who is incapable of socially approved behavior is unlikely to experience the acceptance from the teacher that he would have if he displayed appropriate behavior. Lack of social skills can also handicap the child with his peer group; when seeking friends, he may not be concerned with the desires of the teacher.

In stimulating the child's abilities and special talents, the cooperative efforts of the parents and school can pay big dividends. They work together in the education of the child. For parents to stimulate intellectual and artistic development, they must have an idea of the ability the youngster possesses. However, even more important than a general ability appraisal is an appreciation of each child's particular strengths and weaknesses. Parents should be encouraged to accept each child individually rather than comparing the siblings. Each child should be encouraged to develop his strengths. It is in these areas that parents and child can enjoy the learning process together. Child success can be positive reinforcement for both parents and child. By understanding that all learning builds upon previous learning, parents provide an on-going readiness for learning.

On-going readiness is a result of parents talking, listening, and reading to the child. Parents stimulate intellectual development by taking time to talk with the child. They also must listen, thereby encouraging active verbalization. Through conversation they stimulate the child to think. Reading to the child creates pleasant and secure associations with words and books, having carry-over value into school. The aim of this activity is to instill in the child a desire to learn because learning is self-satisfying as well as bringing with it valued goals.

Primary value training comes from the home. The counselor serves as a resource in assisting the parents to implement their own value teaching. Parents and school personnel communicate values to the child overtly or covertly. Occasionally the values of the family and school are different and cause a conflict for the child. Usually parents are eager for the school to support their values and it may be the counselor's function to assist in clarifying and interpreting both values.

Grams[7] points out three areas of value orientation involving the parents and the school: values toward learning, toward oneself, and toward others. Certainly there are many others that would fall under these major rubrics. The parents' attitudes toward learning, school, and teachers are significant factors in the child's value system. Whether a child approaches school eagerly and seriously, suspiciously or indifferently is largely a function of

[7] *Ibid.*, pp. 72–76.

attitudes he has learned from his parents. A child also learns appropriate values about himself and others from his parents. Feelings of personal worth emerge in response to the parents' acceptance of the child and their reliability in encouraging and commending his behavior. Parents also implement the value of concern for others and emphasize the importance of devotion to others in healthy self-development.

What do Parents Want to Know?

If we accept the belief that parents really do want to work with the school in order to better understand their children, we must determine what parents want to know. Why are they interested in the school? What is it that brings parents and teachers together?

A basic problem for parents is the discrepancy between their level of expectation for the child and his actual school performance. A better understanding is needed of the child's abilities and achievement. Parents and their child's school experiences differ. Courses, materials, methods, and teaching have changed radically, so that many times parents cannot understand what is happening in their child's learning process. They find it difficult to see how or what their child is learning or what good it will do to learn the material.

Parents are concerned with the differences that may exist between home and school values. The members of minority groups may be sensitive to phases of the curriculum, a school organization, or a specific teacher's practice, placing their children in awkward positions. These may be ethnic or religious groups with whom the teacher must exchange information and feelings; closer harmony between school and home is anticipated.

Parents often seek advice on disciplinary problems, particularly techniques for punishing the child rather than explanations of cause of behavior. It is better for the counselor to explore various possibilities with the parents, leaving decisions to the parents.

Some problems of the elementary school children's parents were studied by McConnel.[8] An open-end questionnaire was sent to the parents of first, second, and third graders in one urban city. The classification of 2,844 statements by 745 parents show the major concerns of some elementary school children's parents.

The three most common concerns were personal and classroom behavior, academic progress, and social behavior; these all ranked close in percentage. Parents showed less concern with home-school relations, individual aptitude or ability, and health and physical condition. There were some socio-economic differences. Parents in higher economic classes were more interested in social behavior and academic progress than in personal and classroom behavior. Parents in low socio-economic classes were more interested in personal and classroom behavior and less in social behavior. There was about the same interest in academic progress except in the lowest socio-economic group which placed it first.

Froehlich and Hoyt[9] give five reasons for parents asking questions. First, parents want information about their child's general learning potential. This information is usually recorded in the cumulative record in the form of an I.Q., but this should not be given directly to parents. The use of percentiles or stanines is the easiest way of presenting this information and helping parents understand their child's abilities.

Secondly, schools may discover special talents previously unknown to parents. These talents should be identified for parents, so that they can provide developmental opportunities for the child. These become most important in planning future education and vocation.

Thirdly, parents are concerned with the level of educational

---

[8] Gaither McConnel, "What do Parents Want to Know," *The Elementary School Journal*, 58, 84 (1957).

[9] Clifford Froehlich and Kenneth Hoyt, *Guidance Testing* (Chicago: Science Research Associates, Inc., 1959), p. 307.

development in various subject areas. The report card usually tells parents of individual class subject achievement. This is inadequate, as it is not a complete interpretation of the child's relative level of educational development. Conferences can be used to share standardized test information, potential, and peer relationships.

Fourthly, parents are interested in the status of counselor-teacher-pupil relationships. Usually academic motivation is the basis for discussion in this area, but other phases of these relationships as well as different relationships may enter into the conversation.

Finally, the status of peer relationships is important. Parents know their children as an individual, but the teacher and counselor see him as a group member. What the teacher and counselor know about a child and share with his parents leads to more competent decision-making.

Guidelines for Parent Consultation

Rotter[10] describes general principles illustrating some implications of social learning for consultation with parents. Initially the counselor helps the parents understand the effect of their behavior on their child's behavior. Although it may be that parents cause maladjustive or undesirable behavior, blaming them only stimulates guilt. It is difficult to help parents understand the interrelationship of behaviors, without placing some blame upon them. The counselor assures parents by recognizing their good intentions and desire to help their child. When appropriate, he might assure them that their behavior may have worked with most children, but not with this particular child.

[10] Julian Rotter, *op.* cit., pp. 427–433.

They may need to be assured that errors and difficulties are normal. Focusing on changing the situation is what is needed.

Another principle emphasizes leading, not pushing, the parent. An interpretation, decision, or suggestion is more likely to be accepted, if the parent feels it is his idea, or that he has had a major part in reaching a conclusion. The counselor presents various types of information and helps the parents see the relation between them. He may ask the parents how they feel the child could be approached and then reinforce the parents' suggestions.

Closely related is the principle of dealing with facts that make sense to the parents. A counselor supports the suggestions or recommendations of the parent with information available to them both. The parent appraises the data and reaches a conclusion in light of his own experience. The counselor clarifies the relationship between the parent-reported behavior and the actual behavior of his child.

The fourth principle, implied earlier, suggests that the counselor does not go beyond the parent's potential ability for acceptance. If the counselor leads a parent toward certain conclusions and decisions but meets resistance, it is better to retreat from the issue, rather than lose all cooperation with the family. The counselor can avoid parental rejection, by allowing the possibility for rejection of one idea, as opposed to the whole process. He states his position in terms of probability.

The success of the conference is determined primarily by the counselor and how he behaves with the parents. An atmosphere is desired in which the parents feel free to express themselves. Emotionally-toned words or facial expressions of the parents may communicate their feelings and attitudes. Alternatives can be suggested. The child's schoolwork can be used as a means for informing parents about the child in general. If decisions are made, the parent should feel he had a part in making them. This process is aimed toward increasing the parents' expectancy that a change in their behavior will result in more effective behavior for his child.

Methods of Consultation with Parents

Van Hoose[11] pointed out four basic tenets in the consulting process:

1. Consultation is a collaborative effort at problem solving or prevention.
2. The purpose of the specific consulting relationship should be clarified.
3. Understanding of individual roles and perceptions is a major goal.
4. Consultation should be a learning process for everyone involved.

Conferences

Individual Conferences

There are many types of conferences between the home and school. There is a one-to-one relationship between the counselor and the parent or a group conference involving parents and teachers. Whichever it is, the objectives, preparation, and conduct of the conference are similar.

The individual conference with the parent is the basis of the two-way communication between home and school. It is here that the counselor can discuss with the parent a child's progress, his work habits, his relationship with his classmates, and the kind

[11] William Van Hoose, "The Emerging Role of the Elementary School Counselor," paper read at American Personnel and Guidance Association Convention, Dallas, March 1967.

of help he may need. They may discuss how to stimulate him, how to encourage him, and how to show him the faith the home and school have in him.

The counselor makes a definite plan or design for the conference. This includes both the purpose and goals. Limits are set as to the length of the conference, in order to keep rambling and inefficiency to a minimum. Parents are prepared for the conference. Every conference carries with it the possibility for improving or impairing working relationships. If it is the first conference, parents should know why the conference is being held and what the counselor has to talk about.[12]

It is sometimes very difficult to establish rapport. Only when parents realize what counselors and teachers are trying to do in school and conversely the school personnel realize what parents are trying to do at home, can they effectively work together. Parents may come to school fearing something is wrong, and defensively criticize something they do not like. The teacher or counselor who can not accept criticism, or who is inclined to speak as an impersonal authority, will alienate parents and fail to engage them in cooperative participation necessary in helping the child.[13] The counselor helps the parents tell their story, listens carefully, and lets them know the school is genuinely concerned. Once the parents have released their negative feelings and the counselor has enlisted their help in solving the problem, there is time for the counselor to present the factual material he has gathered. The counselor, with his facts—not opinions— creates the possibility for emotional involvement. If the conference is successful, new insights, ideas, and perceptions are made evident for the parent and the counselor. They see a child's behavior in a new light. Parents gain insight about their attitudes

[12] Willis Vandiver, "Preparing Parents for the Conference," *Parents and the Schools, Thirty-sixth Yearbook, The National Elementary Principal* (Washington, D. C.: National Education Association, 1957), pp. 218, 219.

[13] Richard Anderson, "A Social Worker Looks at the Parent-Teacher Conferences," *Exceptional Children,* **28,** 433, 434 (1967).

and their child's behavior. Allowing the parent to express his feelings tends to make him feel accepted and a good working relationship between the school and home begins.

Group Conferences

Guidance conferences for parent groups are based upon the philosophy that parents, teachers, and counselors share common interests in child welfare. When parents come to school for a group conference, they usually look for two things. First, they want to know better methods of handling their child. Second, they want to better understand their child and his growth and development, so that they will be more capable in child-rearing.[14]

Careful preparation is taken in selecting a topic for group discussion. Pure information-giving is not advisable; however, stimulation of thought and attitude formation is commendable. A common procedure is sending an invitation to the parents which includes a check list of possible topics of interest. It gives the parents an opportunity to select meaningful discussion topics for themselves.

The conference leader is skilled in conducting discussions, as well as using other group techniques. Much of the leadership comes from the parents in the group, but the bulk of the responsibility remains with the counselor. The counselor draws comments from the group by asking questions, and he summarizes and evaluates the discussion periodically. Many of the parents' questions are directed to other parents. To utilize parental leadership, the counselor divides the large group into small "buzz" sessions and allows them to discuss topics. Another method is to ask parents in advance to be prepared to lead discussion on certain topics.

The program for the group conference may be formal or infor-

---

[14] Roy Willey and Melvin Strong, *Group Procedures in Guidance* (New York: Harper and Brothers, 1957), p. 258.

mal, featuring panel discussions by pupils and parents, or films used to begin a program followed by a group discussion. Socio-drama or role-playing are other means of influencing parent groups.

Another specific use of the group conference is the pre-school orientation period. Most schools do not have the time or person-nel to conduct an extensive preschool orientation program. Be-cause there is a need for such a program, the P.T.A. or other community groups take this as one of their functions. The usual plan is for very informal orientation meetings, where parents sit down and discuss mutual problems. A teacher or principal may be asked to offer leadership or consultant services. Resource personnel may be recommended, discussion leaders secured, and a program prepared to teach parents how to help children make the transition. The school counselor and psychologist discuss normal growth patterns and common adjustment problems, while doctors and nurses discuss physical development. Again, films benefit discussion.

Parents become acquainted with the community resources available for their child's health and guidance. Children who are well-integrated emotionally, socially, and physically find the transition from home to school a pleasant one. Parents, teachers, and counselors are better able to keep up with the children if they meet regularly to discuss the child's growth. It helps identify areas in which the home and school can work together; confer-ences with parents identify the family attitude toward the school and the child for the school personnel.[15]

Family Group Consultation

Parent discussions prove fruitful for parents with a common problem. They experience the fact that all parents have problems

---

[15] Francis Rosecrance and Velma Hayden, *School Guidance and Personnel Services* (Boston: Allyn and Bacon, Inc., 1960), pp. 30–32.

with their children, and that parents have the power and confidence to work out solutions. These group discussions relieve parental anxieties, especially when the participants realize that the group discussion is a form of therapy in itself. The goal of the family group conference is to improve the parent-child relationship, by better understanding the dynamics of their relations and child development.

Family consultation or family group consultation is a form of counseling receiving recent attention. The term consultation is used because it describes the communication involved. A family or group of families meet together to consult with the counselor as well as each other. The advantage of a group of families is that parents and children discover a broader range of alternative solutions than that encompassed by the limited approaches within a single family.

Zwetschke and Grenfell[16] describe the purposes of family consultation as establishing better understanding between individuals in the family, reduction of the cultural encapsulation of members of the family, expression of affection and regard for each other, and greater openness in their behavior with each other.

Families interested in resolving some problems within their family constellation meet weekly with a counselor or counselors. For the first hour the entire family and counselors work together. During the second hour the adults meet separately. In consultation, individuals are encouraged to let others know their problems and needs. They receive reinforcement from the counselor and other members of the group.

Individual family members learn the necessity for behavior change through self-exploration, group discussion and evaluation. Alternative behavior, conceived through group discussions, is

[16] Earl Zwetschke and John Grenfell, "Family Group Consultation: A Description and a Rationale," *Personnel and Guidance Journal*, 43, 974–980 (1965).

tried in regular family life. Results are reported at a subsequent group meeting and discussed. When families are able to report consistent successes, they are ready for termination.

Home Visits

Because of increased school size education has become more and more detached and powerful in the eyes of some parents. This is an unfortunate gap that needs to be reduced. Use of the school's visiting teacher or social worker as liaison between the home and school is a great help; however, it may be necessary for the counselor to accept some responsibility himself. The visit to the home is a two-way communication, but the counselor is the primary learner. This is because the parents feel comfortable in their own surroundings, enabling uninhibited conversation. The counselor observes the parents and the physical environment of the home first-hand. He learns a great deal from a home visit which is not recorded or available at school. The counselor more realistically learns the points of view of the parents with respect to the educational program, and the counselor may help the parents learn the philosophy, objectives, and activities of the school. The home visit provides an opportunity for developing better public relations, because much of the hostility and attacks upon the school program is due to a lack of public relations.[17]

When the counselor visits the home, he learns a great deal about the physical surroundings of the home. He can learn if there is an opportunity for the child to study and if the parental help given reflects the attitude of the parents toward study. The counselor learns how parental attitude toward the child's education has affected the child's attitude. It may be possible to observe whether or not the child can share his interests and ideas

[17] Karl Douglas, "Why Visit Homes?" *Parents and the Schools, Thirty-sixth Yearbook, The National Elementary Principal,* **37** (Washington, D.C.: National Education Association, 1957) pp. 239, 240.

with his parents, which is to say, whether the child is encouraged or discouraged. Clues to the acceptance of the child within the home may be evidenced.

It is important to inform both the child and the parents of the plans for the home visit. If they know the purpose of the visit, it relieves their anxiety and also leads to more positive feelings of anticipation of the visit with the parents having some positive things to share. The counselor learns as much as he can about the child and his family before making the visit. Parents feel that they know the counselor from the child's reports, and they will expect the counselor to know something about the child's program and behavior in school.

The counselor looks for parental reactions to information he presents. It is important that the parents understand the information and do not misinterpret what the counselor says. The counselor tries to have the parents incorporate the information into their own conceptions of their child.

Casual, unhurried conversation is more conducive to a good working relationship than a highly structured conference. Parents also feel more comfortable when they introduce a subject rather than when the counselor brings it up. Both the counselor and the parents should feel, at the conclusion, that the meeting has been successful in helping the home and school work together.

Other Methods of Communication

The oldest and most common type of contact between the home and school is the written report. In the past, the report card was often the only communication between them. Today, even though parents, teachers, and specialists meet in group conferences, the written report is still used.

The Report Card

The most widely used method, the report card, gives grades achieved by the child, an estimate of the child's endeavor, and a rating of his school citizenship. The information must be factual, even if disappointing, so the parents can use it to understand and help their child.

The educational philosophy in the school system governs the instructional program and the content of the report. If achievement in subjects is a central goal, the report card reports the child's standing in knowledge of his subjects. If behavior according to growth and development is a goal, then a description of the relevant behavior is reported. If progress in work habits and skills is desired, then the report indicates status or progress in specific skills and habits. As the instructional program serves more than one of these goals, the report gives a mark in subjects and a check on various behavior traits and work habits.[18]

Letters

In many schools, the letter is used as a replacement or supplement to the report card. This allows teachers and counselors to report the child's progress in all areas without being confined to following a form. The two main drawbacks to this method are: (1) it is difficult to write without repetition in each letter, and (2) writing is time consuming.[19]

Occasionally schools make effective use of letters to parents to state the general purposes of specific school programs, such as guidance, music, and athletics. Other letters to a group of parents prepares them for a conference about their children. This may be a letter of explanation and/or a list of questions, pre-

[18] William Alexander, "Reporting to Parents—Why? What? How?" *National Education Association Journal,* p. 16 (1959).
[19] Herman Peters and Gail Farwell, *Guidance: A Developmental Approach,* 2nd Ed. (Chicago: Rand McNally and Company, 1967), p. 439.

ceding the conference. Another letter variation deals with specific activities a child could carry out at home. A communiqué is sent home to inform parents concerning new information about child development or the transfer from elementary to junior high school. Still another letter summarizes or interprets a program that has been carried on through the semester or year, with the aim of helping parents better understand some aspects of the school program.

Letters from the school may improve school relations, therefore encouraging parents to work out problems with the school and to look on the school and home as a partnership. The strength of a letter lies in the writer's creative ability to write a cogent, personal interpretation of the program.

Telephone

The telephone interview between the counselor and the parent is a convenient method of communication. When conference time is not available, he carefully establishes rapport and is sympathetic and understanding of the parent's problem, conducting the interview the same as if it were a private conference. Many parents will express complaints on the telephone that they would not say in person. A telephone call is an excellent method for setting a personal conference time or in making an initial contact. The phone call always is a good way to pass on a positive note to parents.[20]

Consultation with Teachers

Second to the home, the school provides the greatest influence on child development and helps the child make the transition

[20] *Ibid.*, p. 419.

from the home to the larger society. Perhaps the main importance of the school is to help the child attain a feeling of security and an expectancy for success.

The school can also be a source of problem behavior. A child who experiences frequent failure or criticism in school has low expectancy of school achievement and, if these negative reinforcements are frequent or important enough, the low expectancy generalizes to other areas of his life. The grading system is a major contributing factor in this process. Besides setting up academic standards, a school frequently sets up standards of social behavior that may discourage some children and lead to a feeling of worthlessness and inadequacy.

The teacher is the counselor's chief professional ally in the attainment of guidance objectives. The teacher identifies children in need of counseling, contributes to the student appraisal, and assists the child in understanding himself and his environment through manipulation of the classroom environment.[21]

Teachers who positively reinforce or reward a child's efforts build up satisfaction for the child which leads to constructive behavior. The teacher helps the child set goals appropriate for his ability. Thus, by meeting these goals he is reinforced by the teacher and himself. The teacher praises the child for what he can do, rather than comparing him with the group. It is, therefore, important to recognize different needs, previous experience, and background of the children, as well as their unique abilities. In order to provide time and special attention, the teacher uses the counselor as a consultant.

Although the need to understand each child is evident, many teachers have not received sufficient preparation in child development and educational psychology. Teachers may have difficulties because they misinterpret children's behavior, underrate

[21] Kenneth Hoyt, "Guidance: A Constellation of Services," *Personnel and Guidance Journal,* **40,** 690–697 (1962).

their abilities, and misunderstand their interests and goals. Frequently teachers are not aware of individual differences of children or the differences that exist in attitudes and values of different social classes.

An attempt to understand the child leads the counselor and teachers to a systematic study of children. They focus on the developmental tasks of children and the personal and social variables in their school performance.

Understanding the learning process is equally as important as understanding the child. Teachers have little preservice education in motivation, reinforcement, or other principles of learning related to the classroom. However, much of the literature does not deal directly with real-life teaching and learning situations. The teacher is interested in understanding the learning process as it applies to a particular subject or class. The interrelationship of learner and learning is complicated, because children achieve differentially in various subjects, and patterns of achievement reflect varied developmental histories. Teachers, children, and the .learning process are unique and, therefore, so must the process be in which they are related.

Consulting Services

An elementary school counselor focuses his skills on assisting the teacher to help children in the classroom. A counselor consults with teachers about the behavior of a specific child, provides teachers with insights into the nature of the problems, and helps decide ways the teacher can control the classroom environment to assist the child. The advantage of consulting with a teacher over counseling with a pupil is that a counselor may see the child a few hours a week, while the child is under the supervision of the teacher for twenty hours a week. The counselor has a great impact on the child by concentrating on helping the teacher make the twenty hours more beneficial.[22]

The teachers in a California study reported that counselors gave them the most help by testing individual children, counseling with children, helping them with classroom problems, and participating in parent conferences.[23] The activities developed by another group of counselors include: consulting with teachers, providing in-service education programs, providing case conferences, observing children in classroom situations, and assisting in curriculum development.[24]

The counselor provides a number of consulting services for the teacher. He collects, organizes and synthesizes information relevant to a child. He uses test data, conducts pupil or parent interviews, observes the child, reviews the school records and then meets with the teacher. The counselor and teacher interpret the relevant data and work toward a solution for the child.

A major activity of the elementary counselor is assisting teachers in clarifying the expectations they hold for the child and in modifying their treatment of him. He assists teachers in evaluating their relationships with the children and with other staff members, as well as evaluating the child's relationships to school and his peers. He helps teachers in understanding the socio-psychological climate of their classroom. Teachers can be helped in understanding their influence on a child's development and in modifying their behavior and attitudes toward a child, leading to more effective behavior by the child.

The counselor assists in the early identification of problems and, when necessary, refers parents to outside agencies. He needs to know the school and community services available for

[22] D. W. Brison, "The Role of the Elementary Guidance Counselor," *National Elementary Principal*, **43**, 41–44 (1964).
[23] William McCreary and Gerald Miller, *op. cit.*, pp. 494–498.
[24] Status of Elementary School Guidance Pilot Projects in New York State, *op. cit.*, pp. 4–14.

referral. The counselor also helps prepare the parents and child for referral.

A counselor provides in-service training for teachers in child development and learning. Such services stress the interrelationship of the teacher, the child, and the learning process. Another area of consultation with teachers involves assisting with curriculum. This subject will be covered in Chapter 6, Guidance and the Curriculum.

Methods of Consultation

The counselor assists teachers by providing additional information about children and the learning process and helping them apply their new understanding to change their behavior. The counselor carries out these functions through in-service study programs, individual case studies with teachers, and group discussions with teachers.

Case Study

One of the most valuable cooperative techniques is the case study and case conference, in which the counselor, teacher, and others who have knowledge of the child pool their information and interpret it. Through this method, a better understanding of the pupil is gained; helpful recommendations follow. When a problem persists and it is believed that a mutual sharing of information will contribute to a better understanding of the pupil, then a case study is initiated.

Two valuable purposes are served by a case conference. The participants pool their knowledge of the child which they have gained from their various contacts with him. The combined thinking builds a deeper understanding of the child than is possible by an individual. If a plan for helping the child is decided upon and administered by the members of the conference, they will act more effectively. Secondly, the case conference provides an excellent form of in-service training. The case at hand affords the opportunity to understand human behavior, learning, and cooperative education.

The case study does not end with the collection of data, rather the discussion with the teacher leads to a plan of action carried out in the classroom. Parents and other significant persons are also consulted regarding a plan of action. An extensive description of the development and use of a case study is given in Chapter 9, Guidance Instruments and Techniques.

Individual Consultation

A teacher seeks assistance from the counselor for a particular child. The counselor aids the teacher in developing means of collecting and interpreting information that is helpful in working with the child. He also counsels with the child. Following the counseling interviews, the counselor sits down with the teacher, and they cooperatively devise a plan of action.

In-Service Education

Emphasis in in-service education should be on helping teachers help pupils. A program helps teachers to understand the guidance viewpoint and to learn to use guidance techniques in the classroom. Other areas in child development and learning may help them understand certain children and their problems. The counselor talks to the teachers or has other consultants discuss specific topics. Meetings focus on a case study, role-playing, tape recorded interviews, audio-visual aides or other resource materials.

In organizing an in-service program, it is imperative that it be based on the needs and interests of the teachers. Where possible, part of the program is carried on during the school day. This means the counselor will have the assistance of the school administrator in organizing the program. If an in-service program is to be successful, it should be a systematic, year round program. Continuous evaluation enables the counselor to determine the effectiveness of the program and the teacher's attitude toward it.

A Team Approach

Most teacher-training institutions give teacher trainees very little, if any, training in getting along with peers, administrators, and pupils in an interpersonal relationship. As teachers spend a great amount of time with children during the children's formative years, improvement in the educational output and effectiveness of our school is insured by helping teachers get training in effective communication and in understanding of interpersonal relationship dynamics.

School counselors who have been trained in the area of communication and the dynamics of interpersonal relationships make a contribution to the total school climate by involving the school personnel in a team effort in improving the school climate. Teachers and the counselors work together as a team, giving the pupils the best possible educational experience. The counselor involves interested teachers as co-counselors in counseling groups of pupils; the teachers are involved in in-service workshops in interpersonal dynamics; and the teachers and administrators regularly meet in informal discussion or process groups. Teachers learn to use the counselor as a tool to observe the dynamics of the classroom. The teacher and counselor then discuss possible changes from the standpoint of "I wonder what would happen if we tried. . . ."

If a teacher feels that the counselor is doing something with him, not to him, that the counselor is also a teacher possessing unique skills, and that together they learn from each other to make the school situation more productive, the total climate of the school becomes more open and productive.

Summary

Many people share responsibility in working with the elementary school child. A major role of the counselor is in keeping others aware of their contribution and serving as a consultant. The idea of consultation is based on the concept that the behavior of the child is influenced by the reinforcements he receives from others; parent and teacher behavior change results in changes in the child's behavior.

Consultation calls for a collaborative relationship in which the teachers, parents, and counselor work together in understanding the child and his environment. The child is best understood in terms of his unique social environment and his interpersonal relationships. The counselor provides insights into pupil behavior and possible methods of meeting problems. The counselor does not have all of the answers, but works with parents and teachers in modifying the situation.

The counselor contributes his psychological skills to the efforts of the teacher. When the teacher and counselor combine their knowledge and skills, a more effective educational environment is developed for the pupil. The counselor assists parents in understanding the impact of their behavior on the child. Through a better home-school relationship both agencies will be able to provide a more conducive environment for child development.

SELECTED REFERENCES

Don Dinkmeyer, "The Counselor as a Consultant to the Teacher," The School Counselor, **14,** 294–297 (1967).

Armin Grams, *Facilitating Learning and Individual Development* (St. Paul: Minnesota Department of Education, 1966).

Julian Rotter, *Social Learning and Clinical Psychology* (Englewood Cliffs, N.J.: Prentice-Hall, Inc., 1954).

CHAPTER

6

GUIDANCE
AND THE CURRICULUM

Early 20th-century classes were well-disciplined; children sat
rigidly in silence, hands folded on their desks, waiting to be
called upon by the teacher. One subject was engaged in by the
entire class under strict teacher supervision. In reading class, all
pupils read from the same text at the same time, with the teacher
calling upon fast readers and slow readers to breeze or stumble
through a designated line or paragraph. All too often the pre-
vailing emotional climate of the elementary classroom during
those "good old golden rule days" led to pupil boredom and
embarrassment.

Ragan[1] cites three developments since the turn of the century

---

[1] William Ragan, *Modern Elementary Curriculum* (New York: Holt,
Rinehart, and Winston, Inc., © 1966), pp. 138–139.

that have been particularly influential in creating dissatisfaction with the regimented, discipline-oriented, authoritarian, classroom system. One is the increasing amount of information about the wide differences existing among children at any given grade in school. Pupils entering the first grade generally differ in mental age by approximately four years; by the time children reach the sixth grade, the spread amounts to five or six years. The second development is the increasing acceptance by educational leaders of the continuous growth philosophy, that is, each child grows according to his natural pattern. The bright child should be given the opportunity to learn as much as his ability and effort permit and the slow child should not be forced to perform to standards not intended for him. The third development is called "the quest for excellence" emphasizing efforts to identify the gifted child and to capitalize on his talents. The space race heightened the intensity of this pursuit.

Each of these developments points out the necessity for some type of pupil ability grouping for instructional purposes. Shane[2] lists thirty-five approaches to grouping that have been developed and discarded, modified, or made part of common practice. The central aim of grouping plans is to break away from the traditional authoritarian classroom atmosphere and move toward more individualization of the learning environment and meet the needs and abilities of each pupil. There is an increasing trend toward student oriented curriculum structures.

Concept of Curriculum

The term curriculum has been traditionally thought of as a listing or patterning of the subjects taught in school. The recent

[2] Harold Shane, "Grouping in the Elementary School," *Phi Delta Kappan*, 41, 313–319 (1960).

trend is to broaden its meaning by encompassing the whole life and program of the school. It now includes all the child's experiences for which the school accepts responsibility. Instructional content is important, but curriculum includes much more. It includes the teacher-pupil relationship, the provision of opportunities for pupil participation in group activities, school assemblies, and the use of the local environment in learning; in short, it involves all the experiences under the direction of the school.

Initiation of a developmental approach to the elementary school curriculum means using the meaningful degree of the learning experience to each child, as the final criterion for all school practices. This principle implies that every aspect of the curriculum considers the data of developmental child psychology. It implies that at each level, every effort is made to adjust schoolwork to the abilities, interests, and needs of the child.

Ragan[3] lists the following implications of this broader curriculum concept:

1. The curriculum exists only in the experience of children; it does not exist in textbooks, in the courses of study, or in the plans and intentions of teachers. . . .
2. The curriculum includes more than content to be learned. . . . The human relations in the classroom, the methods of teaching, and the evaluation procedures used are as much a part of the curriculum as the content to be learned.
3. The school curriculum is an enterprise in guided living. Instead of being as broad as life itself, the school curriculum represents a special environment that has been systematized, edited, and simplified for a special purpose.
4. The curriculum is a specialized learning environment deliberately arranged for directing the interests and abilities of children toward effective participation in the life of the community

[3] William Ragan, *op. cit.*, p. 5.

and the nation. It is concerned with helping children to enrich their own lives and to contribute to the improvement of society through the acquisition of useful information, skills, and attitudes.

Dutton and Hockett[4] view curriculum organization as a continuous process, constantly modifying itself to meet the changing needs of children, society, and instructional methods. They point out that the modern elementary school teacher must grow as the curriculum grows; one cannot advance without the other. The counselor stimulates teacher growth by working with them to improve the curriculum and better meet the needs of the children.

Factors Affecting the Curriculum

School personnel have become increasingly attentive to the significant contributions of research in the area of intellectual development. Early childhood is demonstrated to be the crucial period for intellectual development. Studies of the culturally deprived indicate that the quality of perceptual and verbal experiences of a young child determines, to a great extent, his later achievement. Worth[5] reports data supporting the "critical years" hypothesis. He states that approximately 50 per cent of general school achievement attained at grade 12 has been reached by the end of grade 3. In terms of intelligence measured at age 17, about 50 per cent of development takes place between conception and age 4, about 30 per cent between ages 4 and 8, and about 20 per cent between ages 8 and 17. He found that the

---

[4] Wilbur Dutton and John Hockett, *The Modern Elementary School Curriculum and Methods* (New York: Rinehart and Company, Inc., 1959), pp. 41, 42.
[5] W. H. Worth, "The Critical Years," *The Canadian Administrator,* 1965.

language structures and speaking habits of many children almost completely establish themselves in the early years. The period between the ages of 6 and 10 is particularly crucial for boys in crystallizing the desire for task mastery and intellectual competence.

Kagan and Moss,[6] in summarizing a 30-year longitudinal study, point out that, "The most dramatic and consistent finding of this study was that many behaviors exhibited by a child during the period 6 to 10 years of age, and a few during the age period 3 to 6, were moderately good predictors of theoretically related behavior during early adulthood." The importance of the early development of positive attitudes toward academic achievement is clearly illustrated. Many core-area teachers complain about the fifth- and sixth-grade ghetto boys who have already given up in school.

Waetjen[7] cites several studies which reveal a discrimination against boys in the present elementary school program. He points out that it is not accidental that we have considerably more nonreading or poor reading boys than girls; that 98 per cent of the youngsters who are in speech clinics for functional disorders such as stuttering and articulation problems are boys; that youngsters referred to counselors by teachers, not on a self-referral or parent referral basis, are in the majority, boys; that a large percentage of the pupils "held back" each year are boys; that the majority of eventual school dropouts are boys.

Moustakas,[8] in discussing children needing psychotherapy, states that the submission and denial of the self is the root of difficulty for many children. "Somewhere along the line of his

[6] Jerome Kagan and Howard Moss, *Birth to Maturity* (New York: John Wiley and Sons, Inc., 1962), p. 266.

[7] Walter Waetjen, "Research from Educational Psychology that has Implications for Elementary School Guidance," paper read at The Invitational Conference on Elementary School Guidance, Washington, D.C., March, 1965.

[8] Clark Moustakas, *Psychotherapy with Children: The Living Relationship* (New York: Harper and Brothers, 1959), p. 3.

growth and development, he has given up the essence of his being and the unique patterns that distinguish him from every other person. The growth of the self has been impaired because of his rejection in important personal relationships." Understanding the meaning that experiences have for children, how they feel, and what they believe about themselves, is essential. School personnel are primarily responsible for assisting pupils in developing realistic and wholesome attitudes toward themselves.

Sociological research underscores the changing conditions in our society, influencing the nature of the elementary school program. The following conditions reported at the 1960 White House Conference on Children and Youth indicate some of the influences that must be considered today: (a) There will be an increasing mobility of our population with a definite trend toward the urban pattern of living. It was estimated that approximately 32,000,000 people move each year, with 70 per cent of our population living in urban areas at the present time and an estimated 85 per cent by 1975. The mobility is resulting in a large portion of our population being confronted with situations where values and expectations are different from those they have known. (b) There is a development of the concept of the world-wide interdependence of man. (c) There is an increase of both parents working; in many instances with limited opportunity for family interaction. (d) There is a larger number of broken homes. In 1960 13 per cent of all youth under eighteen years of age lacked the guidance of two parents, because of broken homes caused by death, divorce, or desertion. (e) There are increasing pressures for higher achievement, especially pressures upon the gifted. There are pressures for youth to be channeled into areas requiring skill in mathematics and science, and pressures for student acceleration. (f) Social expectations, formerly valued at more mature levels, are being moved to the elementary school. This includes planned, formal social events and increased emphasis upon competitive sports for elementary school boys.

(g) There is increasingly consolidation of school districts, producing changes in learning environment for pupils.[9]

These, and many other changes and influences, mandate that all who have responsibilities for child development know more than ever before about their needs, abilities, and interests and about the concerns and expectations of society.

Lachman[10] studied the level of aspirations phenomena in the classroom. The results of his studies confirm the long-suspected notion that the level of aspiration (goal-striving behavior) tends to rise with success and to fall with failure. The consistently poor achievers apply themselves less and less; yet, all too often, their apathy is met with threats of punishment and lectures to "get on the stick," rather than a restructured learning environment, allowing them to experience some success.

Other effects of classroom environment on motivation have been investigated. As a result of research dealing with mental health consultation in the elementary schools, Cutler and McNeil[11] state that the global picture is one in which the classroom screws gradually tighten as the year progresses. Teachers increasingly concentrate on content communication, but fail to provide the appropriate climate in which the content may be learned. At the same time, pupils respond by losing motivation, being less cooperative, feeling less accepted by teachers and peers, becoming less adequate group members, and becoming anxious about school and standards of performance.

The information expansion constantly creeping into "material to be covered" subject-matter units pushes the intermediate grade teacher into crash lecture periods during the last half of the

[9] Eli Ginzberg, *The Nation's Children*, Vol. 1, "The Family & Social Change" (New York: Columbia University Press, 1960), pp. 24–49.

[10] Sheldon Lachman, "Level of Aspiration: A Classroom Demonstration of Phenomena and Principle," *Journal of General Psychology*, **65**, 357–363 (1961).

[11] Richard Cutler and Elton McNeil, "Mental Health Consultation in the Schools," unpublished Research Report (Ann Arbor: University of Michigan, 1963).

year. Such teaching at the elementary level is grossly ineffective. Considering the frequency of this practice, coupled with its inherent emotional dangers, the degree of mental health in the elementary school environment is very questionable.

Research in intellectual development, sociology, and educational psychology point out the very urgent need for meaningful learning experiences for each pupil in the elementary school. Learning is facilitated through individual attention. Each child's physiological make-up and experiential background give him a quality of uniqueness, assaulted by societal and educational pressures for conformity. Knowledge about the preadolescent's development, needs, and vulnerability cannot allow the clashing of individual uniqueness and "the demands of the school" to be left to chance. The counselor serves as a reconciliation agent.

The basic concern of administrators is to "run the system;" the teachers' primary task is to instruct; the counselor helps each pupil to use his maximum potential. He assists each child in understanding and accepting himself in relation to his abilities, his needs, and the environmental demands.

In working with the individualization of the curriculum, the counselor's function becomes truly developmental. He may help with the remedial work of pupils in academic or emotional difficulty. However, the much broader goals are concerned with anticipating developmental difficulties and attempting to provide curriculum services that will help each child meet his developmental tasks.

An integral part of the total educational process emphasizes the early identification of assets and liabilities, the interpretation of these observations to parents, teachers, and curriculum specialists, and the provision of a counseling relationship for all children. Encouragement nurtures the development of special talents.

Thus, although guidance continues to serve remedial and diagnostic functions, a primary focus is in the area of curriculum development. Again, its purpose is to facilitate learning through individual attention. Although people act and react in terms of different learned behavior patterns, nonetheless, all people respond positively to respect and sincere interest. The ultimate goal of a guidance program is an educational atmosphere where every child feels respected and the object of real interest.

The Emerging Grouping Plans

Grouping children in elementary school, i.e., homogeneous, nongraded, for team teaching, has certain definite structural influences upon the learning environment. Due to the many existing grouping plans, a discussion of the counselor's role only in relation to a school program where the self-contained classroom plan still persists is deficient. Below is a review of some of the more widely used plans, focusing on specific counselor responsibilities pertinent to each.

Self-Contained Curriculum

The most widely used plan for forming elementary school instructional groups is the self-contained classroom. This plan grew out of conditions existing in the nineteenth century and the establishment of public school systems in this country. Infatuation with factory-like precision, the necessity of maintaining large classes, the development of carefully graded textbooks, and the relative simplicity of giving a single assignment to an entire class were some of the factors leading to the graded, self-contained classroom. Today, with the comparatively recent advent of better prepared teachers, more abundant instructional materials, and improved teaching techniques due to a better understanding of child development, this plan is still used most often.

The typical self-contained classroom follows this description:

Twenty to thirty pupils are assigned to a teacher and placed in a classroom where she (or he) does most of the instructing. She is expected to have the skills and the knowledge for competent instruction in virtually all subject matter areas. She provides the best she can for a range of individual needs and abilities of pupils in her group. In addition, she ordinarily performs a variety of clerical and supervisory duties of a noninstructional nature. Under typical conditons, she has little "professional" contact with other teachers in the building, and she receives little supervision.

As the self-contained classroom calls for the placing together of one teacher and a group of pupils for the major portions of the school day, this plan's major advantage is that it enables the teacher to learn a great deal about each pupil by observing him throughout the entire school year in a wide variety of learning situations. It has long been argued, by administrators in favor of this plan, that this child-teacher exposure is more beneficial to learning experiences than the teacher's mastery of the subject-matter. They believe the scope and depth of subjects taught in the elementary school are not so great, that they could not be adequately handled by regular classroom teachers. These administrators feel that other teacher competencies, such as an understanding of child development and formulating and reorganizing learning experiences, are of greater importance.

Under the direction of the same teacher, and as members of the same group, pupils in self-contained classrooms have more quantative and qualitative opportunities to learn to participate effectively in group enterprises. Without predetermined class-switching, there is more flexibility in the use of time. Important lessons are continued for as long as necessary, and significant learning experiences, involving more than one period in the daily schedule, are easily arranged. The competent teacher in the self-contained classroom is in a much better position to help her pupils see the inter-relatedness of subject-matter fields.

The importance of the environment is apparent in realizing that all learning takes place through the interaction of the individual with his physical, social, intellectual, and emotional environment. The school day includes opportunity for several types of activities and experiences. The sequence provides alternation between periods of vigorous physical and mental activity and relaxation intervals in which group and personal experiences (pupil initiated activity) are shared. A daily schedule may contain fixed periods and routines which provides security, but it is also flexible as to timing and time allotments, allowing deviations that may yield greater returns in learning, interest, and stimulation.

The teacher attempts to teach a group of children. Although it is desirable, as well as necessary, that children work and learn together in school groups, such work and learning are effective only insofar as they are relative to the abilities and interests of the individuals in the groups. Hence, the classroom teacher's greatest challenge is to identify and meet the needs of each of her unique pupils.

COUNSELOR ROLE. The elementary guidance counselor in the self-contained classroom organization facilitates each teacher's knowledge of the needs, abilities, and interests of her children. Such knowledge is imperative, since the teacher is mainly responsible for planning and establishing the appropriate, effective learning and developmental experiences for her children. Not only is the level of difficulty and range of subject-matter important, but the pattern in which this material is presented must also be considered (flexibility, etc.).

Most classroom teachers do not have the background in human learning, developmental sequence, and child psychology required of counselors. Counselors assist teachers to utilize these disciplines in relation to curriculum formation and reorganization, in order to meet the needs of their children. The counselor, acting as a consultant, renders such assistance to teachers individually or in groups, i.e., in-service guidance or curriculum meetings. Working individually with the teacher, the counselor interprets pupil data, classroom observation of pupil learning behaviors, information obtained from tests and counseling sessions, referrals to other "special services," explaining to the teacher what assistance can be expected from the service, discussion of guidance or teaching techniques the teacher can utilize with individual pupils, and discussion of human relations with the teachers.

One of the biggest disadvantages of the self-contained classroom structure is its lack of professional communication between teachers. Working to improve communication channels is another counselor task. With the increasing number of elementary counselors, helping teachers, social workers, attendance workers, psychologists, and health services personnel, the typical elementary teacher is forced to become more "open" and communicative, as to what she hopes to accomplish and as to what really occurs in her classroom. There is, however, a continuing tendency among many teachers, especially the more "experienced," to stick to themselves, "to concentrate on their own jobs," rather than attempting to work closely with other teachers in an inter-grade or inter-level helping relationship. The counselor facilitates a greater sharing among teachers of pupil and curriculum information. Recent research points out the usefulness of knowledge about the individuals developmental sequence, as an aid in organizing proper instructional techniques and materials, as well as providing a better basis for predicting adequate classroom behaviors. Much stronger relationships between pupil and teacher result, if the child realizes the teacher recognizes him as the fastest runner in the class, not simply the slowest reader.

Homogeneous Grouping

Homogeneous grouping is an attempt to form instructional groups composed of pupils who are near enough alike in respect to one or more traits to justify reaching them as a group and to reduce the task of adapting instruction to individual differences. Pupils at the same grade level are assigned to various teachers based upon learning ability. Measures of intelligence are used as the bases for group formation by many schools, while others have based grouping on achievement (chiefly in reading), social maturity, and special abilities or disabilities.

An advantage claimed for homogeneous grouping is that each child is challenged at his own level and, therefore, has a realistic chance to succeed. Children have an opportunity to successfully compete academically and socially; average and slow pupils become leaders in their own groups. Teachers have a better opportunity to work with individuals, when the range of ability in the class is reduced. Differentiated ability instruction offers able students an opportunity to move through the skill areas at their own speed. Teachers have fewer preparations to make, allowing more planning time.

Theoretical limitations state that the plan may violate the pupil's right to be different. When labeled bright, slow, or average, he begins to think of himself in these terms and begins to try to be like others in his group. Some plans pay little attention to any pupil characteristics, other than that trait which is used as the basis for grouping; there is evidence that pupils with similar scores on intelligence tests differ widely in respect to other characteristics. There is often a lack of data to allow for successful grouping.

Studies show that ability grouping is physical assembling of pupils with similar ability. Gains in achievement are influenced more by teacher and group differences in individual classrooms than by the presence or absence of gifted pupils, the ability range in the class, or even by the intellectual ability of the pupils.

COUNSELOR ROLE. Proper curriculum revision to complement a homogeneously grouped plan is imperative, if added learning benefits are to materialize. While the direct leadership for reorganization does not fall upon the counselor, he is involved. He participates in the curriculum committee, hopefully insuring that appropriate instructional material and techniques are planned for the groups which he has helped form. His duty is to make sure that true revision is being considered, that it is not just frill alteration. In working with parents, teachers, and pupils, the counselor stresses the concept of individual differences as one that has given positive, rather than negative, direction in education. Self-concept, attitudes toward school, friendships with pupils in other groups, and parent-child relationships are possible areas of exploration in the counseling interviews. The counselor helps the pupils formulate challenging, but realistic, immediate and long-range goals. He is a source of encouragement to each pupil. Research shows the powerful role of reinforcement in the learning process. Many times youngsters feel that new goals and challenges are formulated too quickly, depriving them of the praise and satisfaction deserved for reaching the "old" goal.

The counselor works with individual teachers, making them more aware of the complete "being" of each of their children. Actually, this information is reciprocal. As the physical school building and classroom is the same as the self-contained classroom organization, here too, the counselor encourages teachers to establish professional working relationships with one another. Teachers of the average and slow groups should be assisted in seeing the importance of their own particular roles. Unfortunately, many homogeneously grouped elementary schools give the impression that their "top" groups are taught by the system's expert teachers.

The counselor plays a very critical role in the homogeneously grouped organization plan. Although effectively run programs have their advantages, the plan is potentially very dangerous if mishandled. As a protector of individuality, the counselor acts as a sensitive safety indicator. It is his responsibility to shout the first alarm, if rigid groupness sets in.

Team Teaching

Team teaching provides for two or more teachers, with complementary skills and abilities, assuming the joint responsibilities for directing the learning activities of a group of pupils. Together, the members of the team take charge of planning lessons, developing appropriate methods and materials, and teaching a program of studies for their group. The number of pupils in the total group usually corresponds to a one to thirty ratio, i.e., two-member teams with approximately sixty pupils, three-member teams about ninety pupils, and so on, with teaching team membership seldom above five. Team teaching is not a method intended to reduce the number of teachers in any given school. It is a redeployment or different utilization of the existing teaching staff.

The teaching team is a formally organized hierarchy whose basic unit is the teacher. The team teaching position carries comparable prestige and status as that of the self-contained classroom teacher. The next hierarchical step is that of senior teacher. Large teams may have more than one senior teacher, and small teams may have none. He (or she) is an experienced teacher with special competence in a particular subject or in a particular skill or method. He assumes responsibility for instructional leadership in the area of his special competence, both for his team and, if necessary, across several teams.

At the top of the team hierarchy is the position of team leader. The team leader is a specialist in the subject-matter area that complements the areas of his senior teachers. His general administrative and coordinating functions include directing the continual reexamination and development of the curriculum, training and supervising the unexperienced team members, assuming the primary responsibility in his team for the identification of pupil needs and readiness, and for the assigning of pupils to groups.

Most team leaders are released from classroom teaching responsibilities for at least one-third of the day.

A basic tenet of team teaching is that the teacher receives more professional and personal stimulation working on a team than working in isolation. Better communication among staff members enhances motivation for continuous curriculum improvement and cooperative planning. The team places a premium on unusual ability, skill, and exceptional leadership qualities.

Some advantages of this plan include: practical and effective in-service education through frequent team meetings, marked success in inducting new teachers into school systems by using interns as team members, use of aids to release teachers from routine duties, teachers' involvement in planning and developing curriculum as a result of team structure, improved guidance from the planned exchange of information about pupils, improved correlation of subject matter because of cooperative planning in team meetings, and more effective use of space, material, and equipment. Due to team structure, there is the possibility of grouping and regrouping frequently according to achievement, ability, or interest levels. There is opportunity to exchange teaching responsibilities among the team teachers, in order to exploit teachers' special talents, knowledge, and training.

The success of the plan depends to a great extent on the ability of team members to work together harmoniously; if friction develops in interpersonal relations, the program suffers. There are numerous indications that not all teachers make good team members. Research indicates that differences among teachers need to be recognized, equally as much as do variations among teams.[12]

Members of the team spend a great deal of time working on plans for scheduling group activities and individual projects. The

[12] Robert Hanvey and Morton Teneberg, "University of Chicago Laboratory School Evalutes Team Teaching," *The Bulletin. National Association of Secondary School Principals,* **45,** 189–197 (1961).

problems of selecting superior teachers to serve as group leaders is complex; teachers who are very successful at working with a group of pupils may experience frustration, when they are faced with semi-administrative tasks involving team leadership. Team leaders are particularly adept at encouraging new teachers or new group members to contribute new materials, suggestions, and procedures, but too much leadership may stifle teacher initiative and creativity.

COUNSELOR ROLE. Elementary school team teaching is receiving more and more backing from education leaders. The main drawbacks of this plan center around the possible breakdown of a favorable human relations environment. The counselor's role as a consultant seems appropriate in a school setting using this plan. The counselor generates a climate for warm personal relations. Consultants must concern themselves with seeing that individuals, whether pupils, teachers, or administrators, are protected. When teachers feel threatened, they cannot love enough to properly facilitate a developing self.

The frequency of team member meetings gives the counselor an excellent chance to work closely with the teaching staff. This plan, more than any of the others, allows him the opportunity to function as the leader of a comprehensive in-service guidance program.

Nongraded

The nongraded program attempts to maximize opportunities for each child to fully develop his potential capacity. It is designed to provide continuous growth and learning opportunity for each child through flexible groupings. The curriculum is tailored to meet the needs of the children.

The plan minimizes the traditional grade lines. The range of children's ability in any given year of school is so great that it is virtually impossible to make them conform to specific grade levels. Levels are established through which pupils pass, based upon the development of all aspects (social, physical, and emotional), not just the intellectual.

Generally, however, progress through the early levels is based primarily on the pupil's advancement through prescribed reading tasks. There are usually eight to ten such levels, encompassing the traditional grades K–3 including level overlap; pupils move up or down within their own classroom. Transfers to other levels in other classrooms are easily made as well.

The ungraded plan is consistent with recent psychological findings concerning child growth, development, and learning. Subject matter content is designed in terms of the child's readiness and need for more functional learning and is organized on the basis of an individual's growth and motivation pattern. Pupils advance step by step at their own rate, without worrying about "failing" the grade.

Although elementary school programs which utilize the non-graded plan vary from one school to another, there are some basic features common to most of them:

1. Annual promotions are eliminated; the content of the curriculum for the first three years in school is divided into eight or nine sequential levels; and pupils progress from one level to the next in terms of their ability and rate of learning.
2. Most pupils remain in the primary unit three years, but a few may complete the work in two years and a few may require four years to complete it.
3. Progress levels are frequently geared to reading achievement.
4. The plan involves an extensive use of tests and other evaluation procedures to determine when a pupil has completed one of the levels.
5. Schools using the plan generally form instructional groups consisting of pupils who do not vary more than two progress levels in achievement.

6. Pupils can move up or down easily within their classrooms and transfers to other levels in other classrooms can be made at any time.[13]

This plan appears to be gaining popularity, as more and more emphasis is centered around efforts to develop various types of "continuous progress" programs in elementary schools. One study, which reports on a small sample of a little over 600 out of a total of 85,000 public elementary schools in the nation, indicates that 6 per cent used some nongraded sequences in 1956 and that 12 per cent were doing so in 1961. Twenty-six per cent of the principals reporting said they looked for such programs to be in use by 1966.[14]

An advantage claimed for the nongraded plan includes continuous pupil progress without predetermined barriers. Each child is accepted at his maturity level and is helped to grow as fast as his rate of development permits. Many slow starting children, who could flunk a regular first grade, subsequently make up for it and finish the primary unit in the regular three years. A child does not repeat materials he already knows, as he begins a new year from where he left off. The system is well adapted to lags and spurts, which psychology shows are typical of growing children. The nongraded system encourages flexibility in grouping and promotes more faculty teamwork. Pressures to achieve end-of-term goals are eliminated.

Disadvantages include establishing nongrading without curriculum reform, which results in simply replacing levels for grades. Difficulties are encountered when pupils from a nongraded elementary school move into a graded junior high school. Ex-

[13] William Ragan, *op. cit.*, p. 138.
[14] Project on the Instructional Program of the Public Schools, *The Principals Look at the Schools* (Washington, D.C.: National Education Association, 1962), pp. 39, 40.

tensive records are kept for each child. Nongrading nearly always results in the need to plan new reporting practices to parents, as the traditional marking systems are not consistent with the aims and methods of nongrading. The nongrading plan does not give the teacher a group of pupils who are alike in every respect; it gives the teacher a group of pupils who are more nearly alike than pupils in a conventional grade with respect to one factor— rate of learning.

COUNSELOR ROLE. The counselor's competencies in child development, learning theory, human relations, and curriculum design are challenged by this program. He assumes a leadership role in the areas of diagnosing children's levels of development, planning learning experiences to complement developmental stages, initiating comprehensive school-to-parent reporting plans, and reorientating curricular patterns for alignment with the nongraded "continuous progress" structure. Upon his shoulders fall much of the planning responsibilities for the elementary to junior high school transition, placement of transfer students, school to community reporting, and development of in-service programs in learning theory, child development, and pupil-oriented evaluation procedures.

An inherent danger in this plan is teacher susceptibility to "teach for tests." The counselor sensitizes teachers to the whole child evaluation approach. If completing the levels in the primary unit consists mainly of demonstrating mastery of basic skills in reading, language, and arithmetic, other subjects such as social studies, health, science, music, and art may suffer.

A visitor to a nongraded "open-school" elementary building is impressed by the aura of "doing" that permeates the learning environment. The counselor becomes actively involved in this challenging plan. This is certainly not the school setting for a guidance person who finds security in operating behind closed doors.

The Counselor's Role in Implementing
the Curriculum Goals

The broad curriculum goal is established as the provision of a learning environment where youth attain academic knowledge, intellectual skills, and personal development. This is based upon the democratic premise that every individual should be given the chance to gain as much academic knowledge as he is able to acquire. He is provided the opportunity to learn about himself, his own psychological world, and the specifics of the world in which he must make life-course decisions.

Counselors are designated several roles which facilitate the curriculum goals. Frequently, these designated roles emphasize "counseling back to normal" those pupils who apparently did not know enough about themselves to be able to function adequately in the school setting. Perhaps it is what these pupils face in the school that they could not understand as being meaningful. More knowledge about the pupil's environment and what it does to him is necessary in order to treat the environmental causes, as well as the resulting disorders. There is a need for more "guidance involvement" in the pupil's learning environment: the curriculum.

Elementary school curriculum is moving to individualization of instruction. Guidance workers assist teachers in better understanding pupils as individuals. Research in education shows that children's thinking is different at different levels of development. The "new math" and science programs focus on developing the cognitive structure of the child. Working together, the teacher and counselor recognize and provide for the various functioning levels of their pupils.

The goal of the elementary school curriculum is educational and personal development. The counselor works as a consultant confering with teachers in an effort to help them skillfully and comfortably understand various kinds of developmental tasks. He is resourceful in helping teachers to know and use techniques, that enable them to recognize and meet each child's academic and personal needs, as determined through counseling, testing and teacher-counselor observation of classroom behaviors. He offers each child the opportunity to know more about himself and his relation to his world. He is an expert in child development and the elementary school program, helping plan for and maintain an educational atmosphere where each individual can engage in meaningful learning.

The guidance person develops considerable competence in the area of coordination. He builds upon his knowledge of the importance of peer groups, family, school, church, and community forces as they seem to bear on immediate problems. He learns how to marshal these resources in aiding the development of a curriculum, which meets the needs and abilities of the pupil and which aids the development of a realistic, positive self-concept.

Curriculum Consultant

More and more school districts are initiating new positions under the general heading of curriculum-planning specialist. This new staff member has the basic duties of orienting the faculty to the nature of curriculum planning, assisting faculty in the formulation and definition of objectives for their local program, and providing leadership in bringing about the reorganization of programs to more effectively meet these objectives. This person works closely with the counselor and elementary teachers, to learn the nature of the students and the instructional facilities, materials, and techniques available to achieve curriculum objectives.

The teachers implement curriculum daily. Their own recognitions of individual behavior or curricular approaches are important elements in curriculum revisions. Counselors and curriculum specialists proceed through the teachers, when wholehearted teacher support is desired. Teachers' expert experience and perceptions are heavily relied upon when instructional experiences are improved.

For the establishment of better working relationships, the curriculum specialist is a staff, rather than line member, in the specific school unit. Similar to the counselor, he is easier to support, if he is perceived by the teachers as a consultant rather than a supervisor.

Cooperation between guidance and curriculum consultants results in improved curricular patterns for individuals and groups of pupils. The curriculum specialist's extensive knowledge of the current developments in instructional approaches, techniques, and materials make him a great asset in designing instructional programs for those groups or individuals who are perceived by the counselor and/or teachers as needing more meaningful curricular experiences.

The counselor is a communication channel between teachers and the curriculum specialist. The counselor's close working relationship with individual teachers keeps him well informed of curriculum areas teachers feel need reevaluation and adjustment. He brings their ideas and revision plans to the specialist.

The counselor knows the individual pupils through counseling relationships, record-keeping, and classroom observation. As a repository of pupil information, he is potentially the curriculum specialist's best asset for curriculum planning. He knows the pupils collectively and individually. The value of the exchange of this information is obvious, when considering the curriculum specialist's main function as tailoring the curricular program to fit pupil needs.

The counselor's background in child development, human relations, and learning theory adds sophistication to the curriculum specialists' functional knowledge of curriculum theory, design, and patterns, and his approaches for assessing, building, and re-organizing curriculum.

On-going curriculum coordination meetings, which bring together teachers, counselors, and curriculum specialists, set the stage for high quality planning activities leading to instructional patterns designed to meet school-wide, class-wide, and individual learning objectives. Each representative carries to the meeting expert experiences with, and perceptions of, those for whom the planning is being formulated, the pupils.

Summary

The curriculum includes all pupil experiences under the direction of the school. The way in which the pupils are grouped affects their experiences. The pupil's interaction with course content, teachers, and peers differs in the various grouping plans. The counselor's role is influenced by different grouping plans. In any plan, he still meets with individual pupils, consults with teachers regarding their pupils, class environment, and inter-staff communication, and works with the curriculum specialist in improving curricular patterns for teachers and pupils.

SELECTED REFERENCES

Maurie Hillson, *Elementary Education, Current Issues and Research* (New York: The Free Press, 1967).

William Ragan, *Modern Elementary Curriculum* (New York: Holt, Rinehart, and Winston, Inc., 1966).

Benjamin Sachs, *The Student, the Interview, and the Curriculum* (Boston: Houghton Mifflin Company, 1966).

GROUP PROCESS
IN ELEMENTARY GUIDANCE

Most human experience involves interaction with other persons. Whether these interactions are part of a formal or informal structure, individual competency in interpersonal activity leads to adjustment in modern society. This does not mean that the only goal of guidance is adjustment. It does imply that the utilization of various group guidance and/or counseling arrangements have valuable meaning to children at all school levels.[1]

There is some controversy in the guidance field concerning group processes. There is the belief that counseling is the major

[1] Herman J. Peters and Gail F. Farwell, *Guidance: A Developmental Approach,* 2nd Ed. (Chicago: Rand McNally & Company, 1967), p. 249.

153

Figure 4.

Interaction of Content and Process in Group Guidance, Group Counseling, and Group Therapy

	Process		
	Level I	Level II	Level III
Content	Leader plans topics	Leader and group members collaborate in planning topics	Topics originate with group members
	Lecture and recitation	Discussions, projects, panels, visits	Free discussion, role-playing
	Facts and skills emphasized	Attitudes and opinions emphasized	Feelings and needs emphasized
	Units in regular classes	Separate guidance groups meet on schedule	Groups organized as needed, meet as needed

Figure 4. (Continued)

	1	2	3
Type A Usual school subject matter: mathematics, English, etc.	1	4	7
Type B School-related topics: the world of work, choosing a college, how to study, etc.	2	5	8
Type C Nonschool topics: dating behavior, parent-child relations, handling frustrations, etc.	3	6	9

155

task of the school counselor and this can be accomplished only in a one-to-one relationship. Others suggest counseling is possible with more than one counselee at a time. Still another alternative suggests that group guidance occurs didactically, that is, very similar to classroom teaching but with the subject matter closely related to some guidance topic.

The range of activities in group activity is illustrated by Figure 4.[2] Goldman[3] uses this method to demonstrate the various dimensions and processes necessary to these areas.

> (This) shows the two dimensions: content across the rows and process down the columns. In each instance, the total range is divided for convenience of discussion into three parts, but this is arbitrary. Each dimension should be seen as a continuum which could with equal logic be divided into two parts or ten.
>
> *Content.* Going down the rows, we move from the usual academic subjects, i.e., mathematics, literature, and all the others which are universally accepted as school curricular content—to topics at the other extreme which are in many places considered to be off-limits, topics such as dating behavior or parent-child relations. Between the extremes are the school-related topics such as educational and vocational opportunities, which, though not academic subjects, are usually accepted as belonging somewhere in the school's total curriculum.
>
> *Process.* Moving from left to right we go from the more traditional, teacher-directed methods to those which give pupils more responsibility for planning and conducting classroom activities. Also as we go across the columns,

[2] Leo Goldman, "Group Guidance: Content and Process," *The Personnel and Guidance Journal,* **40,** 519 (February 1962). © 1962 by the American Personnel and Guidance Association.

[3] *Ibid.,* p. 518–522.

there is decreasing emphasis on cognitive elements and increasing emphasis first on attitudes and opinions, and later on deeper feelings. The manner of forming the groups is also seen to differ. Finally, perhaps the best indicator of differences among these processes is the kind of evaluative questions one asks. At Level I, the questions are likely to be: How much does he know? How much skill has he developed? At Level II, the questions are more likely to be these: Does he have well-developed and well-substantiated opinions? Have his attitudes changed or developed? And at Level III the questions would be: How does he behave in relation to peers or parents? How realistic a degree of self-acceptance does he have? It seems clear that Levels II and III contain more of the elements of guidance and counseling, while Level I has more of those which are appropriate to instruction.[4]

Goldman establishes some baselines for describing group activities. As the reader will note the lines between the content and processes are difficult to establish. However, the extremes do illustrate that the activity in cell one dealing with school subject matter in a traditional classroom approach is different from cell nine in which topics of interest to and initiated by group members are discussed and followed as necessary without particular regard to academic progress or a pre-planned approach. This helps differentiate the terms group guidance and group counseling as being related to the source of the topic, i.e., from inside or outside the pupil. In addition the activity of the leader is altered when group counseling is in operation as opposed to the more didactically oriented group guidance.

Groups play an important part in most elementary school

[4] *Ibid.*, pp. 518, 519.

activities and thus are a natural vehicle for achieving some elementary guidance goals. It is important to recognize that group methods are valuable only to the extent that the group member receives unique assistance exclusive of other situations. To organize a group on the basis of extreme client numbers without regard to whether the group becomes a profitable experience is outside the authors' guidance concept. The group provides a unique experience fostering positive growth of each member.

Purposes of Group Guidance

Groups are formed for any of several purposes. The group is a vehicle for assisting the members to make certain orientational transitions throughout their school careers. It prepares the pupils for a new experience within the present school environment. The pupil learns to understand the environment and his relation to it and thus views the school and guidance program more positively. The counselor meets many pupils, and in addition to the orientation activities he accomplishes many public relations activities.

In elementary school it is necessary to provide opportunities for pupils to involve themselves in various specialized learning experiences, e.g., dramatic activities, music, or sports. These extra class activities critically extend the living-learning situation. The counselor utilizes these activities in promoting increased participant self-understanding. The informal atmosphere of these activities naturally promotes guidance and counseling services.

A third group purpose relates to activity in pre-individual counseling. In this situation, the pupils discuss general concerns of their age group. The counselor or leader simply allows each participant to think about the subject-matter and to contribute when appropriate. By allowing the pupils to discuss common concerns, individuals seek help for a particular manifestation of the problem. This can lead to individual assistance by the elementary counselor.

A fourth group function concerns the use of groups for counseling endeavors within this group. Specialized training and supervised experience is needed. Experiences in group counseling help pupils learn that other pupils have similar concerns. Often peer-attempted solutions mean more than the counselor's suggestions and threaten less than the unknown variables facing the pupil. Finally group counseling supports and reinforces group member needs attainable only in the less autonomous group setting.

Principles of Group Guidance

Group processes are an integral part of the guidance program. Without acceptance of this basic principle attempts to utilize groups are predestined to limited, if any, success. Group processes aid in achieving those guidance objectives which cannot be met in strictly one-to-one counseling. This does not preclude the use of group processes in achieving purposes accomplishable in individual sessions. It does suggest that unless there is a clearly defined advantage to working with groups of pupils, individual interviewing remains the center of counselor time and attention.

Groups supplement individual guidance. Thus, when a number of individuals manifest similar concerns a group aids in achieving the objectives of the guidance program. Groups, *per se*, without clearly defined and meaningful goals are not acceptable under these principles. Groups also complement individual counseling. The group provides a vehicle through which the pupil examines himself without immediate personal application or need for defensive action. He projects into the group situation his feelings, without clearly identifying these feelings as an unacceptable part of his behavior pattern. On the basis of this trial examination the pupil may decide that further, more depth-oriented assistance is valuable and, thus, seeks the counselor's assistance on an individual basis.

In terms of the individual, the group provides important adjustive, therapeutic and developmental assistance. The meeting of needs is determined in large measure by the skill of the group leader. The counselor should have prior experience and training in group processes. Finally, in group guidance the focus is on the pupil as an individual. The group gives additional assistance to individual pupils.

The Behavioral Approach

In this book the basic orientation to working with pupils is the behavioral approach. The group leader (counselor) needs to understand behavioral theory. Chapter 4 presents a basic coverage of the subject. Several processes are utilized in behavioral group work. The first process is reinforcement. The counselor determines the kinds of remarks he wishes to reinforce, i.e., respond to. Usually these include information gathering remarks and positive self reference statements. By responding to the predetermined type of remark the counselor assists group members to move in socially desirable directions, meeting their educational or vocational goals.

A second process is modeling. A model pupil, with concerns similar to the counselor's, is presented to the group. This sets a pattern for group reaction and the counselor reinforces those statements or activities relating to the predetermined group goals. Numerous modeling methods are used. The actual pupil comes into the group; video or audio tape recordings are played to give visual and audio cues to the group members; role playing to a prepared typescript is used with members of the group playing one or several roles. Generally the use of live models is less desirable since the conversation or interview is not as concentrated as an edited version presented on tape or a role-playing situation.

Expectations

Persons normally seek out counselors in order to meet certain needs. Whether or not these needs can be stated in specific terms by the counselee does not change the fact that he seeks something. At the elementary level the nonspecific is generally the case. The pupil often is not aware of his needs nor his resultant behavior, and it becomes the job of the counselor to provide first, the orientation to counseling and second, counseling assistance. When dealing with more than one pupil this need is compounded, and the counselor establishes the reason for group formation, expectations and group functioning. As the elementary school includes a rather wide range of pupils, groups formed at various levels have a variety of rationales. First-grade pupils learn more effective interpersonal relationships with the help of the counselor. Sixth-grade pupils need to understand the meanings of the transition to Junior High. In addition, in most groups, anxieties are proper topics for discussion. Group formation during the counselor's initial year may be from outside, i.e., through teachers, incumbent counselors or other persons. However, the counselor realizes that voluntary involvement is more meaningful than involuntary attendance and he actively fosters this within the school.

Application to Group Tasks

In terms of group activity specified earlier and under the general methodological rubric of the "behavioral approach," the elementary school counselor operates in the following manner with the pupil groups.

ORIENTATION.   Children tend to be anxious about the unknown. Developmental efforts to alleviate these anxieties are varied and they are designed to provide the pupil with increased competency and confidence in handling new situations. The elementary counselor is available to pupils whenever this activity is necessary.

Many times the modern school is called upon to initiate new programs for the pupils. Whether these are designed to meet specific needs of a small group of pupils or to meet more general needs of the pupil population, the children and parents need to become better acquainted with the program. The counselor arranges groups of pupils, parents, or mixed groups and assists them in better understanding the rationale for the new offerings. Other persons who have experienced the activity provide models for the pupils. This includes carefully directed group interaction allowing pupils to voice their opinions and concerns. The counselor listens and reinforces those behaviors or statements which increase the movement toward understanding the new curriculum or toward reducing anxiety. When simple lecturing, teaching, or a letter home would not suffice, the counselor increases the involvement of the persons who will be affected by the program.

Another common orientation problem is transition between segments of the school. Pupils are often quite apprehensive about leaving the secure atmosphere which they enjoy in the elementary school and facing the diverse extensions of junior high school. Adding to this anxiety are the stories which the junior high students relate to the elementary pupils, increasing their psychological tension. The counselor provides the opportunity for the pupil to learn about the new situation and to be more aware of himself. This involvement differentiates the proposed activity of the elementary counselor from a film tour or visit to the school. External information is meaningless if the pupil does not have greater self-understanding about his own concerns and his own behavior and feelings in new situations. Group discussion focusing upon the movement into the next segment is valuable if the counselor reinforces those statements and behaviors positively related to the move. Finally he gives individual assistance to certain pupils in the group.

SPECIALIZED LEARNING. The counselor assists pupils to greater self-understanding as applied to specialized areas. For example, the pupil needs to understand present and future meaning of extracurricular activity. Too often the pupil is given an opportunity to make a decision while he has relatively little information from which to decide. The counselor, in a group setting, assists the pupils in making more meaningful decisions. Likewise when a parent decides for a pupil or adopts a "do what you want" attitude the counselor creates an opportunity for a meaningful dialogue. The counselor establishes general goals and discusses those statements related more directly to these goals. The objective is to help pupils make better decisions and to ease the way for any future necessary alterations.

INDIVIDUALIZED COUNSELING. The discussion on orientation includes a reference to individualized counseling. Once a group is formed the counselor tunes in to the needs of the group and of each individual in the group. If necessary the counselor initiates individual counseling. Though this is not a primary focus for the counselor in the group, it does occur. Group members with inadequate self-concepts require this attention. Self-rejection is more apparent in a small group than in other settings within the school. Thus, the counselor reinforces those activities and statements which are positive and growth producing.

GROUP COUNSELING. Finally, of course, is the group counseling situation. In this case the counselor counsels a group of pupils. This involves the greatest counselor skill for he is dealing with a variety of pupils in a counseling relationship. Preceding discussions advocate a behavioral change approach. The reader is referred to the chapter on counseling for a clearer understanding of the goals and processes of counseling. The counselor applies this understanding within the group in an attempt to counsel group members. Krumboltz and Thoresen[5] report the application of this process to a discussion of future plans and decision-making with a group of pupils. The counselor reinforces any information gathering remark of any of the four group members. A model-reinforcement method was used. The general results suggest that the reinforcement process tends to increase the number of information-seeking behaviors of the pupils. Many other types of group counseling occur. The basic requirement is that the counselor has a prior idea of the general group goals and utilizes reinforcement techniques within the group. The counselor establishes specific processes resulting in behavioral change. He responds to the group members in enhancing behavior change.

The reader is cautioned to examine carefully the precepts of behavioral counseling. There is a need to be aware of the rationale established for the behaviorist and its limitations. Finally it is essential that the counselor be trained to provide the assistance suggested above. Group processes are difficult under the most favorable conditions and thus the better prepared the person the more valuable the process is for the pupils.

Initiating and Continuing Groups

Groups begin in several ways. They may form when the same group of pupils eat lunch together or play together during recess or be a product of formal structure and control from outside sources. They may occur as a result of several factors related to either of the above. Regardless of the process by which elementary groups begin, some structure by which the group continues

---

[5] John D. Krumboltz and Carl E. Thoresen, "The Effect of Behavioral Counseling in Group and Individual Settings on Information-Seeking Behavior," *Journal of Counseling Psychology,* 11, 324–333 (Winter 1964).

to grow and function is necessary, particularly at the elementary level. The following topics are guidelines for the elementary counselor in the process of initiating and continuing groups.

IDENTIFICATION FOR GROUPS. One of the tasks facing the group leader is establishing the group for some type of operation. This occurs in several ways. First the pupils are informed that there is an opportunity for this type of activity. Those who wish to become involved are encouraged to volunteer and the group is scheduled.

Another method is to have various persons refer pupils who need assistance. The pupil is sent to the counselor and he arranges a time for meeting the individuals. It is obvious that a combination is used where some are self-referred and some are referred by others.

The counselor determines the criterion for placing pupils in a group. One possibility brings pupils with similar concerns or problems into a small group with the expectation that the situation existing among the individuals is alleviated by the process of group interaction. Such diagnostic problem categories as under-achievement are appropriate for this group.

Another method includes individuals having varying personality patterns. These people become part of the group in an attempt to understand themselves and to learn new behaviors.

Some persons need careful screening before becoming group members. Pupils using group psychodynamics to attack others are removed and given individual help. The extremely aggressive or hostile individual destroying the group atmosphere by fulfilling his own needs within the group is also removed. There is some question whether persons continuously in contact with each other outside the group ought to be included in the same group. Finally a person monopolizing the group is also excluded. Thus, any person upsetting the opportunity for group members to interact and to learn from the interaction probably is not a good prospect for group guidance activities.

In any case the counselor provides information concerning the structure and content of the group so that the group can function. The various rules and regulations facilitating the group are made clear to the members. There is a major difference between groups at various levels. Communication, structure of the group, length of operation, all relate to the grade and age level of the pupils.

SIZE OF THE GROUP. The size of the group depends on the maturity of the child, his problems, the competency of the counselor, and the general characteristics of the group members. At the elementary level, the size is small, approximately four to six. This provides each pupil more opportunity for interaction and at the same time allows the counselor greater involvement, mandated by the fact that the pupils are not as verbal or as concerned as they might be. Also, under our rationale the counselor utilizes a behavioral approach suggesting the need to selectively reinforce the responses of the group members.

LENGTH OF SESSION. As with most school activities any extracurricular activity generally fits into the classroom schedule. This is even more necessary for elementary pupils, as the span of attention and activity precludes long sessions. Generally the length is about twenty to twenty-five minutes for most groups. The group has a special meeting place with decor conducive to group interaction. Circular seating is necessary and the materials in the room are not more interesting than the group. This simply suggests that there is a need to keep the setting relatively simple and uncluttered so that the group can progress toward accomplishing its selected goals.

LENGTH OF TIME. The group continues only as long as the group members receive benefit from attendance. One session does not realistically serve the purpose. However, extending it over several weeks without some indication of individual and group progress meets the needs of the counselor as opposed to the needs of the group members. Evaluation is necessary so that the progress or lack of progress is noted.

R U L E S.   The elementary school counselor establishes rules under which the group session is held. Whether these come strictly from the counselor or from a cooperative endeavor depends upon the counselor's personality. However, without this structure the group is predoomed to minimal success.

The following illustrates some rules which provide a necessary structure for beginning a group:

1. Group guidance and counseling is a cooperative job.
2. Group members must be willing to examine their problems honestly. Any refusal to do this will decrease the group's and each member's movement toward solution.
3. Listen to what the person next to you is saying and expect him to listen to you when you have something to say.
4. Stick with the current topic. The time to change is when most of the group members seem to be willing to examine another topic.
5. Speak whenever you have something to say. If you are not completely clear about your idea the group can assist you in the clarification process.
6. If you have had a similar experience tell the other person. Often you understand yourself better as you find yourself talking to others about how they feel.
7. The purpose of the group is to explore problems together. Any solution or decision which occurs, however, must be your own.
8. Group discussion is enhanced when everybody trusts one another. The more quickly you get to know the others and to trust them the more quickly the group is going to have value for all members.

The language used in presenting these rules is determined by the age and developmental level of the pupils.

Group Roles

Within any group there are a variety of roles assumed by various people. Benne and Sheats[6] have classified these as follows:

1. Group Task Roles—Participant roles here are related to the task which the group is deciding to undertake or has undertaken. Their purpose is to facilitate the coordinated group effort in the selection and definition of a common problem and in the solution of that problem.
2. Group Building and Maintenance Roles—The roles in this category are oriented toward the functioning of the group as a group. They are designed to alter or maintain the group way of working, to strengthen, regulate and perpetuate the group as a group.
3. Individual Roles—This category does not classify member-roles as such since the "participants" denoted here are directed toward the satisfaction of the "participant's" individual needs. Their purpose is some individual goal which is not relevant either to the group task or to the functioning of the group as a group. Such participations are, of course, highly relevant to the problem of group training, insofar as such training is directed toward improving group maturity or group task efficiency.

During the course of any group interaction various roles may be assumed by the leader or members in each of the three areas. Illustrative of the group task roles are the following:

"The *initiator-contributor* suggests or proposes to the group new ideas or a changed way of regarding the group problem or goal."

[6] Kenneth D. Benne and Paul Sheats, "Functional Roles of Group Members," *Journal of Social Issues*, **4**, 42–47 (Spring 1948).

"The *information giver* offers facts or generalizations which are 'authoritative' or relates his own experience pertinently to the group problem."

"The *energizer* prods the group to action or decision attempts to stimulate or arouse the group to 'greater' or 'higher quality' activity."[7]

Group Building and Maintenance Roles are related to building group-centered attitudes. These include the following and may be part of the role of member or leader.

"The *harmonizer* mediates the differences between other members, attempts to reconcile disagreements, relieves tension in conflict situations through jesting or pouring oil on the troubled waters and so forth."

"The *standard setter* expresses standards for the group to attempt to achieve in its functioning or applies standards in evaluating the quality of group processes."[8]

Finally, the Individual Roles which are used to satisfy individual needs include some of the following:

"The *blocker* tends to be negativistic and stubbornly resistant, disagreeing and opposing without or beyond 'reason' and attempting to maintain or bring back an issue after the group has rejected or by-passed it."

"The *help seeker* attempts to call forth 'sympathy' responses from other group members or from the whole group, whether through expressions of insecurity, personal confusion, or depreciation of himself beyond reason."[9]

The counselor is aware of the variety of roles played by the group members. He utilizes this knowledge to keep the group working. This is especially true if the basic approach is behavioral. Any reinforcement takes into account the verbal report or physical activity of the group member along with some notion

[7] *Ibid.*
[8] *Ibid.*
[9] *Ibid.*

of the motivating factor behind the behavior. If the pupil responds continually from an individual need point of view the leader carefully avoids reinforcing this behavior since it usually does not facilitate group oriented goals whether they are initiated within the group or are products of the counselor and/or society.

Role of the Counselor

The effective counselor is most often characterized by richness of personality and capacity for perceptiveness and flexibility. He understands group processes and group dynamics. He is a student of human behavior, especially child behavior and can accept, within the group, whatever deviations might be exhibited in the group. He provides the psychological and physical climate for the group. He utilizes the group and individual members to generate positive relationships. The counselor is a catalytic agent who uses his knowledge of behavior, group dynamics, and behavior change to stimulate verbal and non-verbal responses toward positive behavior for group members.

Training

Examination of the training of group workers is necessary with reference to the preceding statements. Although the teacher works with groups every period of the day there is enough uniqueness about group counseling or guidance to warrant specialized preparation. Krumboltz[10] describes the preparation used for the counselors in his group. All were assigned to a school during October prior to the experimental efforts. They "participated in weekly seminars, read various assignments and spent one half day per week in their respective schools as part

[10] Krumboltz and Thoresen, *op. cit.*

of their training."[11] The rationale of behavioral counseling was discussed and role playing situations were devised during the weekly seminars. They were provided with interview rating sheets on which to categorize verbal information-seeking responses and other responses during the interviews. Each counselor practiced exercising the rapid judgment needed in deciding whether or not a given statement was to be classified as an information-seeking response.

Counselors selected subjects from the pool of volunteers in their high school to practice interviewing prior to the beginning of the experiment. These practice sessions were tape-recorded and used for discussion during the seminar. Regularly scheduled individual interviews were also held between each counselor and one of the instructors.[12]

This process prepared the counselor for a specific type of group work. With dimensions of the group specified the counselor was given work in group precesses during the preparation program. Many counselor education institutions are attempting to integrate group practice in their preparation programs.

Teacher Involvement

Teacher involvement in guidance activities is clearly established. By the nature of the classroom arrangement, the teacher extends his opportunities for contact with pupils. Thus the counselor utilizes the teacher in various guidance activities. When group activity is discussed involvement of the counselor and the teacher needs to be delineated. As was stated earlier, guidance and counseling focus upon the individual as opposed to

[11] *Ibid.*, p. 327.
[12] *Ibid.*, p. 327.

subject matter content, and the teacher is assisted in understanding the objectives of the group. The teacher is utilized in the selection process. He is in a more favorable position to know the pupil and to be able to describe his behavior, personality factors, or ability level. Once the group is formed and operative the teacher is kept informed of the meaningful data emerging from the group. This creates a problem since some of the material within the group may be confidential and not relatable to the teacher. The counselor does have an obligation to keep contact with the teacher concerning the general aspects of the group. Briefly stated the counselor consults with teachers prior to establishing groups and communicates, generally, the progress of the group. Unless the teacher feels and actually is involved the chances of successful program operation are slight.

What Outcomes Might Be Reasonably Expected

Some research suggests the various outcomes possible through group activities. Relatively little of the research is reported at the elementary level.[13] The descriptions are of value in terms of illustrating potential areas of counselor and teacher involvement in elementary schools. They also indicate the need for further investigation and research with elementary age youth.

Kranzler[14] et al. report that group counseling and group work in the classroom seem to support the hypothesis that behavior modification is possible. However, the gains reported for the classroom group tend to disappear when new situations are

[13] Merville C. Shaw and Rosemary Wursten, "Research on Group Procedures in Schools: A Review of the Literature," *The Personnel and Guidance Journal*, 44, 27–34 (September 1965).

[14] Gerald D. Kranzler, George Roy Mayer, Calvin O. Dyer, and Paul F. Munger, "Counseling with Elementary School Children: An Experimental Study," *The Personnel and Guidance Journal*, 44, 944–949 (May 1966).

observed. This was not true of the counseled group. Ohlsen[15] reports several group projects dealing with gifted under-achievers. Significant growth was noted in self awareness and acceptance of self and others. The group offered an environment for better self understanding and this led to greater understanding and acceptance of others.

Broedel[16] *et al.* provided group counseling with four groups of under-achievers. Three of the groups showed significant growth in achievement test scores, increased acceptance of self and others and improved ability to relate to peers, siblings and parents. Atwell and Odum[17] report success with a group of pupils with behavior problems. The pupils began to act more socially and the group seemed to be of value in working with this type of individual. Smith[18] demonstrated the need for clarity in role expectations. Due to the presence of two silent members the group was not able to make progress and expressions of dis-satisfactions increased.

In short the application of group processes in the elementary school is highly theoretical. Past success at other levels suggests that groups may be valuable for the counselor and teacher at the elementary level. Behavior modification, at least within the given environment, does occur and in some cases this is transferred to other situations. There is a need to provide more research evidence on the types of elementary youth for which group interaction is most valuable. The areas suggested in the

[15] Merle M. Ohlsen, "Counseling Within A Group Setting," *Journal of the National Association of Women Deans and Counselors,* **23**, 104–109 (April 1960).

[16] John Broedel, Merle Ohlsen, Fred Proff, and Charles Southard, "The Effects of Group Counseling on Gifted Underachieving Adolescents," *Journal of Counseling Psychology,* **7**, 163–170 (Fall 1960).

[17] Arthur A. Atwell and Robert R. Odum, "The Guv'nors Venture in Group Guidance," *Elementary School Journal,* **64**, 124–130 (November 1963).

[18] Ewart E. Smith, "The Effects of Clear & Unclear Role Expectations on Group Productivity & Defensiveness," *The Journal of Abnormal & Social Psychology,* **55**, 213–217 (September 1957).

present chapter are starting points offering the counselor or teacher an opportunity to try various group processes in several guidance areas.

Summary

Guidance activities involving small groups of elementary pupils have a place in the total guidance program. The counselor acquires knowledge of group dynamics, child growth and development, and a basic rationale for group work prior to attempting to work with groups. In this book the rationale suggested is a behavioral approach. The range of activities is from guidance activities, e.g., orientation, to counseling. The counselor is charged with clearly establishing goals or objectives and of attempting to aid the group to move in these directions. He must also enlist the aid of teachers in selecting or establishing meaningful groups and communicating to the teachers the general progress of the group. Specialized preparation is essential for the counselor in group work.

SELECTED REFERENCES

Edward C. Glanz and Robert W. Hayes, *Groups in Guidance,* 2nd Ed. (Boston: Allyn & Bacon, Inc., 1967).

C. Gratton Kemp, *Perspectives on the Group Process* (Boston: Houghton Mifflin Company, 1964).

Walter Lifton, *Working With Groups*, 2nd Ed. (New York: John Wiley & Sons, Inc., 1966).

VOCATIONAL DEVELOPMENT IN THE ELEMENTARY SCHOOL

Rapid change universally pervades American society. Automation, civil rights, increased technology, space exploration, to name a few factors, point to the fact that the world of tomorrow will be considerably different than today's world. The pupil in school today is called upon to fill positions unknown to today's labor market. Choice, decision-making, and vocational planning are becoming increasingly complex, and the demands of society pressure the individual as he prepares for future endeavors.

The individual will need to display increased technical competence. The pressure toward more education will continue and only a small percentage of jobs will be available to persons without education beyond high school. Guidance programs provide youth with basic knowledge about themselves and the working world. This is true at the elementary level, as career development begins at this time. Vocational elementary school guidance begins the process of assisting the pupils with vocational development, by increasing the opportunities to learn about themselves and the world of work. Several specific purposes of vocational guidance for elementary school children can be identified:

TO ASSIST IN DEVELOPING THE SELF-CONCEPT. Vocational development is frequently a reflection of one's self-concept. Therefore, vocational guidance helps the pupil in developing an adequate self concept.

One basic aspect of choice is the coming into being with oneself. While the child is forming a concept of himself, he also develops a concept of an ideal self, an image he wishes to become. This one choice of early childhood is possibly more closely related to a concept of an ideal self than to a real self. The child projects himself into the future, imagining what he wants to be when he grows up. Eventually a co-experience between his ideal self and real self-concept occurs.[1]

The 1960 White House Conference on Children and Youth[2] pointed out that guidance and counseling should begin in elementary school with educational and vocational planning based on early and continuous appraisal of each child in order to identify his assets and liabilities. Children learn that interests and abilities enter into an individual's work choice. The child relates what he perceives about himself to his future vocational development.

Grell[3] states that the attitudes toward self begin early in life

---

[1] Carroll Miller, *Foundations of Guidance* (New York: Harper and Brothers, Publishers, 1961), pp. 216–234.
[2] Golden Anniversary 1960 White House Conference on Children and Youth, "Recommendations," *Composite Report of Forum Findings* (Washington, D.C.: U.S. Government Printing Office, 1960).
[3] Lewis Grell, "How Much Occupational Information in the Elementary School?" *The Vocational Guidance Quarterly,* 9, 52, 53, 1960.

and are important in the development of a future worker. The elementary school pupil is helped in developing a positive attitude toward himself. He learns about his assets and liabilities and develops wholesome attitudes about himself. With these attitudes he copes with success and failure and improves his work habits.

TO STIMULATE INTEREST IN SEVERAL OCCUPATIONAL AREAS. "If we accept the premise that attitudes and values are developed in the formative years, then a formalized program of direction to the world of work should be inaugurated in the primary grades."[4] Through such a program children acquaint themselves with new and unfamiliar vocations and develop an appreciation for different kinds of work. Frequently children are aware only of occupations they contact personally.

TO DEVELOP A CONSTRUCTIVE ATTITUDE TO-WARD WORK. This attitude is evident in their school work and subsequent occupation. Children can gain a perception of the relationship of education to work and develop study habits conducive to the development of work habits.[5]

Pupils develop a respect for other people, their work, and their service and product contributions. Children learn that all types of labor are worthy of maximum effort, and all honest labor is dignified. The interaction of work groups permits today's high standard of living. No work is degraded, if it is done well.[6]

TO ASSIST PUPILS TO BECOME AWARE OF A CHANGING WORLD OF WORK. Technological changes rapidly change the world and certainly affect the type of work children see. Wrenn[7] says the elementary school has a more

[4] John Wellington and Nan Olechowski, "Attitudes Toward the World of Work in Elementary School," *The Vocational Guidance Quarterly*, **14**, 160–162, 1966.

[5] *Ibid.*

[6] Grell, *op. cit.*, pp. 52, 53.

[7] C. Gilbert Wrenn, *The Counselor in a Changing World* (Washington, D.C.: American Personnel and Guidance Association, 1962) pp. 150, 151.

urgent need to stress vocational information and counseling than it did in the past. Educational requirements to enter occupations change too rapidly to permit youth to keep abreast of them, unless systematic help is given.

Numerous social and economic factors resulting from a rapidly changing society increase the need for early vocational guidance. Such factors as change in industrial processes, increased number of jobs and shifts in some occupational groups, the mobility of population from rural to urban living, higher standards of living, and decreased employment opportunities for youth are examples.

Children make psycho-social changes as a result of pressure from new technological and scientific advances. When parents lose jobs (are unemployed) because of technological changes, the child feels the effects of adult concern, frustration, and confusion. "Even when parents do have some insight with regard to changing educational and work requirements, they frequently interpret such change to mean increased pressure for higher scholastic achievement without regard for a child's personal needs nor his academic potentialities."[8]

TO ASSIST STUDENTS WHO DROP OUT OF SCHOOL AND GO TO WORK. In *The Counselor in a Changing World,* Wrenn[9] recommended that it is the responsibility of the counselor to provide realistic social and vocational orientation in the elementary school, particularly for pupils who terminate their formal education at this level. More education and training are required for entrance into occupations. In view of this trend, the proportion of children who do not complete high school is extremely high. Studies indicate that unemployment is higher among dropouts than for high school graduates, and the situation is likely to worsen.

The Department of Labor reports that many of the young

---

[8] Goldie Kaback, "Automation, Work, and Leisure: Implications for Elementary Education," *Vocational Guidance Quarterly,* 13, 202–206, 1965.
[9] C. Gilbert Wrenn, *op. cit.,* p. 138.

people who are 16 to 21 years old, and no longer in school, dropped out; high proportions of these (in the labor force) are unemployed. For example, in the fall of 1965 one-third of the 5.6 million 16–21-year-old youths in the labor force, and no longer in school, did not graduate from high school. Sixteen per cent of the boys and 25 per cent of the girls 16 and 17 years old were unemployed.[10]

Wolfbein,[11] and Glueck and Glueck[12] interpret the data on school dropouts, adult unemployment, and juvenile delinquency as showing that these problems could have been reduced during the first four or five years of school, if guidance personnel were available.

Vocational Development Theories

To Frank Parsons, planning one's career was a threefold process. He recommended the individual study himself, study the occupational world, then by "true reasoning" make a choice based on the facts. However, vocational development is considered more complex today. Several theories have been proposed which encompass a variety of variables in the process of vocational development.

Borow[13] believes the identifying marks of present day psychological conceptions of career development fall into four general

[10] Forest Bogan, "Employment of School Age Youth" Special Labor Force Report No. 68, Reprint No. 2493 (Washington, D.C.: U.S. Department of Labor, 1966) pp. 739–743.
[11] Seymour Wolfbein, "The Transition from School to Work," *Personnel and Guidance Journal,* **38**, 98–105, 1959.
[12] Sheldon Glueck and Eleanor Glueck, *Predicting Delinquency and Crime* (Cambridge: Harvard University Press, 1959).
[13] Henry Borow, "Development of Occupational Motives and Roles," In *Review of Child Development Research,* Lois Hoffman and Martin Hoffman, editors (New York: Russell Sage Foundation, 1966) p. 397.

groups: (a) There is more to establishing a theoretical framework for generating vocational hypotheses than interpreting empirical findings. (b) More attention is being given to stimulus variables thought to be associated with vocational development, i.e., types of child-rearing climate, patterns of course work and school experience, avocational experiences, and opportunities for counseling. (c) There is greater interest in the childhood roots of vocational development. (d) Acceptance of responsibility for personal planning, knowledge and use of sources of occupational information, overt personal planning for the future, and sequence of the decisions in career development add to the variables of aspiration and choice in occupational behavior of pre-employed youth.

A review of some widely accepted theories of vocational development shows the complexity of the process and the significant aspects affecting elementary school children.

Ginzberg's Theory of Vocational Development

Ginzberg's[14] theory of occupational choice contains four basic elements.

First, occupational choice is a developmental process, typically taking place over a period of ten years. Second, the process is largely irreversible. Investments of time, money and ego during the process, although they may not be regarded as absolute mandates in themselves, do make it increasingly difficult to change the direction of the developmental process as the decision-making process continues. Third, Ginzberg makes it clear that compromise is an essential aspect of every choice. This compromise exists between interests, capacities, values and opportunities. Acknowledgement of this aspect of vocational choice was made as far back as 1909 by Frank Parsons, when he described

---

[14] Eli Ginzberg, Sol Ginsburg, Sidney Axelrod, and John Herma, *Occupational Choice: An Approach to a General Theory* (New York: Columbia University Press, 1951).

vocational counseling as a process during which an individual is helped to study both himself and occupational opportunities, while, at the same time, being encouraged to compromise between his abilities, interests, and opportunities.

Ginzberg, in his fourth element, postulates three periods of occupational choice: a period of fantasy choice characterized by the wish to be an adult; a period of tentative choice beginning at about eleven, first determined by interests, and subsequently by the individual's capacities and then by his values; and, finally, a period of realistic choice beginning at about age seventeen. This third period is divided into substages labeled exploration (in which the individual realistically looks at possible vocations), crystallization (in which the individual focuses on one or a few specific occupational areas and eliminates others), and specification, (which involves the devotion of energies to one specific occupation).

Super's Theory of Vocational Development

Donald Super[15] stresses the concept of vocational development as being synonymous with the development of a self-concept; the process of vocational adjustment is the process of implementing a self-concept, with the degree of satisfaction attained proportionate to the degree of self-concept realization. Work is a way of life, and adequate vocational and personal adjustment result, when both the nature of the work and its concomitant way of life are congenial to the aptitudes, interests and values of the individual.

The following is a brief summary of Super's theory of vocational development. People differ in their abilities, interests and personalities. Thus, they qualify for a number of occupations, each of which requires a characteristic pattern of abilities. In

[15] Donald Super, "A Theory of Vocational Development," *American Psychologist,* **8,** 185–190 (May 1953).

addition, vocational preferences, competencies, and environments, and hence self-concepts, change with time and experience. Vocational development is a series of life-stages and substages. The two stages, according to Super, are the Exploratory stage and the Establishment stage. The Exploratory stage refers to the period when the individual seeks the occupation which implements his or her self concept. This period has three substages: Fantasy, Tentative, and Realistic. Similar to Ginzberg, these are defined as: (a) a period of fantasy choices, governed largely by the wish to be an adult; (b) a period of tentative choices determined largely by interests, and (c) the period of realistic choices beginning about age seventeen, during which exploratory, crystallization, and specification phases succeed each other.

The Establishment stage is divided into trial and stable phases. First, the individual locates himself in a career, and via a process of acculturation and insight, he sees a possible place for himself in the world of work. Second, the individual, who now knows more specifically what he wants to do and where he may be able to do it, studies his work to see how he can succeed and institutes such goal-directed behavior.

Super clearly understands that the nature of the career pattern is determined by the individual's parental socio-economic level, mental ability, personality characteristics and opportunities, but he also feels that development through life-stages is guided by: (a) aiding in the process of maturation, (b) aiding in reality testing, and (c) aiding in the development of a self-concept. The process of compromise between individual and social factors, between the self-concept and reality, is one of role-playing, whether in fantasy, the counseling interview, or real-life activities. Finally, work satisfactions and life satisfactions depend on the extent to which the individual finds adequate outlets for his abilities, interests, personality traits, and values. His type of work,

work situation, and way of life influence how he plays the role which his growth and exploratory experiences tell him are congenial and appropriate.

Tiedeman's Theory of Vocational Development

David Tiedeman[16] views careers in terms of vocational development, but he feels an explicit statement of the process of decision making in vocational development is needed. Individual and social congruence, as expressed in vocational behavior, is effected within a set of decisions. This set, and the context or relevance for the anticipation and implementation of each, constitutes the essence of vocational development.

According to his theory of decision and vocational development, the latter is oriented by each of several decisions with respect to school and work. With regard to each decision, decision making is divided into two periods: the period of anticipation and the period of implementation or adjustment.

The Period of Anticipation has four subaspects or stages:

1. Exploration is characterized by random acquisitive activities in which a number of possible goals are considered. The relevant goals set the field for choice, but the mind is open. Conditions of relevance are given order and meaning only in relation to the goal. The fields are highly imaginatory and transitory—unassociated. In this period there is the least reflection on aspiration, opportunity, interest, capability, and distasteful requirements of the job.

2. Crystallization, in which the organization and ordering of all relevant considerations in relation to each of the goals, takes place. Opportunity, interest, and capability, as well as distasteful requirements—relevant aspects of the field set by

[16] David Tiedeman, "Decision and Vocational Development: A Paradigm and Its Implication," *Personnel and Guidance Journal,* **40**, 15–20 (1961).

each goal are important, and the person measures himself in relation to each alternative.

3. Choice or decision becomes imminent as crystallizations stabilize. Degrees of power vary and these degrees are a function of the complexity of the situation and the antagonism of the alternatives involved in the ultimate crystallization.

4. Specification occurs when choice readies the individual to act on his decision. Further elaboration of the image in the future ensues, and former doubts concerning the position dissipate.

The Period of Implementation or Adjustment has three sub-aspects or stages. These are:

1. Induction—in which imaginative concerns come face-to-face with reality on the day of initiation. The goals of the individual and society come into contact. The individual is at first receptive and eventually perfects his individual goal. By this time, the individual has gained acceptance and fulfilled the expectations of co-workers and superiors.

2. Transition—in which a metamorphosis occurs. The mood of reaction changes from responsive to assertive. The group goal and field is attacked in order to incorporate the modified goal and field of the person.

3. Maintenance—in which the assertive need subsides and equilibrium is reestablished. This phase is initiated with the modification of both the individual and group goals.

Although the decision is in the maintenance stage, it is possible to disturb the "status quo" by changes in goals, the field, further vocational development, or ensuing disintegration. Furthermore, the course of events relevant to decision making unfolds with regard to several simultaneous decisions.

These decisions relate to a wider context of decisions past, present, and future, and the individual organizes these diverse sets. Systems of secondary order specify vocational development. Anticipation influences a person's action with regard to past, present, and future decisions.

Vocational counseling enhances the operation of reason and frees the person to act upon a particular decision as well as to view decisions in relation to those made and unmade. The client views his educational-vocational decisions as a means-end chain, an earlier end becoming a means for a later goal. Behavior is purposeful and elaboration of self ensues. Furthermore, no goal becomes so compelling in conflicting situations that it cannot give way to a later, more compelling goal.

Roe's Theory of Vocational Development

Anne Roe's[17] approach to vocational choice includes hypotheses about the relationship between early experience, attitudes, abilities, interests, and other personality factors affecting an individual's ultimate vocational selection. Her theory is based in part on Maslow's hierarchy of prepotent needs, which suggests that higher order needs cannot appear until lower order needs are relatively well satisfied. Whereas essential lower-order needs (e.g., physiological needs such as those reflected in hunger and thirst) show less variability, Roe primarily concerns herself with the more variable higher-order needs, such as the need for understanding, beauty, or self-actualization.

According to Roe, early experience determines the direction of the eventual pattern of psychic energies and results in primarily unconscious needs. The intensity and organization of these needs is the major determinant of the *direction* of motivation, as seen

[17] Anne Roe, "Early Determinants of Vocational Choice," *Journal of Counseling Psychology,* **4,** 212–217 (1957).

in chosen vocational fields, and the *degree* of motivation as expressed in accomplishment.

The significant areas of early experience involve patterns of early experience with parents. The individual's basic orientation with respect to persons later ramifies into patterns of special interests and abilities. Emotional concentration on the child, as seen in both overprotection and overdemanding behavior on the part of the parents, increases the degree of social interest in the child's eventual vocational choice. In the case where the parents are cold and overdemanding, the major orientation toward persons may be regarded as a defensive mechanism to reduce anxiety associated with nonperson orientations. Such needs fulfill occupational groups classified as "General Cultural" (i.e., lawyers, librarians, reporters). On the other hand, parent-child relationships characterized as overprotective (warm) result in a major orientation toward persons which is only partially defensive. Occupational groups termed "Arts and Entertainment" (i.e., performers, teachers, photographers) meet these needs. The parent-child relationship characterized as warm, loving, and accepting results in a major orientation toward persons which is not defensive. Occupations classified as "Service Occupations" (i.e., counselors, social workers, policemen) fulfill these needs.

In contrast, warm casual acceptance of the child by the parent results in a nonperson, nondefensive orientation and is fulfilled in occupations in the group labeled "Technology" (i.e., engineers, dentists, technicians). Parent-child relations characterized by cold avoidance whether rejecting or neglecting result in the choice of occupations such as outdoor occupations or those associated with the group labeled "Science" with a major orientation not toward persons.

As the degree of motivation relates to the level sought in the occupational group, she further hypothesizes that needs satisfied routinely as they appear do not develop into unconscious motivators, and higher-order needs, for which even minimum satisfaction is rarely achieved, become expunged, or if they are lower order, prevent the appearance of higher-order needs, and become dominant and restricting motivators. Finally, delayed need satisfactions become unconscious motivators, depending largely on how much satisfaction is felt. In other words, their strength as motivators depends upon the strength of the basic need within the individual, the length of time elapsing between arousal and satisfaction, and values ascribed to the satisfaction of this need in the immediate environment.

In summary, the pattern of special abilities is primarily determined by the directions in which the psychic energy is involuntarily expended. These directions are initially determined by the patterning of early satisfactions and frustrations. The eventual attention pattern is the major determinant of the field or fields to which a person will apply himself. The degree of motivation depends on unconscious needs and their motivation, and it is evidenced in terms of accomplishment.

Holland's Theory of Vocational Development

Holland[18] integrates existing knowledge about vocational choice theories. He classifies occupations into six major groups, each having somewhat distinctive tasks, and characterized by a distinctive occupational environment. The Motoric Environment is an example used to describe occupations such as laborers, machine operators, aviators, truck drivers, or carpenters; the Persuasive Environment describes salesmen, politicians, and business executives. Other environments include: the Intellectual Environment, the Supportive Environment, the Conforming Environment, and the Esthetic Environment.

[18] John Holland, "A Theory of Vocational Choice," *Journal of Counseling Psychology*, **6**, 35–45 (1959).

At the time of vocational choice, a person is the product of the interaction of:

1. his particular heredity.
2. a variety of cultural and personal forces, including peers, parents and significant adults, his social class, the American culture, and physical environment. From this experience the individual gradually develops a hierarchy of preferred methods of dealing with environmental tasks, referred to as the individual's adjustive orientations. The individual satisfies his adjustive orientations through occupational choice.

Orientation represents a somewhat distinctive LIFE STYLE or developmental pattern characterized by preferred methods of dealing with the environment, it corresponds to the occupational environment. Values, interests, interpersonal skills, and other personal factors determine the LIFE STYLE; the LIFE STYLE heading the hierarchy determines the major direction of choice.

Ordering vocational preferences effects the person's *range* of vocational choice. For example, a hierarchy in which one LIFE STYLE dominates all others results in vocational choice without conflict or hesitancy. An ambiguous hierarchy (one in which there are two or more competing developmental patterns), results in vacillation, making or not making a choice.

The blocking of the hierarchical choice by economic factors or rejection by would-be employers results in the selection of the next highest developmental pattern, if such a pattern is available.

Research indicates that patterning of vocational choices influences the stability of choices, the success encountered in the vocation chosen, and the individual's resistance to deterring factors.

Within a given class of occupations, however, the individual also chooses the level at which he wishes to operate. This choice level is a function of (a) intelligence and (b) self-evaluation, including status needs and an estimation of existing and potential competence, as well as an estimate of relative self worth. Self-evaluation, moreover, is a function of the individual's life history; the primary determinants are: education, socio-economic origin, and family influences.

A person's ability to make discriminations among potential environments in terms of his own attributes is described as his self-knowledge. Self-evaluation, in distinction, is the worth a person attributes to himself. Holland hypothesizes that persons with a limited or inaccurate self-knowledge make inadequate vocational choices with respect to both range and level. Likewise, persons with more information about occupational environments make more adequate choices than do persons with less information. This, of course, is partly a function of age, and it is hypothesized that the amount of knowledge about any occupation is positively correlated with the individual's developmental hierarchy. In other words, the person will know more about the occupations heading his hierarchy.

Vocational environments characterized by distinctive tasks and the individual, characterized by distinctive LIFE STYLES are described above. The process of vocational choice describes the way in which the two interact.

In summary, the influence of: (a) a series of personal factors including self-knowledge and evaluation, knowledge of occupational classes and familiarity with the tasks characteristic of the classes, and the orderliness of the developmental hierarchy, and (b) a series of environmental factors including the range of potential occupational environments, social pressures, evaluations of employers or potential employers, and limitations imposed by socio-economic resources and the physical environment, determine the major occupational class toward which the individual directs himself. Within this major class of occupations the particular occupation chosen is a function of the individual's self-evaluation and ability.

Summary

Having summarized the theories of Ginzberg, Super, Tiedeman, Roe, and Holland, it is possible to draw together a consensus of opinion applicable to vocational choice and the elementary school child.

First, Roe has emphasized the determining influence of early experience (particularly with the parent-child relationship) on the eventual pattern of psychic energies, in terms of direction and strength. These energies result in primarily unconscious needs; the ways these needs are satisfied, mainly in the parent-child relationship, is a major determinant in the degree of motivation expressed in accomplishment. The child's major orientation with respect to persons resulting from these needs later ramifies into patterns of special interests and abilities. These special interests and abilities then determine the general group of occupations into which the individual goes, as well as the level toward which the individual is motivated to move.

Inasmuch as Roe's theory is based on early childhood experiences, it is concerned primarily with the elementary or pre-elementary school child. The concepts of Super and Ginzberg view vocational decision-making as a process extending over a considerable period of time, including the pre-adolescent period when the child is in elementary school. In addition, Super's emphasis on the development of a "self-concept" during the life stages in vocational development emphasizes the importance of the experiences of the elementary school child in the Fantasy stage, the first substage of Super's Exploratory Stage and the first of Ginzberg's three periods of occupational choice.

Period and stage analysis characteristic of Ginzberg, Super, and Holland provide teacher and counselor with better norms than have previously been available, for estimating whether the young person approaches his occupational choice in a manner commensurate with his maturity. In addition, such theories help to identify individuals who encounter abnormal difficulties with the problems of occupational choice and suggest the type of help to offer at different developmental stages. Furthermore, such theories emphasize the limitations attached to offering help prematurely, help more effectively utilized at a later stage. Finally, such theories carry with them a strong warning against an over-evaluation of objective tests and suggest that the child needs outside help, whether from the family or some guidance source, in delimiting the unknown with reference to vocations.

Role models and role-playing critically effect the development of a self-concept. Normal play, for example, provides opportunities for playing roles learned through observation and hearsay; satisfaction-producing roles are played again and, eventually incorporated into the player's behavior pattern or personality. Although the child's first experience with people is in the home and it is the source of various roles for the child, the school now functions as the home did formerly. It is now an important exploratory institution in which the curriculum is a means of formal exploration. The pupils familiarize themselves with a variety of subjects so that later a wise choice of school curricula can be made. School activities, assembly programs, and group activities have indirect exploratory value. Primary social groups also play a major part in the attitude formation of the child. The school also provides new role models for the child and adolescent, so that the individual's behavior is modified and developed by a broader social environment than the home. To be sure, conflict results if the attitudes at home make different evaluations than those encountered in the school environment, but, given adequate role models outside of the home, it is possible for children to develop new personality integrations, allowing them to capitalize on aptitudes and personality traits. Contact with new key figures makes it easier for the child to visualize his real self in a variety of roles, rather than restricting the number of roles to those presented in the home.

Tiedeman is primarily interested in the process of decision-making in vocational adjustment. As such, its implications for the elementary school pupil lie in the ways in which this decision-making process is implemented in school, at home and in other information-producing activities. Although it is the period of anticipation in vocational decision-making that occurs in the elementary school, the passage from the stage of exploration with its random acquisitive activities to crystallization, when alternatives begin to emerge and relate to consequences, cannot be accomplished without thought in relation to aspiration, opportunity, interest and capability, and distasteful requirements of occupational choices. Elementary school encourages this thought.

Finally, Holland, in attempting to integrate knowledge about theories of vocational choice, emphasizes the "wholistic" view of occupational choice. His treatment of "adjustive orientations" and choice levels within given occupational environments, depending primarily on intelligence and self-evaluations force recognition of the fact that the totality of the individual and his environment is pertinent to the decision-making process.

Both Arbuckle[19] and Borow[20] offer a precautionary note regarding vocational development theories. Because the theories integrate many aspects, there is a tendency for a counselor to misconstrue postulates and hypotheses as if they were fact. The body of research from these theories is modest and not altogether consistent. However, the theories lead to research and point out numerous aspects of vocational development important to the counselor.

---

[19] Dugald Arbuckle, "Occupational Information in the Elementary School," *Vocational Guidance Quarterly*, **12**, 77–84 (1963).
[20] Henry Borow, *op. cit.*, pp. 395–417.

Relevant Research Findings

Much of the research involving elementary school children is not related to vocational development theories. However, many studies contribute information about children's occupational knowledge and choices, as well as the influence of socio-economic class, sex, and the school.

Occupational Knowledge and Choice

Simmons[21] felt that the idea of elementary school children being "ignorant and fantasy ridden" in their occupational thinking was not true. The correlation of 0.868 between fourth-grade males' prestige rankings and adult prestige rankings implies a high degree of awareness. The girls in fourth grade were much lower in their agreement with adult prestige ranking. However, most of the occupations were not typically identified as feminine. Simmons concluded that elementary school children have a prestige frame of references and may be able to integrate occupational information. There was also a tendency for occupations ranked high in prestige to be ranked high in interest.

An investigation of twelve-year-old sixth graders' vocational choices and the reasons for their choices showed that 60 per cent of the students made tentative choices. Tentative choices were defined as decisions based on capacities, interests, and values of the individual. More mature choices were correlated with intelligence and feminine sex. Reading retardation seemed to be related to immaturity of occupational choice. Race and socio-economic standing did not seem related in any significant degree with maturity of occupational choice.

[21] Dale Simmons, "Children's Rankings of Occupational Prestige," *Personnel and Guidance Journal*, **41**, 332–335 (1962).

Gunn[22] asked children to rank jobs in order of their standing in the community and to report what they thought the term social class meant. Boys in grades 1 and 2 described the work largely in terms of what it personally meant to them. They typically ranked their expected job and/or father's job highest. Frequently they identified the top one or two jobs, and the others were about the same. Third graders were characterized by wider horizons and a tendency to view jobs in terms of importance to the community. Characteristics which began in the third grade were accentuated in grades 4, 5, and 6. Boys no longer ranked jobs in terms of what they meant personally. Service criteria were used to judge occupations, i.e., good for the community and country. Father's job carried no particular prestige, simply because he performed it. By the seventh grade, the boys saw a definite ladder of occupational prestige.

DeFleur[23] reported that as age increased from six through thirteen, knowledge of roles and status increased as a linear function of age. However, even young children acquired a basic idea of prestige ranking and had considerable information about the labor force. Personal contact was the most effective source of occupational information, and television was the second most important source of learning.

Gifted children in grades 3 through 6 were asked to select from a list the most important characteristic for job satisfaction. The children listed having an opportunity to be helpful to others as the most important. Their parents listed having an opportunity for their children to use their special abilities as most important. The parents and the gifted children included the same requirements in the highest three.[24]

[22] Barbara Gunn, "Children's Conceptions of Occupational Prestige," *Personnel and Guidance Journal*, 42, 558–563 (1964).

[23] M. L. DeFleur, "Children's Knowledge of Occupational Roles and Prestige: Preliminary Report," *Psychological Reports*, 13, 760 (1963).

[24] Walter Barbe and Norman Chambers, "Career Requirements of Gifted Elementary Children and Their Parents," *Vocational Guidance Quarterly*, 11, 137–140 (1963).

Socio-Economic Influence

Socio-economic status operates almost at birth in terms of how parents react to the child. The process and goals of acculturation differ for families from different socio-economic levels. The importance of social class differences in child rearing influences the early formation of occupational attitudes and values. The relationship between social class status and occupational attitudes of elementary school children is unclear. In a longitudinal study Tyler[25] found few career-related differences in interests appearing between students of different social classes, until the eighth grade. Davis, Hagen, and Strouf[26] compared the maturity of vocational choices of sixth-grade children from middle- and lower-class neighborhoods and found no difference.

Galler[27] conducted a study to determine the extent socio-economic class influences a child's choice of occupation and the reasons behind the choice. Upper-middle-class boys and girls gave more intrinsic reasons for occupational choice than lower, possibly because adults find intrinsic interest in their work. The upper-middle class boys gave more altruistic reasons than lower class; there was no difference between the girls. Comparison of self esteem reasons (self-evaluation in relation to the job) yielded no significant difference. Within each group, jobs of all ranges of status were chosen. However, upper-middle-class children chose more occupations, having higher social status than lower-class children. Age appeared to be a factor, as older groups chose higher status occupations than younger children. Clark[28] re-

---

[25] Leona Tyler, "The Antecedents of Two Varieties of Vocational Interests," *Genetic Psychological Monographs,* **70,** 177–227 (1964).

[26] D. Davis, N. Hagen, and J. Strouf, "Occupational Choice of Twelve-year Olds," *Personnel and Guidance Journal,* **40,** 628, 629 (1962).

[27] E. Galler, "Influence of Social Class on Children's Choices of Occupation," *Elementary School Journal,* **51,** 439–445 (1951).

[28] Edward Clark, "Influences of Sex and Social Class on Occupational Preference and Perception," *Personnel and Guidance Journal,* **45,** 440–444 (1967).

ported that middle-class boys expressed a greater preference for professional occupations than do lower-class boys. He believed the fundamental difference in occupational orientation of middle- and lower-class girls was that the lower-class girls did not perceive of homemaking as a separate occupation, whereas this was the third-ranking occupational choice of middle-class girls. He described these as middle class, although the middle was 100 per cent white and the lower was 90 per cent Negro. Stewart[29] reports that social class was a factor in the occupational attitudes of fifth-grade boys. Interest scores were related to occupational preferences of upper status boys and not to those of boys from lower status homes. Lower status children respond to personal reference items such as a wish, i.e., they would like many things which they cannot afford. Nelson[30] reports that children from higher socio-economic families, with higher IQ's, and from urban areas, knew more about occupations and discriminated better among occupations of different status than children of less favorable circumstances.

The occupational development of Negro children is stunted, because they have few high-level job-role models in their community. The importance of models was emphasized by De-Fleur's[31] finding that personal contact was a more effective source of occupational information than television or the general culture. Deutsch[32] described both Negro and white elementary school boys, as aspiring in an unrealistic way to high prestige occupations. The high aspiration level expressed by some lower

[29] Lawrence Stewart, "Relationship of Socio-economic Status to Children's Occupational Attitudes and Interests," *Journal of Genetic Psychology,* **95,** 111–136 (1959).

[30] Richard Nelson, "Knowledge and Interests Concerning Sixteen Occupations Among Elementary and Secondary School Students," *Educational and Psychological Measurement,* **23,** 741–754 (1963).

[31] DeFleur, *op. cit.,* p. 760.

[32] Martin Deutsch, "Minority Group and Class Status as Related to Social and Personality Factors in Scholastic Achievement," *The Society for Applied Anthropology Monographs,* 1960.

class children involves only the appearances, rather than the substance, of aiming high. The lower-class child may not perceive the eventual reward of striving and self-denial as actually attainable and he may fail to acquire a delayed-gratification behavior pattern.[33]

Sex Differences

In a study of elementary school children's occupational choices, O'Hara[34] found differences between reasons reported by boys and girls. For boys in grades 4, 5, and 6, interests were clearly the dominant basis for choices by the sixth grade. Values remained fairly constant throughout the grades. Capacity was mentioned infrequently at each grade level. For girls in grades 4, 5, and 6, values were of primary importance with interests secondary. The girls were highly altruistic. They paid little attention to capacity in making their choices. The choice of teacher, nurse, secretary, and mother accounted for two-thirds of the girls' choices. Because of the limited choices and their experience with these areas, the girls' choices were more realistic than the boys'.

Children's occupational preferences are described as their projected self-image. Tyler[35] studied the interests of first-grade children and found definite sex differences. She found the development of interests related to the sex roles being learned, and that these roles did not exist in isolation from the beginnings of other roles and attitudes. From his review of earlier research, Miller[36] concluded that as a group, preadolescent boys progres-

---

[33] D. Ausubel and P. Ausubel, "Ego Development Among Segregated Negro Children," In A. Passow, editor, *Education in Depressed Areas* (New York: Columbia University Press, 1963).

[34] Robert O'Hara, "The Roots of Careers," *Elementary School Journal,* **62,** 277–280 (1962).

[35] Leona Tyler, "The Relationship of Interests to Abilities and Reputation Among First-Grade Children," *Educational and Psychological Measurement,* **11,** 255–264 (1951).

[36] Carroll Miller, *op. cit.,* pp. 225–234.

sively narrow their range of occupational preferences, while girls seem to have a more limited range at all grade levels. Clark[37] also found that girls limited the variability of their preferences with teacher and nurse, accounting for two-thirds of both lower and middle-class girls. There was little overlap in the occupational preference of boys and girls, when given open response choice.

School Influence

Lifton[38] asked teachers to list which occupation they could illustrate in the classroom. They were limited to only those jobs in which they knew the training requirements, salary levels, and job opportunities. Professions led the list by far, followed by sales and clerical tasks; skilled trades barely showed. The job distribution was almost the exact reverse of the distribution of jobs resulting from census data. Teachers were asked to go through all their classroom books and list the occupations. They found a heavy emphasis on service occupation in the primary grades, followed by a rapid shift to the professions in the upper grades. Again, skilled trades were barely represented. Lifton concluded that children receive a distorted picture of the importance and type of jobs available from both teachers and textbooks. Tennyson and Monnens[39] analyzed the occupations presented in the reading series of six publishing companies. Their analysis found that only a small fraction of the many types of work were given consideration. The workers in reading texts are engaged in the professions and service occupations. The infrequent inclusion of clerical and sales workers and the

---

[37] Edward Clark, *op. cit.*, pp. 440–444.
[38] Walter Lifton, "Vocational Guidance in the Elementary School," *Vocational Guidance Quarterly*, 8, 79–82 (1959).
[39] Wesley Tennyson and Lawrence Monnens, "The World of Work Through Elementary Readers," *Vocational Guidance Quarterly*, 12, 85–88 (1963).

lack of attention to skilled workers shows little consequence with the distribution these occupations now maintain.

Summary

These studies indicate that elementary school children do have knowledge of prestige rankings of jobs and that they tentatively choose higher level jobs. There appears to be some socio-economic class influence in their vocational interests, aspirations, and choices. However, the relationship between these variables is unclear.

Most elementary school children limit their range of choices. This is particularly true of girls. Apparently the educational system influences a child's limited range of occupational considerations. If pupils' interests in several occupational areas are to be stimulated, a program of occupational information is necessary.

Vocational Information

Various methods of presenting vocational information may stimulate interest in several occupational areas, develop a constructive attitude toward work, and help children become aware of the changing work world. However, the majority of methods are carried out by the teachers. The counselor stimulates their interest in this area and enlists their participation in the program.

The counselor serves as a consultant, assists in the development of units, or integrating occupational information into the curriculum. He provides resource people, reading materials, and audio-visual materials. He arranges field trips and accompanies the pupils on the tours. The counselor and teacher cooperate in presenting a vocational orientation to the pupils.

Observation

Elementary school children learn about many occupations through observation. Children casually observe workers daily without appreciating what the worker does or the contribution he makes to society. Guided observation and discussion of the work and workers most frequently seen by the children assists them in understanding the occupational world.

To broaden the child's perspective, special contacts are made through visits and tours. Touring a factory, children see, hear, feel, and smell the worker's environment. Their attention is focused on the worker, rather than on his product. In a factory, business, or company, the children observe different types of work relating to the same general area. They realize the interdependency existing among all workers, and they develop respect for the products and services workers provide.

A meaningful tour requires guided observation. The place visited is appropriate to a child's level of development. Arrangements and preliminary discussions set the stage for meaningful questions and observations. Following the visit, discussion focuses on abilities and skills required for the job and the type of work they would enjoy. The discussion provides an opportunity to correct misunderstandings and to initiate discussion of abilities, aptitudes, interests, and job satisfaction.

Curriculum

Certain areas of the curriculum integrate material on occupations. Teachers, counselors, and curriculum coordinators cooperate in developing materials and integrating them into the curriculum; text books do not provide a diverse coverage of occupations.

Occupational exploration develops into most areas of the curriculum, however, science and social studies receive the major emphasis. Studying famous Americans or vocations of people in foreign lands serves as stimuli for children. Norris presents a program of incorporating some of these ideas into a social studies course.

> Kindergarten. The child learns about the work activities of his mother, his father, and other members of his household.
>
> Grade 1. The child learns about work in his immediate environment—his home, school, and neighborhood.
>
> Grade 2. The child learns about community helpers who serve him as well as about familiar stores and businesses in the neighborhood.
>
> Grade 3. The child studies the expanding community. Emphasis is placed upon transportation, communications, and other major industries.
>
> Grade 4. The child learns about the world of work at the state level, including main industries of the state.
>
> Grade 5. The child's studies broaden to cover the industrial life of the nation. Major industries of the various sections of the United States are selected for study.
>
> Grade 6. The child's program is expanded to include the entire western hemisphere. Life in Canada and in South and Central America is contrasted with life in the United States.[40]

These sources also provide enough knowledge about the occupations to allow in-depth role-playing.

[40] Willa Norris, *Occupational Information in the Elementary School* (Chicago: Science Research Associates, Inc., 1963) p. 56.

Reading

Reading about various people in occupations is an important source in learning about the world of work. Children's magazines, books, and pamphlets provide specific stories about occupations. The elementary school counselor includes these in the school library and supplies bibliographies for the teachers. Norris[41] lists complete series of books and pamphlets by industry and by approximate grade level.

Audio-Visual Aids

Numerous audio-visual aids, including movies, film strips, radio, television, and bulletin boards stimulate occupational exploration. Many movies and film strips are available to add to the vocational orientation of elementary children. Movies and film strips are worked into the curriculum during recess or after lunch on days when weather prohibits going outside. Suggested viewing of selected television programs followed by discussion are also beneficial.

A counselor may establish a central bulletin board which includes materials designed to help children study occupations. Teachers may devote a bulletin board in the classroom to occupations and change them frequently. By having the students in charge of the bulletin board, they look for pictures in magazines and assume responsibility for the task.

Resource People

Scheduling speakers to discuss their vocational experiences provides children with first hand information about an occupation and give them personal contact with the worker. Speakers should bring the tools they work with enabling them to demonstrate, rather than just talk, about their job. The counselor informs

[41] *Ibid.*, p. 150–195.

teachers of available resource persons and assists with arranging the program.

Children also meet with resource people individually, interview them, and report to the class. If the weatherman, for example, lives in the neighborhood, a youngster could interview him. Such experiences not only provide occupational information, but help in learning to meet people and assume responsibility.

Counselor Competencies in Vocational Guidance[42]

In order for a counselor to appreciate the meaningfulness of vocational guidance, the social meaning of work must be meaningful to him. It is necessary that he understand the complexity, pervasiveness, and influential aspects that work has on the people's lives. Work reflects personality, value structure, and economic status.

Thinking about, selecting, and entering an occupation are not isolated activities, but rather a part of total human development. Though there are no definite descriptions of vocational development, a counselor is assisted through a knowledge of theories of vocational development. The theories and the research assist him in understanding children. A counselor needs to understand the relationship between the theories of vocational development and the use of occupational and educational information.

Changing technology and work patterns necessitate that a counselor understand the occupational structure of his community, state, and nation. He familiarizes himself with the description and characteristics of the major jobs in his locality. In

[42] Gilbert Moore, editor *Counselor Competencies in Occupational Information.* Mimeograph (Washington, D.C.: U.S. Office of Education, 1966), pp. 1–50.

order to be helpful to elementary school children, the counselor understands the relationship of present trends in the occupational structure and the implications of a rapidly changing technology for occupational groups and future career patterns. He is aware of potential educational changes inherent in the value of rapidly changing technology.

A counselor begins a file of occupational information and keeps an up-to-date file. He is aware of occupational information resources and acquainted with directories, guides, and catalogs of current materials. A counselor evaluates the materials to be sure they are appropriate for his pupils. Many materials have only limited applicability. Therefore, the counselor needs techniques to extract information for an abstract, or adapt materials for the level and locale of his students. The counselor establishes a filing system to facilitate quick retrieval of the occupational information, and he needs to understand systems and types of classification, i.e., the United States Employment System including the Dictionary of Occupational Titles and the Entry Occupational Classification System and the Standard Industrial Classification System.

Occupational information by itself is only a means to an end. It is important that the counselor be competent in using occupational information and in helping others to use it. The counselor has responsibility in providing information for individuals and groups, and he needs skills in using a wide variety of group techniques. This may be more prevalent than using occupational information in individual counseling. The counselor bears in mind the purposes in presenting occupational information to elementary school children.

He can act as a consultant. He assists in developing units or integrating occupational information into the regular curriculum. He serves as a liaison between the school and community, assisting with tours or securing speakers. A counselor develops exhibits using occupational information either independently or in cooperation with local business and industry.

Summary

Vocational planning is becoming increasingly complex and the demands of society are becoming greater upon the individual as he prepares for the future. Vocational guidance begins in the elementary school, as career development commences during those years. Theories of vocational development and research involving elementary school children suggest that children are interested in the world of work. Vocational guidance begins the process of assisting pupils with vocational development through increased opportunities to learn about themselves and the working world. The counselor and teachers cooperatively stimulate pupils' interests in various occupations, develop a constructive attitude toward work, and help them become aware of the changing world.

SELECTED REFERENCES

Henry Borow, "Development of Occupational Motives and Roles," In *Review of Child Development Research,* Lois Hoffman and Martin Hoffman, editors (New York: Russell Sage Foundation, 1966).

Henry Borow, editor *Man In A World at Work* (Boston: Houghton Mifflin Company, 1964).

Willa Norris, *Occupational Information in the Elementary School* (Chicago: Science Research Associates, Inc., 1963).

Herman Peters and James Hansen, editors *Vocational Guidance and Career Development* (New York: The Macmillan Company, 1966).

GUIDANCE INSTRUMENTS AND TECHNIQUES

The counselor plans, uses, and evaluates the school's measurement program. Measurement refers to a broad spectrum of possibilities including the testing program. Both standardized and nonstandardized instruments are part of the measurement program. In addition the techniques involved in maintaining and using anecdotal records, sociograms, or scattergrams, are subsumed under this term. The user of the tests or processes described under the rubric measurement has the responsibility to understand the instrument or technique. In the case of standardized tests manuals are available and are important in administering and interpreting the tests. For nonstandardized instruments, understanding and use involves acquiring this information from other sources.

Purposes of Testing

Testing assists the pupil in understanding and gaining a more realistic picture of himself. Other purposes are for selection decisions or classification decisions on the part of the test giver. When test results are used to provide meaningful assistance to pupils directly or indirectly, testing is most relevant in the school. Appraisal helps the individual assess his strengths and weaknesses so that reasoned decisions about himself can be made. It also assists his movement toward self-established goals. The present chapter investigates the process of data gathering activities. The next chapter examines the use of data in the appraisal process. It is necessary to develop these as continuous entities. Separated for purposes of investigation, they supplement each other in practice. Stanley[1] suggests that any testing program must be "cooperative, practical, and definite." Program development is accomplished with the assistance of teaching, administrative staff, and pupil personnel staffs, if the school has the autonomy to devise its own program. If this is not the case, the counselor works toward this goal.

The testing program attempts to solve practical school problems. Although tests lead to such decisions as classification, grouping, and promotion; the teacher and counselor use the results in assisting pupils to a clearer self understanding.

Finally, the program delineates what tests will be given, when they are given, and the rationale underlying the use of the test.

---

[1] Julian C. Stanley, *Measurement in Today's Schools*, 4th Ed. (Englewood Cliffs: Prentice-Hall, Inc., 1964), p. 300.

Decisions such as the time of the year, the concurrent administration of related tests, the scoring and profiling process, and the interpretation or use of the test are made. Various members of the school staff under the leadership of the counselor should become involved and the latest in research must be available to assist in decision-making.

Cronbach[2] suggests that testing aids in improving the following:

1. Selection decisions—The test provides additional insight into the selection of various special programs or admission into other school levels. These decisions are not made only on the basis of test data.
2. Classification decisions—Once a person is selected for a particular program or grade level, within class placements may be necessary. Tests assist in making this decision.
3. Evaluation of Treatments—When care is taken in this area, tests assist the school personnel in knowing whether the individual's progress is in the desired direction. Teachers often see this as an evaluation of their activity. This is possible but it is not the primary use for tests in treatment evaluation. Counselors can alleviate these fears for teachers by communicating the real use for which tests are given.
4. Verification of Scientific Hypotheses—This is similar to the Evaluation of Treatments with one important difference, namely, experimental and control groups are established to ascertain whether one treatment is "better" than another. Experimental bases and related hypotheses established prior to the onset of the treatment and experimental control are maintained so that the final evaluation is valid.

[2] Lee J. Cronbach, *Essentials of Psychological Testing*, 2nd Ed. (New York: Harper and Brothers, Publishers, 1960), pp. 18–20.

The basic reason for tests is providing more meaningful assistance and information to pupils. The counselor uses tests to assist the pupil toward self understanding. The following criteria for test selection are necessary: Will the test be meaningful to the pupil and enhance his self understanding? If the answers to these questions are "no," there is a basis for challenging the value of the test.

Some Statistical Concepts

Prior to discussion of specific types of tests, some basic statistical terms and concepts are examined so the potential test user is able to interpret them. At the elementary level the teacher, counselor, and administrator should have this minimal competency. Statistics aid in understanding groups. Although no specific statements can be made concerning an individual, the test supplies information helpful to the pupil, teacher, and counselor. In addition, the test result gives general ideas concerning probabilities within the pupil's life.

Measures of Central Tendency

The mean is the central tendency measure most often reported in technical reports. It is the arithmetic average of all the scores in a given set of scores. It is represented symbolically as $\overline{X}$ or M and is computed by summing all the scores in the set (ΣX) and dividing by the total number of scores (N). Thus $\overline{X} = \dfrac{\Sigma X}{N}$.

The median is the score above and below which one-half of the cases fall. This is measured by arranging the scores from the highest to the lowest. Then, by counting from either end of the column, the score which falls at the mid-point (one-half of the scores) is the median. It may be that this score occurs more than once in the distribution. However, for rough estimates the exact score is used as the median. It will also happen that, on sets of scores where the number of scores (N) is an even number of scores, the median will fall between two numbers. In most cases the problem is solved by designating the mid-point of the scores as the median. Thus the median of the scores 2, 4, 6, 8, 13, 20 is halfway between 6 and 8; 7.

The mode is the score with the greatest frequency in the distribution. Thus, if one score occurs four times in the distribution and the highest number of any other scores is three, the mode is the score appearing four times. The mode, as contrasted to the median and mean, can be any place along the distribution rather than occurring somewhere near the middle of the range of scores. As the mode is the score occurring most frequently, there is the possibility of having multiple modes in any distribution.

Measures of Variability

It is possible to obtain similar means, medians, or modes from highly dissimilar groups of scores. The following sets of scores illustrate this:

A	B
200	**102**
150	**101**
100 Mean = 100	**100** Mean = 100
50	99
0	98
$\overline{500}$	$\overline{500}$

The spread of scores both from highest to lowest and the individual score spread within the distribution must be determined. Related concepts are.

R A N G E. This is the difference between the highest and lowest score. The range is computed by subtracting the lowest score from the highest score and adding one. The convention of adding one indicates that an inclusive set of numbers is being considered as opposed to a simple difference. The range of the scores 3 and 6 is four, as 3, 4, 5, and 6 are included in the set of scores.

STANDARD DEVIATION. The most common variability statistic is the standard deviation. This represents the average deviation of all scores in the set from the mean score. This statistic is related to the normal curve concept in which an assumption is made concerning the general distribution of scores on any set of data. The normal curve is bell-shaped in design suggesting that most scores fall toward the middle of the distribution, and that few scores are located at the ends of the distribution. It is represented graphically by Figure 5.

Figure 5. Normal Curve

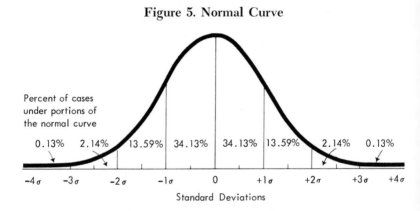

Percent of cases under portions of the normal curve

0.13%   2.14%   13.59%   34.13%   34.13%   13.59%   2.14%   0.13%

-4σ -3σ -2σ -1σ 0 $+1\sigma$ $+2\sigma$ $+3\sigma$ $+4\sigma$

Standard Deviations

The breakdown of the curve is in terms of numbers of standard deviations with about ⅔ or 68 per cent of the cases falling within the limits of one standard deviation above and below the mean. If another standard deviation either direction is included, about 95 per cent of the total cases fall within the limits. Almost all cases (99.74 per cent) are found within 3 standard deviations plus and minus the mean.

The standard deviation is computed by determining the difference between the mean and each score. These differences are negative and positive. To eliminate the negative numbers, each difference is squared and a total squared deviation obtained. By definition the standard deviation is the average deviation, thus, the total is divided by the number of cases (N). As the deviations are squared, a square root is extracted from the remaining number. This is the standard deviation of the group of scores.

STANDARD ERROR. A related measure is the standard error. This concept provides interpretive assistance for an individual score. Whenever a test is given and a score obtained, the resultant score is not necessarily a true or accurate score. It is essential to know the precision of the score. The most common measure is the Standard Error of Measurement. The method used to determine this statistic uses the following formula:

Standard Error of Measurement $= \sigma\sqrt{1-r}$, where σ is the standard deviation of the test as reported in most test manuals and r is the reported reliability coefficient of the test. Assuming that the pupil scored 36 on a particular test, and the Standard Error of Measurement is computed to be 3, the interpretation is that the chances are about 2 to 1 that the pupil's true score lies somewhere between 33 and 39 (1 SE $\pm$ the score). Similar interpretations concerning the chances for additional SE's increase the probability of a true score falling between two specified points. Thus, there is a method for determining the approximate accuracy of the test score. A high SE makes the score more suspect than a small SE, which restricts the range of possible true scores.

STANDARD SCORES. Many publishers of standardized tests now report the norms of the test as standard scores. These are based upon group data and assist test users in having a better foundation for comparing pupils' scores on various types of tests. Standard scores are based upon the normal curve distribution. The mean score is determined and is converted to a standard score, e.g., 50 or 500. However, there is no absolute rule for the conversion of scores. The standard deviation is computed and converted to standard score units, e.g., 10 or 100. Then, scores in between the mean and the standard deviation limit are converted to standard scores. For example, the mean raw score of a group was 28 and the standard deviation 3. Pupil A, with a raw score of 25, has a standard score of 40, mean standard score $50 - 1$ standard deviation $10 = 40$. Likewise, pupil B, with a score of 34, has a standard score of 70, mean standard score $50 + 2$ standard deviations of $10 = 70$. Understanding and interpreting scores with different standard score means and deviations follows the same pattern. One needs to know what the mean and standard deviation of the standard score is prior to examining and using the data.

If pupil A has a standard score of 40 on an arithmetic test and 70 on science, he is slightly below average on the arithmetic and well above average on the science test. By using standard scores the comparison is possible since the norms are prepared on large numbers of similar pupils. Comparison with groups and with other types of tests becomes more meaningful and is easily accomplished when the norms are reported in standard scores as opposed to raw score data. Standard scores are reported in various terms, percentiles, grade equivalents, and T scores and are based upon the specific statistical concepts of mean, standard deviation, and the normal curve.

Measures of Comparison

Comparison of test to test is mentioned above. Comparison between various groups of pupils or between test results is often necessary, especially if any research is involved since it helps in interpreting whether the experimental treatment effected the various groups. The typical measures of comparison used in test manuals and research studies are coefficient of correlation, significance of difference and chi square.

Coefficient of Correlation

Whenever there is test data of more than one kind, it is possible to determine the degree of relationship existing between the sets of data. If the data are numerical, correlational techniques are used. The Pearsonian r is used most often for equal sized groups and is expressed in terms of a number ranging from a positive 1 to a negative 1. Usually the following standards are applied:

Less than 0.20	negligible relationship
0.21—0.40	small relationship
0.41—0.65	substantial relationship
0.66—0.90	marked relationship
0.91—1.00	very dependable relationship

The same type of interpretation is made for negative correlations since the degree of relationship is not affected by the sign; only the direction of the relationship is changed.

The reported "r's" are generally related to the reliability and validity of the test. A high reliability indicates that a test consistently measures what it purports to measure. A high validity suggests that the test relates substantially to an outside criterion, e.g., another test or observed performance. Reliability and validity are more fully discussed in the next chapter, *APPRAISAL IN GUIDANCE.*

Significance of Difference

It is often desirable to know whether groups of persons are similar on certain factors. A common factor concerns the results of various groups of pupils on a test. The "t" test for significance of difference is a widely used method. By comparing the mean score and the variability of the scores within the group it is possible to make certain tentative statements concerning group similarity. This is reported in probability terms such as 0.01 or 0.05, meaning that the possibility of the amount of difference found is due to chance only one time in 100 for a 0.01 probability or 5 times in 100 for a 0.05 probability. Therefore, it is possible to determine various aspects of group make-up or applied techniques by comparing groups of pupils on similar tests.

Chi Square

Many times counselors deal with group factors other than numerical data. For example, an examination is made of the similarities between a group of suburban high income family youth and the youth from a core disadvantaged area. As it is not possible to designate one group as being better than the other, a statistical process is utilized examining numbers of youth rather than numerical value of the criterion under examination. Chi Square is a widely used technique. In this case the final reporting process is still in terms of probability, e.g., 0.01. Interpretation is made of the numbers of youth falling into any given category at greater than chance levels. Thus, a 0.01 result suggests that the numbers in various categories occur only one time in 100 by chance and that there probably is a difference in whatever factors are chosen to use with the groups.

Guidance Instruments

This section discusses various instruments used in the guidance program. A variety of personnel develop and use the instruments. In addition, some of the materials are prepared commercially while some are developed locally. Some are supported by extensive research data and some have no substantiation. The user realizes that the major objectives for use of guidance instruments are related to assisting pupils to do a better job and to helping the school be attuned to pupil needs.

Cumulative Record

The cumulative record is a common instrument for housing pupil information. Although many record.forms exist, the main concern here is the type of information which is included and the use of the record by various school personnel.

There is some compulsory information. Name, date of birth, residence, place of birth, and sex are examples of this mandated type of information. These, with the exception of residence, do not change and one permanent entry suffices for the pupil's school career.

Other information is included so that the development of the child is known. Health data for the child prior to entry and during school often is valuable in pinpointing physical causes for inadequate school or personal performance. As a school staff member the nurse teacher directs the gathering of this information. Family data are also valuable. This occasionally poses some problems if the family situation is not readily discussed by the pupil or the information is unavailable. However, such factors as parent's occupation, number and age of siblings, and general home environment provide insight into understanding many child problems.

The pupil's school record is as complete as possible. Marks and explanation of marks for each year of attendance are noted. Whenever any deviation is recorded the teacher or counselor explains probable causes and the subsequent attempts the school makes in assisting the child. Finally, test data is complete. This gives a record of the pupil's growth during his school career. Deviations are noted and possible causes are listed. The test data in cumulative records includes readiness, achievement, ability, and aptitude test results. When reasonable, personality test results are included. However, since these results require more interpretation it is better to indicate that the test was used and that further information is available from the counselor or other designated school personnel. Other types of data are pertinent to the record. Areas of interest exhibited in class or in interviews are valuable to teachers and counselors for working with pupils in succeeding grades. Similarly recording out-of-school activities assists school personnel in understanding pupils.

All of the above find a place on most printed cumulative record cards. Further information included in the folder, but not written on the actual form, are anecdotal records, rating scales, and in some instances, the case study.

Anecdotal Records

Anecdotal records provide several valuable kinds of data. An experience which occurs in the school life of the pupil is recorded. It is a first-hand account of the pupil's activities, illustrating various facets of the pupil's behavior, rather than just his deviate behavior. School personnel record objective observations of a child. The record continues over a period of years so that the individual's developmental growth is more clearly perceived.

Rules for compiling these records include: The report is short but objective. Only actual events are reported. Anecdotal records report both complimentary and uncomplimentary incidents. To insure this, the recorder establishes a specific observation time rather than waiting for behavioral problems to occur and then recording the incident. All pupils are observed on an individual basis and subsequent records are prepared. Although the record is not long, such statements as "Jimmy talked out in class today" have little value. The dynamics of the situation and Jimmy's involvement are important.

There are limitations. First the observer sees what he wants to see, rather than being strictly objective about the situation. The observer records what occurs. Also, in certain cases, physical appearances, previous knowledge of the pupil, or his ethnic or cultural background cause problems. Statements such as, "he is from Back Street" suggest that the observer is falling into the trap of applying only normative data to understanding the child. It is important to know where the pupil lives but this fact alone is not sufficient in understanding the child. As suggested earlier, negative behaviors are more noticeable than positive activities. Both types are essential in understanding children. Peters and Farwell suggest, "To report child behavior adequately the (observer) must know what to look for, where to look for it, how to recognize it, and proper reporting form."[3]

Rating Scales

Certain characteristics are defined discretely enough to prepare a form and have it completed by school personnel. Rating scales are used for employment or college recommendations. The same principles are applied at the elementary school level. The counselor or teacher prepares the rating scale and circulates it to the staff for completion. A typical form is shown in Figure 6.

As is true with any measurement instrument, certain limitations are accounted for whenever the rating scale is used. As mentioned with the anecdotal record, personal bias often distorts the rating. On the other hand, the effect of desirable activities in one or more areas carries over to all areas resulting in a halo effect. Finally, the extremes of the scale are avoided, reducing by two the possible categories on which the individual is rated. Regardless, the rating scale is potentially strong as a rapid and relatively efficient method of obtaining data from many sources about a large number of individuals.

Case Study

The most extensive instrument discussed in this section is the case study. This is primarily an instrument for obtaining breadth

[3] Herman J. Peters and Gail F. Farwell, *Guidance: A Developmental Approach*, 2nd Ed. (Chicago: Rand McNally and Company, 1967), p. 131.

Figure 6.

Model Rating Scale

	Superior	Above Average	Average	Below Average	Inferior	Not Qualified to rate	Comments
1. Physical Vitality and Health ..							
2. Mental Alertness and Efficiency							
3. Social Adjustment							
4. Emotional Stability							
5. Personal Appearance							
6. Maturity of Judgment							
7. Dependability							
8. Use of Spoken English							
9. Use of Written English							
10. Resourcefulness and Initiative .							
11. Personality Adjustment							

and depth information on a relatively small number of pupils. As such, the involvement of school personnel is wide and, in most cases, more than one member of the personnel team gathers data and prepares the study. The following is an outline of the types of data included in a case study:

I. Preliminary Statement of Situation—apparent problem, probably immediate cause, circumstances surrounding the case

II. Summary of available data (from cumulative records, visits, counselor's record, etc.)

    A. Present status
        1. Age
        2. Sex
        3. Grade—class—teacher's name

    B. Physical appearance and history
        1. General impression made by the child
        2. Obvious physical or mental limitations
        3. Mannerisms, neatness, clothing
        4. Illnesses—general conditions

    C. Educational Status
        1. Present school achievement—kind of work
        2. Promotions—retardations and causes
        3. Relation with individual teachers
        4. Tests or other measures of achievement or aptitude

    D. Personal traits
        1. Personality—general tone
        2. Attitude toward home, friends, self, family
        3. Hobbies, play life, leisure time activities
        4. Educational and vocational ambitions
        5. Marked likes and dislikes, fears
        6. Any special personal problems

    E. Home and family

      1. Individuals at home
      2. Apparent economic level—cultural resources
      3. Relation with home
      4. Record at social agencies
      5. Home cooperation
    F. Work experience
      1. Part time summer jobs
      2. Attitude toward work
      3. Occupational plans and goals
III. Tentative Identification of the Problems and Contributing Causes
    A. Working hypothesis—provisionally adopted from analysis of all available data as a guide to further investigation or action
IV. Additional data needed
    A. From student
    B. From teachers
    C. From home
    D. From other sources
V. Analysis of additional data
VI. Development of plan of treatment or action
    A. Immediate
    B. Long-Range
    C. Desired Outcomes
VII. Progress and results
    A. Reports
      1. Teachers
      2. Others
    B. Observations
VIII. Summary and Recommendations

The *gathering* of data is only one of several steps in a case study. Data are analyzed with special regard to the child-in-situation. Some ideas concerning the problem are formulated. This is parallel to *diagnosis* in the medical profession. The next step involves affecting change in the child or in the situation in which the child finds himself. This is often termed *prognosis*. Different assistance is offered by various school personnel. Prognosis is not limited to one activity. Finally, as with all guidance activities, a *follow-up* on what has occurred is made. This is either a single examination or a sequence of events. It suggests that the concern is sufficiently alleviated so that further action is not required or that more data, diagnosis, and prognosis are necessary. The follow-up process does provide an opportunity for elementary guidance personnel to ascertain the child's growth.

Treatment follows the objective diagnosis of the case study. This is the most difficult stage of the case study. As suggested throughout this section the case study is a team effort. Therefore, the team makes the decisions concerning treatment. Traxler and North[4] offer the following suggestions:

1. A case investigator should not attempt to apply treatment for difficulties that are entirely outside his experience. . . .

2. During the period of treatment the case investigator should keep a careful journal record of the progress of the treatment. . . .

3. If the case is the kind that lends itself to measurement comparable tests should be administered at the beginning and the end of the treatment. . . .

4. After the case has been released from treatment, it should be followed up, and the individual kept under observation for a few months to make sure that a relapse does not take place.

[4] Arthur E. Traxler and Robert D. North, *Techniques of Guidance*, 3rd Ed. (New York: Harper and Row, Publishers, 1966), p. 282.

The limitations of the case study approach relate to time involvement and the small number of persons which can be studied. To gather and utilize the data from a case study, considerable time is spent observing and interviewing various personnel. However, often there is a carry-over from one case study to other pupils in the classroom. The complete generalization from one case to another is, of course, to be avoided. But often the knowledge gained from one case study helps the school personnel develop new educational opportunities for other pupils.

The Sociogram

Another guidance instrument is the sociogram. This determines patterns of interpersonal behavior among pupils. A number of possible questions provides the necessary data for a sociogram. For example, the teacher inquires about persons with whom the children want to work or play. Usually the child is asked to choose two or three persons in each category. Figure 7 illustrates the sociogram and Figure 8 illustrates the tabulation of the data gathered from the sociogram.

Sociogram interpretation leads to several questions:
1. Of the choices made which were expected?
2. Of the choices made which were unexpected?
3. Why are some pupils chosen regularly and almost never rejected?
4. Why are some pupils rejected regularly and almost never chosen?
5. What cliques appear?
6. Are these due to some group factor such as boy-girl or ethnic background?
7. Are there factors which identify the pupils chosen most often?
8. Are there factors which identify the pupils rejected most often?

Figure 7. Sociogram Model

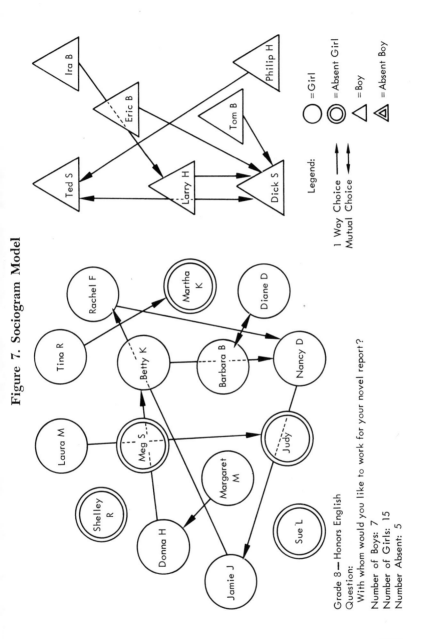

Grade 8 — Honors English

Question:
With whom would you like to work for your novel report?

Number of Boys: 7
Number of Girls: 15
Number Absent: 5

Legend:

◯ = Girl

◎ = Absent Girl

△ = Boy

◮ = Absent Boy

1 Way Choice ⟶
Mutual Choice ⟷

225

Chosen → / Chooser ↓	Eric B	Ira B	Tom B	Barbara B	Diane D	Nancy D	Rachel F	Larry H	Donna H	Philip H	Jamie J	Betty K	Martha K	Sue L	Laura M	Margaret M	Shelley R	Tina R	Judy S	Ted S	Dick S	Meg S	
Eric B	•																				1		
Ira B		•					1																
Tom B			•																		1		
Barbara B				•	1						ʼ												
Diane D				1	•																		
Nancy D						•				1													
Rachel F						1	•																
Larry H								•													1		
Donna H									•		1												
Philip H										•										1			
Jamie J						1					•												
Betty K				1								•											
Martha K													•										Absent
Sue L														•									Absent
Laura M															•			1					
Margaret M						1										•							
Shelley R																	•						Absent
Tina R									1									•					
Judy S																			•				Absent
Ted S																				•	1		
Dick S																				1	•		
Meg S																						•	Absent
Total	0	0	0	1	1	2	1	1	1	0	1	1	1	0	0	0	0	0	1	2	4	0	

Figure 8. Sociogram Tabulation

The sociogram and tabulation show first choices for English working partners by a group of eighth grade honors English pupils. Certain people were not chosen, e.g., Eric B. and Sue L. Sue was absent the day of the sociogram and may have been passed over for that reason. However, Martha K. was absent and was chosen. Absences may not have an effect on the choices which pupils make. Dick S. was chosen most often with four of the other six boys selecting him. Other information can be gleaned from the sociogram and tabulation, e.g., there were two mutual choices. Ted S. and Dick S. chose each other as did Barbara B. and Diane D. No boys chose girls as a first choice working partner and no girls chose boys. This type of schematic representation and the tabulation provide data as a preliminary step in interpretation.

The interpreter locates those pupils who have some difficulty relating interpersonally. Of course the difficulty, as suggested above, relates to the task set in obtaining data. Also the sociogram represents a temporal situation and given similar tasks a few days or weeks later, it is possible for the pattern to change. However, the sociogram assists the teacher or counselor in understanding the group from a point of view within the group. It supplies information for those persons working with individual pupils. During the interview the counselor discusses the results of the sociogram. The ultimate goal is better pupil self-understanding, not conformity to group norms.

Standardized Tests

Standardized tests are available and used in most elementary schools. At the elementary level readiness tests, ability tests, achievement tests, aptitude tests and, in some cases, personality tests are used.

R E A D I N E S S   T E S T S .   These tests measure the readiness of pupils at the primary level (ages 5 to 8) to accomplish certain school related tasks. In general, they measure reading and mathematical readiness. Diagnostic measures are used in conjunction with these tests. There is a need to know more than the state of readiness of the pupil. Reasons why the child is not ready are determined and then assistance is provided to help him move as rapidly as possible toward accomplishing various school tasks.

A B I L I T Y   T E S T S .   Usually known as intelligence tests, these tests measure the mental abilities necessary to thinking and learning. Although there are many abilities which can be listed, in general, ability tests include verbal, mathematical and spatial abilities. There are individually and group administered tests, giving school personnel and the pupil a clearer picture of the latter's expected academic performance. However, it is not unusual for test results and academic performance to be dissimilar; subsequently the pupil becomes identified as a poor or under-achiever. Labeling individuals on the basis of one test distorts the reason for using the test. Any test is valuable only to the extent that it is used to assist the person in identifying and moving toward goals.

A C H I E V E M E N T   T E S T S .   These tests measure the amount of information the pupil has as a result of exposure to various stimuli including his classroom, school, and social environment. Achievement tests measure different kinds of activities, but in general, they are used in the areas of reading, language, mathematics, social science, and physical science, i.e., they are related to school subject matter. These are available in single tests or in batteries covering several achievement areas. They help in pupil diagnosis. They also indicate areas in which the teacher can spend more time and areas in which the pupils exhibit adequate knowledge.

A P T I T U D E   T E S T S .   These tests predict success in some future endeavor. They are usually designed for use at the termination of various programs so that the individual makes realistic choices concerning his future.

PERSONALITY TESTS. In certain specific cases more information concerning personal-social factors of the child is desirable. In these instances it is possible to utilize standard personality tests. These tests are used with more discretion and professional competency than any other test. The rationale for using the test is clearly explained to the persons involved, including parents and pupils. Anything less than that stated above constitutes sufficient reason for not using the test at all. Personality tests are valuable when properly used but are dangerous when used in an unwise fashion.

These tests locate those areas in which the child is concerned over his feelings and his relations with others; parents or peers. Usually the test is a check-list type with the child responding to various statements. Based upon his area and numeric responses, the skilled psychometrist utilizes these to benefit the pupil.

Organization of the Testing Program

Guidance assumes that it is valuable for children to know themselves, their strengths, and their limitations. This assumption implies that there is a systematic means for gathering relevant data. Since the early 1900s standardized tests and inventories have become increasingly popular as one means of supplying this data. Although many test forms have come under criticism in recent years, the value of data comparability taken from standardized tests and inventories has resulted in a steady increase in test use.

Tests are given to children for the primary purpose of helping them to understand themselves. If they fulfill their purpose, tests are meaningful to the children who take them. At the same time, parents and other involved adults acquaint themselves with the rationale behind testing and the significance of the individual test to this rationale. Tests fulfill other purposes in the school. However, for guidance purposes, tests aid the counselor in assisting pupils to become competent in meeting personal and education problems.

Initiating a Program

Maximum effectiveness requires cooperation between faculty, administration, pupils, and parents. As a result, a number of steps are taken in preparation for introducing testing programs to the school. These steps increase the cooperation of the instructional staff and develop a program consonant with school needs and objectives. In most communities these are congruent with community and faculty values. The faculty develops educational objectives and the counselor helps the faculty understand how the guidance program promotes these objectives. The educational staff is familiar with the beneficial uses of test data.

Pupil cooperation is promoted by helping them understand the objectives of the test program. Pupils are given an opportunity to acquaint themselves with the sample test items and approaches to the individual items. A number of studies indicate that test anxiety has a greater influence on test results when given in elementary school than when given in secondary school. This is a result of the fact that secondary school students learn to handle anxiety more efficiently; the fact remains that it is important to enhance the positive values of testing to pupils before the tests are used. Familiarity with the tests probably reduces anxiety. It is also important that tests be administered at appropriate times. The validity of tests administered at times when the pupils are excited for some reason external to the testing situation, e.g., vacations or home situations, is questionable. The effect of fatigue may be greater with elementary school pupils. Tests given to pupils in the lower elementary grades at the end of the day, for example, may not give a true picture of the pupils' capabilities or feelings.

Parents and community groups are informed about the testing program, its limitations as well as its strength. This is done in assemblies to which parents are invited, P.T.A. group meetings, or by a prepared pamphlet distributed to the community. Another potential method is to provide samples of tests to parents in which the test type is clearly illustrated. Some schools give alternate forms of the test to interested parents in the hope that they will better understand the tests, testing program, and test taking processes.

Responsibility for the Testing Program

Responsibility for the testing program rests with one person, although he does not make all decisions regarding the program. As previously indicated, a team approach is necessary for success. Investing program responsibility in one person maintains continuity.

The counselor is logically in the best position to take responsibility for the testing program, because his training is more adequate in tests and measurements than is the training of other members of the faculty or administration. This refers to his familiarity with the variety of marketed tests as well as with their significance, reliability, and validity. The counselor generally has more sophistication with regard to the interpretation of statistical data, and he is in a better position to prepare summaries of test data for the teachers and the administration.

The counselor is in the most advantageous position to evaluate new tests and recommend needed changes in the program. He appreciates the effects on the total testing program, resulting from changes at any level of the program.

The counselor handles the administrative problems associated with the program. Such problems are represented by difficulties in scheduling the administration of tests, giving tests to pupils who are absent when others take the test, and setting up testing programs for new pupils coming in from other areas not having a similar testing background.

The counselor summarizes test findings and interprets them to the faculty, administration, and general public. Inasmuch as it is often inconvenient for parents to come to the school and see teachers, the counselor is more available to interpret test results to parents. Thus, an important aspect of the elementary counselor's role is leadership in the testing area.

The term "continuity" mentioned above applies to two aspects of the testing program. The first is continuity in terms of the types of information sought in the different stages of the program. A testing program is developmental. If test data is received from different instruments, these are interpreted in terms of previous tests so that yearly patterns are discernible. In order to maintain this continuity, the test data is analyzed and appropriate interpretative information provided in the records.

The second type of "continuity" refers to the ways pupils' test scores are recorded on cumulative records. Record keeping takes into account the fact that the testing program is developmental, that each stage provides a foundation for successive stages and that information at any point is understandable only in light of past, relatable information.

Principles of A Testing Program

There is no one test program model which can be prescribed. The testing program relates to the particular system and involves school personnel in any selection process. However, in general terms, the following principles suggest types of tests appropriate for gathering the necessary data in assisting pupils to better understanding:

1. The adequacy and effectiveness of a testing program is measured by the use made of the results.
2. The needs of school and pupil population should determine the testing program.
3. Testing should be a planned and integral part of the school program.
4. Test results should be made available in usable form to teachers, administrators, pupil personnel, and others qualified to use the results.
5. The purposes of testing should be understood by the pupils, teachers, and parents.
6. Ability and achievement tests ought to be given at approximately the same time so that it is possible to relate the achievement level of the pupil with his ability level.
7. It is more meaningful to give achievement tests at the beginning of the year.
   a. The teacher is more likely to use the results for working with pupils.
   b. The teacher is less likely to view the test as a measure of teaching ability.
   c. There will be current test data for all pupils.
8. Achievement and ability tests should be administered on a regular schedule probably at least once each three years.

Summary

Testing and measurement are important aspects of the guidance and school program. Testing contributes to better pupil self-understanding, growth, and development. Many types of measurement devices are available and the teacher, counselor, and other users should understand their theoretical and statistical aspects. If programs of testing and measurement do not contribute significantly to the individual pupil, there is cause to question the personnel and time involvement these programs demand. It is most desirable to utilize the data with pupils. This is defined as assessment and it is the basis for the following chapter.

SELECTED REFERENCES

Lee J. Cronbach, *Essentials of Psychological Testing*, 2nd Ed. (New York: Harper & Brothers, Publishers, 1960).

Walter N. Durost and George A. Prescott, *Essentials of Measurement for Teachers* (New York: Harcourt, Brace & World, Inc., 1962).

Victor H. Noll, *Introduction to Educational Measurement*, 2nd Ed. (Boston: Houghton-Mifflin Company, 1965).

10

APPRAISAL IN GUIDANCE

Appraisal refers to the assessment of personal characteristics and behavioral patterns, in order to better understand the individual and to use this understanding in aiding the individual toward optimum functioning. Appraisal becomes a reactive and active process. It is reactive in the sense that the data are gathered about the pupil in several ways. It is active in that it involves putting the information to work in assisting the individual.

There are several ways in which data can be gathered. The school records contain much information for use in this process. Cumulative and anecdotal records, standardized test data, non-test data, grades, and family background data are part of the information which is available for most pupils. In addition the pupil, teachers, and parents can provide further information. To become meaningful, this information must be put to work with the pupil. The complete appraisal process will be used with small numbers of pupils. However, the counselor's understanding and utilization of the appraisal process will benefit all pupils.

Super and Crites[1] illustrate the essential steps of appraisal as being the identification of the problem, understanding the pupil in the interview situation, and prognosis.

The Problem

The counselor identifies the reason for the counselee's presence in the interview situation. Although in some cases, there is a major problem the individual wishes to alleviate, problems are not the only reason people seek counseling assistance. The degree of seriousness the counselee feels is important. The counselor determines what he is expected to do and whether he can continue to work with the client under the proposed conditions. He develops, in cooperation with the pupil, the approach or approaches valuable in providing assistance to the counselee.

The Appraisal of the Counselee

The counselor attempts to understand the person with whom he deals. This is sometimes called model building and refers to the counselor's attempts to understand the pupil's needs, capacities, and resources and to meaningfully communicate this understanding to the pupil. The pupil is involved in this process for the appraisal process to be valid. If most of the data are invalid the prospects for successful guidance are diminished. Appraisal is a shared experience and both members actively participate.

---

[1] Donald E. Super and John O. Crites, *Appraising Vocational Fitness*, 2nd Ed., (New York: Harper and Row, Publishers, 1962), p. 3.

The Prognosis

Prognosis refers to the prospects available to the counselee. What kinds of behavior seems to be within the client's reach? What new behaviors can be introduced to widen his repertoire? The process of prognosis assists the counselee in moving more rapidly toward optimal functioning.

Limitations of the Appraisal Process for Elementary Youth

At the elementary level the problems of appraisal are limited by several factors. First the nature of the individual is sufficiently different to preclude certain techniques and activities. For example, future educational or occupational prospects may have little, if any, meaning for the pupil. However the need for accurate appraisal is as important at the elementary level as at any other level. Perhaps it is even more important, because the counselor has the opportunity to assist the individual to smoother problem adjustment identified through appraisal processes. Second, elementary school children have difficulty expressing themselves and relating to adults. The communication process is probably extremely one-sided since the counselor carries the major responsibility of obtaining the necessary information for appraisal from the child. Finally, providing the pupil with information for utilization in his own personal life requires increased skill, as the elementary school child has minimal ability in relating to himself. In fact the counselor teaches the counselee new skills. The limitations do not preclude involvement in the appraisal process but they do foster the need for the counselor to understand the pupil more fully and to find ways of working with the elementary age youth. Based upon developmental growth patterns the counselor helps the counselee build a foundation for more effective future behavior. Therefore although appraisal is time consuming and difficult it will be meaningful when the future behavior of the pupil is examined.

Principles of Appraisal

The individual is the focus of appraisal efforts. Although the counselor or teacher has an acute knowledge of group activity or test norms, he cannot fall victim to the tendency of appraising in terms of numerical, chance statements of success. Nomothetic data aid in understanding groups of children but when dealing with one child data relating to the idiographic aspect of the appraisal process are gathered. Objective and subjective data are necessary. It is essential to rely heavily on those data which have been shown to have well established significance and validity. It is important to understand the child's behavior as gleaned from self or teacher reports. The counselor clarifies and objectifies these types of subjective data. Failure to gain this goal does not mean that subjective data are not valuable. The counselor recognizes this fact and he realizes that he may be dealing with nonobjective data.

All hypotheses or influences concerning the individual come from relevant information and are tested continuously for accuracy and meaning. The counselor does not infer or hypothesize simply on the basis of ethnic group, location of the home, or previous behavior of brothers or sisters. Although these may be important they do not represent all the relevant information concerning the personality, attitudes, and probable future prospects of the individual. Such factors as classroom behavior, playground peer group, and self-report of feelings are relevant to appraising pupil characteristics.

Describing the hypothetical or projected situation for which behavior is predicted is valuable. Some time is spent describing the behavioral situation into which the individual is to place himself. In some cases this is relatively simple since it means describing a setting already in existence, e.g., the fourth-grade classroom of Miss Smith. However if the individual is not aware of the setting this is communicated to him.

Once this is accomplished, i.e., client data understood, the future setting described, and prediction made, the perception of others, including pupil personnel specialists, help ascertain the accuracy of the appraisal. A potential contributor to perception testing is the pupil. His observations and understandings are important and are included before a final decision is made. In addition the observations of teachers, specialists, administrators, and perhaps parents play an important part in successful prediction and preliminary movement toward a defined goal.

Alternatives are included in the predictive aspects of the appraisal process. If one direction, placement, or activity commands the major attention of the pupil it is essential to point out the range of possibilities during the appraisal process. This is especially true for the elementary pupil since he has more opportunities to try various possibilities. Decision-making is not as critical for the elementary school pupil as it would be for the high school student.

The degree of intensity varies from individual to individual. Certain elementary school pupils need to gather much data and spend relatively large amounts of time in the appraisal process. Retention, change of classroom environment, or special class placement decisions require extreme care in gathering and utilizing data. Other decisions such as achievement-ability discrepancies necessitate spending less time in the appraisal process and giving more effort to remedial or teaching activities.

Appraisal is a continuous and active process. Data are gathered throughout the schools' contact with the child. Cumulative records are used in the appraisal process if the school personnel record accurate data. Teachers and counselors develop a picture of the pupil's growth pattern with the help of the cumulative folder. If the record is solely a storehouse of required data school personnel limit their effectiveness in serving the pupil. Data are not static. The child is an active participator in life and data reflect this dynamic state. The appraiser parallels the active nature of the child by continuously reinterpreting the available data. This is not an easy process but the results are meaningful to the extent that the appraisal process reflects the active and continuous progress of the pupil toward his goals.

Rationale for Appraisal

As suggested earlier there are several techniques, factors, or variables to consider in appraisal. One of the most important is test data. Cronbach[2] suggests two philosophies of testing, impressionistic and psychometric. Psychometric testing provides numerical estimates on single personal or performance factors. Impressionistic techniques require that a sensitive observer look for cues by several means and integrate these into a *gestalt* or total impression. Both practitioners are interested in understanding the individual or factor being studied so that certain meaningful projections can occur. When dealing with elementary school youth, all relevant data are gathered and used when working with the pupil. The counselor is aware of and competent in both areas.

Psychometric Techniques

Tests are valuable tools in appraisal. The value of an individual test or a testing program depends on how they are used.

---

[2] Lee J. Cronbach, *Essentials of Psychological Testing*, 2nd Ed. (New York: Harper and Brothers, Publishers, 1960), p. 24.

Often the pupil is not aided in any way by the test. A young pupil once commented to his counselor that there wasn't much use taking tests unless you learn the outcomes. He used the following analogy. "It is no fun throwing a stone into a dark room. If you don't know what you might hit what's the use of throwing." Too often tests are given without any preparatory explanation and the results are filed into the cumulative record folder and seldom, if ever, used. The pupil never finds out what he threw at or if he hit anything.

Appraisal helps in solving school or individual problems by providing individual data and assistance in the process. Careful observation, selection, and use of the data are necessary.

Impressionistic Techniques

Impressionistic involvement suggests that other factors are important. The counselor and teacher observe pupils in order to gather data on their total response pattern. The counselor helps the pupil make decisions on the basis of test scores but when this occurs many important facts are overlooked. The counselee can fail even though it appeared that he was properly placed and a wise decision made.

The difference between the two methods is not polar. Each is suited to different purposes. The skilled counselor understands and utilizes each in its proper place. If evaluation or measurement is necessary tests often give the most meaningful data. If understanding the counselee's concerns is necessary, the impressionistic method is more advantageous.

Testing is one form of appraisal. Several others are important. The interview is a widely used method for obtaining appraisal data. The interviewer can have a structured, well planned method and follow this closely, or he can be less formal and determine, through interview techniques the kinds of concerns which the pupil expresses by himself. In either case the data are subjective and are so treated whenever any interpretation is made of them.

Another device in common use is the questionnaire. Closely related to the structured interview it is less useful in gaining insight about attitudes and feelings for all but very open individuals. Rating scales are used in appraisal. Although the rating scale appears to be an objective device the rater is often subjective in his presented impressions. The pupil sometimes prepares an autobiography or writes an essay on some event or aspect of his life. Used properly they are part of the data gathering process. Counselor and teacher are aware that the pupil is continually changing, and these written statements reflect a transient mood rather than a literal statement of the pupil's personality.

Regardless, the techniques above are valuable in most cases and provide the pupil with important data for more complete understanding of himself, his potential, and future possibilities. In order to be as meaningful as possible, appraisal procedures should provide information on typical behavioral patterns and on the meanings of stimuli which elicit behavior. The process should provide the counselor, teacher and pupil with large amounts of information on the individual under observation.

Types of Appraisal

Stewart and Warnath[3] point out that there are at least three types of appraisal; abilities, interest, and life style appraisal.

---

[3] Lawrence H. Stewart and Charles F. Warnath, *The Counselor and Society A Cultural Approach* (Boston: Houghton Mifflin Company, 1965), pp. 150, 151.

Abilities

The elementary counselor is interested in understanding the pupil's ability level. Often this is determined by a series of tests given over a certain period of time. Test consistency provides the appraiser with the ability level of the pupil. If the teacher, counselor, or pupil realizes what the test measures then each can use it with some rationality. The ability test does not identify creative pupils and the test usually discriminates against the pupil from a disadvantaged environment. However, the results on ability tests contribute data for decision-making.

A closely related concept is the relative comparability of achievement and ability tests. Test publishing companies, e.g., Harcourt, Brace, and World have correlated their ability and achievement tests so that a measure of anticipated achievement can be determined. Education emphasizes evaluation and significant status is given those earning high grades. Pupils have widely different ability levels creating given situations where intense effort by a low ability pupil results in failure while moderate effort by a fairly able pupil results in high honors. Of course motivation on the part of the able pupil is of concern but most importantly for the present discussion there is a need to examine the relative achievement-ability factor in order to determine whether the pupil is doing what is reasonable. Perhaps we should not expect students with average IQ's to get other than average grades.

Previous performance is another source for data on ability and achievement. The pupils past accomplishments are valuable. Although this is not absolute, it helps the pupil understand himself.

Finally, self-report is valuable. It provides answers to two questions. First, does the pupil have an idea of his ability or potential? Second, is his perception relatively realistic? Appraisal data become meaningful because the child is being assisted to examine his own behavior in light of several other norms. The counselor aids in integrating all the data so that the pupil begins to understand his own ability levels and opportunities.

Interests

Appraisal identifies interests, what one likes or dislikes. With the elementary pupil these factors are more tenuous than with adolescents or adults. Many things interest the child and these can have long or short life spans, or themes can re-occur throughout the first few years. In many cases the period of elementary school is one of seeking and solidifying the pupil's interests. Thrust as he is into kindergarten or first grade, he widens his previous contacts. No longer are the parents the main identification model. His general model is his peer group which exerts pressure on him and whose parents are often more exciting and less demanding than his own at least from his perception. His friends reward him for certain interests and discourage him from others. Another adult, usually a female, begins to affect the pupil's life. Thus, the pupil has three primary foci structuring his interests, his parents, peers, and the elemenatry teacher.

The pupil is physically more able to attain satisfaction from certain dimly understood interest areas. He comprehends rules and regulations of life whether in sporting activities or in daily activities. He involves himself physically in many things which earlier he observed. He reads, he plays baseball, he acts in plays, and he begins to understand the functioning and mechanical aspects of various machines. He now has the opportunity to explore and widen his interests. The elementary educator expands the process of interest identification. Interest inventories have little meaning at the elementary level, but exploration of classroom related interests is pertinent. The child examines many areas of interest, identifies his interests and relates these to his ability level or aptitude.

The elementary counselor offers a situation in which reflection of ideas, values, and interests, is possible. The counselor helps teachers create the same kind of environment in the classroom. Curriculum specialists advocate this approach, and in many social study areas the child learns more about the world of work leading to positive attitudes about the meaning of work and education in their lives.

Life Style

A third important area of appraisal is the interrelationship of the individual with his total environment. Included here is the concept of role models. After whom does the child choose to pattern himself? Psychological studies suggest that several persons are generally chosen. During the first few years the parent is the model. The teacher during the first few years of schooling becomes the second important model. Older playmates and/or peers gradually gain importance for the child. The methods by which the child copes with his environment are partially determined by the significant role models he is exposed to or chooses.

The individual's environment influences his ability to relate to various situations or stimuli. If his background is disadvantaged culturally or financially he enters school with an attitude different than his schoolmates. Efforts to improve this entrance have increased in the past few years and such projects as operation Head Start or the Higher Horizons Project assist disadvantaged youth in having a better foundation to begin their educational and social careers.

The elementary counselor assists the entering pupil, in coping with today's multifaceted world. Information concerning the child's background helps the teacher promote positive, pupil growth. If necessary, the school can provide an environment facilitating certain behaviors. The elementary counselor assumes major responsibility for the identification and interpretation of these data for each pupil. The teacher applies the data and gives feedback.

Interpretation of Data

Prior to a discussion of the use of appraisal data several factors need to be discussed, clarifying the meaning of objective and subjective data. In all cases the appraiser is aware of certain limitations or degrees of value which the data have.

Validity

Validity refers to the degree to which a test measures what it purports to measure. It also refers to the degree to which the data represent a true picture. Test validity is often available, especially for standardized tests and is ascertained more readily than validity of subjective data. For the latter the counselor continuously looks for internal data consistency. For example, if the pupil reports a given interest, the counselor listens for manifestations of the interest in the pupil's life determining the degree to which the interest is real. When the pupil relates more information about himself and his interests, the counselor ascertains the validity of the reported interest. Cronbach[4] lists four specific types of test validity related to the basic reason for which the test was devised.

Predictive validity refers to the relationship between the test performance and some future success. Many of the present readiness tests are based upon some prediction of how well the pupil will be able to perform certain tasks. Although placement or grouping usually precludes the follow-up of the predictive data, nevertheless, the test has predictive validity.

[4] Cronbach, *op. cit.*, pp. 103–105.

Concurrent validity specifies the degree to which a test discriminates or predicts for the immediate situation. The test may be given during which an observer simultaneously rates the test taker on the desired criterion. The degree to which these two or more measures correspond represents concurrent validity. Two tests given at very nearly the same time would provide concurrent validity. Predictive and concurrent are differentiated mainly by the time interval in this case.

Content validity is well known to teachers because it is the basis of most subject matter achievement tests. Simply the question is: Does the test measure what I have taught, the activity under consideration, or the general goals which have been established? Although relatively few subject matter tests have prepared validity data, it is an intricate part of the test.

Construct validity refers to the degree to which the test measures some theoretical concept. For example if the tester wants to know why the test results are significantly different for some pupils, he may hypothesize that fear is a factor in the test-taking situation. He then determines what effect this construct "fear" has on the test taker and his score. He manipulates the environment to control "fear," and if he finds that there is a relationship between these efforts and the score on the test, he makes a statement concerning the validity of the test as related to the construct "fear."

In most cases the elementary teacher or counselor is primarily concerned with the use of the predictive validity of standardized tests. As the test publisher has prepared data concerning how well people who score at a given level do in various situations, the teacher or counselor uses the tests to aid the pupil in obtaining the most advantageous placement in the school. A major limitation exists; validity data is never completely accurate. It ranges from 0.60 to 0.90 indicating a fairly good prediction but this still does not account for major factors. The outcome is that certain children for whom the data predicts positively may, in fact, not perform adequately. Those for whom the prediction (placement) is low may achieve quite well. This suggests there is a need for prediction to be flexible.

Reliability of Data

Reliability is a second concept which has relevance in the use and interpretation of test data. This is generally defined as the extent to which the test or data consistently measures or describes whatever is under investigation.[5] Usually this is determined by observation, e.g., giving the test at different times and comparing the observations. The observations can be scores for the two points in time or some other objective measure of performance. In the case of tests it may be handled by comparing the first half of the test with the second half of the test. Split-half reliability provides an immediate reliability estimate. Although the validity and reliability of the test or observation are interrelated each is a separate concept and the counselor or teacher examines both when using the data. A high reliability does not mean that the process is good unless the process also measures what it purports to measure; has validity.

Whenever the interpretation of assessment data is undertaken there are at least two specific considerations. These deal with objective and subjective data. The first are those data obtained through specific measuring devices such as standardized tests or grade reports. Although not completely objective they are as objective as possible and not as affected by the personal biases of the counselor or teacher as subjective data. The subjective area includes data obtained primarily by observation from the pupil or from someone who represents a meaningful person in the pupil's life. In each case a different process is necessary.

It is possible to provide a case study in which data or a pupil is subjected to analysis. However, these are available and the

[5] *Ibid.*, p. 126.

reader is referred to these for specific case studies.[6] Below are some of the steps in the processes.

Objective Data

Goldman[7] suggests four steps in interpreting objective data. These he lists as utilizing appropriate norm data, profile comparison, score discrimination, and prediction.

UTILIZING APPROPRIATE NORM DATA. Standardized tests manuals contain a variety of norms which assist in the interpretation of test data. The norms are usually stated in terms of a converted score such as a standard score, a grade equivalent, or a percentile. In any case, placement along a continuum is possible when the pupil's score is compared with the norm group.

PROFILE COMPARISON. This is not always possible in the interpretation process. However, when the test norms also include a profile for several test scores, profile interpretation is meaningful. Such tests as the Academic Promise Test (APT) or the Differential Aptitude Test (DAT) utilize these kinds of norms. At the adult level the General Aptitude Test Battery of the Employment Services uses a three-score profile for job selection. Simply stated, the closer the match of the pupil's scores to the profile norm the better the prediction of success or satisfaction for the pupil.

SCORE DISCRIMINATION. At the elementary level it may be that the pupil is very strong in one academic area while not performing adequately in others. When these types of differences occur, immediate action by the staff remedies extreme variations in performance. Further investigation ascertains causes for low performance.

---

[6] Donald G. Mortensen, Seymour P. Stein and Fred G. Rhodes, *Guidance Casebook and Study Materials* (New York: John Wiley and Sons, 1960).
[7] Leo Goldman, *Using Tests in Counseling* (New York: Appleton-Century-Crofts, Inc., 1961), pp. 218–222.

PREDICTION. An expectancy table or prediction of future success is tentatively developed. This step is fostered by utilizing data from groups preceding the particular pupil through school. What can be expected, on the basis of previous pupils, of a pupil who has low reading scores at the second or third grade level? Will he continue to be low, will reading ability weaken, or will he generally improve his performance? These questions are answered on the basis of data compiled from other pupils rather than upon a generalized notion of what occurs to poor readers or poor spellers.

To obtain data about pupils and allow it to remain unused in file cabinets with no attempt at further analysis is perhaps worse than not gathering the data. The elementary counselor leads the school in utilizing available data. He is not the sole user of these data. Teachers, other personnel workers, and the administration are involved in the proper utilization of objective pupil data.

Subjective Data

The process of interpretation is increasingly more difficult when dealing with subjective data. Although the subjective data obtained for a pupil can be most meaningful, it is eventually necessary to insure that bias or distortion does not appear. With certain children the lack of any subjective data indicates certain dispositions to the guidance staff. Why, for example, has not the teacher, the counselor, or any other staff member ever noticed the quiet little girl at the back of the room? Lack of information can be an important reason for further investigation by the guidance worker. In order to effectively use subjective data, certain guidelines are suggested. These guidelines relate to gathering and interpreting data.

Several techniques are used in gathering data. One technique is observation. The teacher or counselor watches the child in various situations and records what is seen. Some general guidelines for observing behavior are:

1. Behavior occurs in a total environment. At the same time that the child is affecting the environment it also is affecting him. Accurate observation demands descriptions of both factors.
2. Although part of the environment may be other children, it is best to focus upon the individual pupil and record his activities rather than attempt to include all behavers in the observed environment.
3. More than one observation period is desirable. The classroom, schoolyard, formal and informal periods are meaningful in understanding the child and are accounted for during the process of gathering observational data.
4. The observer is accurate and objective. However, since the observer is human he also realizes that his own values and biases color his reporting.

Once data are gathered, it is used meaningfully with the pupil. It is not as easy to establish rules or steps for this process as it was for test data. However, it is possible to describe a general process corresponding to that for objective test data.

DESCRIPTION OF ACTIVITIES. First, there is the simple description of activities, what occurred, when did it occur, who was involved, has it happened before? These questions establish the facts of the behavior. There is a need to verify the data to be sure that the accuracy is as great as possible.

COMPARISON OF BEHAVIORS. Second, observed behavior is compared with the child's previous behavior and behavior norms for the child's age and sex group. This is similar to the profile comparison in tests and gives a better idea of the total behavior rather than simple discrete behavior descriptions. The individual is of primary importance and is not generalized to a greater population and forgotten because he fits a "norm" group.

DISCRIMINATION OF BEHAVIOR PATTERNS. Third, a discrimination of meaning from the behavior pattern is included. Just as with tests, it is necessary to examine whether certain areas are extremely strong or weak. The manifestations of pupil behavior are meaningful when it is discovered that certain things occur more or less frequently than expected.

PREDICTIONS. Fourth, an examination is made of what predictions can be made and what, if anything, can be done with the pupil. Any prediction is tentative especially when the pupil is in early elementary school. However, as a basis for assisting pupils, teachers, and parents to understand the present and future, the counselor is involved in prediction or at least description of future possibilities.

It is obvious that in certain areas of an elementary pupil's life the assessment process is not as crucial as other areas. In certain areas, such as reading, assessment is most crucial. As prevention of long-range problems is part of the elementary program, behavior difficulties are identified, assessed, and hopefully adjusted as quickly as possible. It is true that the complete assessment technique listed above precludes a wide utilization of the method. However, the fact that there is work and effort involved does not eliminate the need to be as diligent as possible whenever needs arise. The teacher, counselor, and pupil involve themselves in the assessment process. The degree of involvement varies between individuals and, in most cases, relatively few pupils need intensive, long-range assistance of the type described in this chapter. For those who do, the counselor and teacher become deeply involved. For many other pupils parts of the process are valuable. For example, all pupils should know what tests are designed to accomplish, what the scores mean, and what the individual's test results suggest. If the counselor and/or teacher do not become involved in the assessment and appraisal process there is some question concerning the relevance of guidance. Likewise for any part of the process the relationship of the activity to the pupil dictates the value of the process. When tests and other appraisal data are not used there is a reasonable basis for eliminating the activity. Hopefully this is not the case in fully functioning elementary guidance programs. Rather the personnel keep in mind that the ultimate use of data relates to the provision of assistance to the pupil toward more optimal functioning and growth toward maturity.

Idiographic vs. Nomothetic Assessment

Alluded to earlier it is necessary to focus on the individual. Although guidance personnel know and understand nomothetic or group norms they also examine the idiographic or individual implications. Unless the focus is upon the individual's behavior and its relationship to him, there is no justification for guidance. By definition the individual is of paramount importance. Thus, the counselor keeps firmly in mind that he is dealing with an individual who has adapted and adopted the commonalities of others in arriving at his present position. In addition, he is also in the process of becoming an individual and has this right in our society. Prediction, control, or manipulation is possible but is only carried out in light of human idiographic factors.

Summary

There are many methods the counselor or guidance worker uses in better understanding the individual. Each has its strengths and limitations which need to be understood and accounted for when dealing with the individual pupil. The greater the range of information examined the more meaningful is the guidance process. Each person involved with assessment needs to be highly skilled in using objective and subjective data. To this end the counselor leads in demonstrations, competence, and assisting others in enhancing their competencies.

SELECTED REFERENCES

Leo Goldman, *Using Tests in Counseling* (New York: Appleton-Century-Crofts, Inc., 1961).

John Horrocks, *Assessment of Behavior* (Columbus: Charles E. Merrill Books, Inc., 1964).

Bruce Shertzer and Herman J. Peters, *Guidance: Techniques for Individual Appraisal & Development* (New York: The Macmillan Company, 1965).

EVALUATION IN THE ELEMENTARY SCHOOL GUIDANCE PROGRAM

School personnel evaluate various aspects of the school program. This process helps make decisions concerning the program's scope and direction. Teachers utilize achievement tests in determining pupil progress and in deciding whether to continue a particular unit or to move into the next segment. Administrators evaluate activities within the school in considering effectiveness or making budget decisions. In fact, as Hatch and Stefflre point out:

> School systems cannot escape making value judgments about their various services since even the continuation

of the present situation implies an evaluation—that concludes "What we are doing is all right. Let us continue our present course."[1]

The Importance of Evaluation

A service growing as rapidly as guidance needs check points in assessing whether the foundation, direction, scope, adequacy of service, and personnel aspects of the program give maximum assistance.

Foundation

In any program the philosophical foundation upon which the program is built is delineated. Whether this is concerned with a broadly conceived philosophical base, such as the democratic approach, or a more narrowly developed philosophy dealing with a specific function, such as the behavioral base for counseling, the meaning and relevance of the base is determined. This involves the identification of the philosophy governing the actions of the personnel and the program's activities. Statements describing the philosophy are developed in such a way that their relevance can be evaluated. A foundation gives the program builder an opportunity to identify his beliefs concerning elementary pupils, guidance, and the interrelationships between the two. This is most important prior to the beginning of the program, for it helps the school staff choose the type of program and personnel to be employed. In short, the foundation aspect sets the stage for subsequent activities. Evaluation of the program's philosophical base clarifies those factors which are not as well defined as they could be. For example, a behavioral approach to counseling

[1] Raymond N. Hatch and Buford Stefflre, *Administration of Guidance Services,* 2nd Ed. (Englewood Cliffs: Prentice-Hall, Inc., 1965), p. 259.

is advocated. The philosophical foundation flowing from this approach suggests that behavior is learned and that modification of behavior is possible. If the counselor espouses this approach, he affects counselee behavioral change, a predetermined philosophical goal.

Direction

The school serves the needs of pupils. The population's characteristics determine, to some degree, the program's point of emphasis. Sometimes the program originally designed does not take into account the pupil population. Also, when the population differs from the original, the direction of the guidance service is changed. Simply stated, the question is, are the original objectives still relevent in terms of the present situation?

Scope

It is suggested above that counseling, consulting, curriculum involvement, and measurement are proper services to include under the rubric elementary school guidance. Examination of whether these represent the total range of elementary guidance services or whether certain of the services fall under another service area is important. Efficient services are the most desirable. The evaluation of the scope of guidance services supplies information illuminating the need for facilities and personnel.

One of the special problems related to evaluating elementary guidance is service initiation. The stages of program development are clearly stated. Thus, the counselor designs a general program of guidance services prior to beginning the job. Usually he cooperates with the principal, representatives of the teaching staff, and other special personnel in the building. The program is affected by existing school-wide policies, especially in large urban and suburban systems. The counselor creates the best program for his school. He systematically determines whether the program is offering the breadth of necessary services. A structured examination at specific times during the year informs the counselor on this subject, which relates highly to broadening or decreasing the scope of the program.

As it may be impossible to initiate a fully functioning program, the counselor establishes priorities of services. He can de-emphasize the counseling aspect at the start of the program, working first through teacher consultation and the curriculum. However, this does not mean that counseling does not occur.

Adequacy of Services

This topic refers to the degree to which the guidance function is adequate to the task set for it. Are the materials and methods tailored to meet the needs of the pupils? The basic question is: How good a job is being done? The evaluator examines the relationship between the services provided the identified needs. A checklist or scaling device is often employed. The evaluator completes the instrument and judges the program's effectiveness. During the evaluative process new services can be suggested. However, evaluation in relationship to adequacy is generally concerned with present services, rather than program expansion.

Personnel

This is a difficult area, as the evaluation is concerned with individual members or groups of guidance personnel. In general, evaluating the performance of persons in education is cautioned. The literature on merit pay scales evidences the resistance to teacher evaluation for pay differentials. The available methods are not sophisticated, and definite evaluation of personnel is more difficult than dealing with the nonpersonnel aspects of a program.

Regardless, this is an important area of evaluation. One method has the pupil personnel staff involved in self-evaluation. How effective is the counselor in providing services and assistance within the school? Results within the pupil population can be observed. The results relate to the predetermined philosophical objectives. For example, if a goal fosters a greater achievement-ability balance for underachievers, the counselor examines data on these factors from year to year in order to determine if this outcome occurs. The counselor can evaluate his own counseling effectiveness. By tape recording sessions, he requests others from the guidance or personnel staff to listen and critique his performance. These two suggestions illustrate possibilities for self evaluation in the personnel area. External evaluators may assess the personnel aspect of the guidance program. The outside team is given directions as to what objectives the evaluation is to determine. It is relatively easy to find weaknesses in any program, but of little value unless changes are made. Restrictions of finance, personnel, or school-wide philosophy make this difficult. The ingenuity of the evaluative team is evidenced in the personnel area. They develop ways and means of obtaining necessary information. The personnel area is the most important part of evaluative observation. Without qualified and adequately functioning personnel, the rest of the guidance program is mediocre.

Other areas are included in the evaluative process. The guidance budget and the available facilities are examples. They may be included under other areas, but are considered during any evaluative effort.

Purposes of Evaluation

The above discussion outlines some specific areas for evaluation. Depending upon the school and the personnel involved, some are emphasized more than others. However, the following seem to be purposes relevant to a general evaluative program.

The evaluative process measures the efficiency of the philosophical foundation, the techniques, and the services offered within the guidance program. Do they enhance the personnel's ability in accomplishing desired goals?

The evaluative process measures the effectiveness of the guidance program. Do the services which are provided meet the pupil's needs? Are the pupils involved? To what extent are they involved?

Evaluation gives objective and positive support for the efficient and effective parts of the total program. What activities are most efficient and effective? What can be done to strengthen these? What should be done about those services presently not highly rated?

Evaluation supplies comprehensive data, linking programs at several levels. What demands are made on pupils as they progress through school? What can be done at specific levels to improve this movement?

Evaluation offers public relations materials. Do definite services suggest the program's value to the community? Is a program, publicly supported as an experimental program, successful? Does any of the data suggest that the services decreases the cost to the public for other or similar services?

Limitations in Evaluation

Several factors limit the evaluation process. The limitations described below are those most often identified during evaluation studies. Listing them has two values. First, if there is pre-understanding of the existing limitations, the evaluator more accurately interprets the data resulting from the process. Second, in many cases, it is possible to promote those practices which eliminate or negate the limitations. For example, if the program relates to an incomplete statement of goals, a more comprehensive statement prior to evaluation can be formulated.

The objectives of the guidance program often are not precisely defined. The behavioral outcomes anticipated for the guidance program need specification. However, a counselor may be involved with a multitude of tasks and fails to spend time specifying objectives.

The terminology is not uniform. The term guidance means several things at the elementary level. It refers to advice giving, directive activities of teachers, or the one-to-one counseling activities of the counselor. Another terminological problem relates to the use of different words describing essentially the same type of specialist. The counselor may also be known as a child development specialist, a consultant, or a guidance worker. The evaluator is aware of the task areas and the range of possible titles. A school may employ a counselor, but unless he is performing guidance and counseling activities the evaluation must be negative.

Means are often assumed to be ends. The activity of the counselor is occasionally examined in light of the degree to which he is accepting, warm, and knowledgeable, when, in reality, the ultimate outcome is the assistance provided. The mere existence of counseling is often quoted as positive evidence of a functioning guidance program. Description and evaluation need to be stated in relation to behavioral outcomes.

Cause and effect is difficult to determine. Often changes or positive results occurring to pupils are a result of long-term guidance and counseling, or due to outside stimuli or normal maturation of the individual. Positive results stimulate the question: How do you know that guidance really made the difference?

Many of the variables, education in general and guidance specifically, are quality variables. Quantification is impossible, and evaluation is changed from an objective process to a subjective activity.

Certain significant tasks are overlooked in the evaluative process. For example, the counselor spends a number of hours preparing for a single individual conference. This preparation fails to appear in the evaluative report of the work of this counselor.

The limitations described above are important in understanding the evaluation process. These do not limit or preclude involvement in evaluation, but rather attempt to make the evaluation process meaningful. In discussing limitations, the authors of the booklet *Guidance Counseling and Testing* suggest:

> These (limitations) should not present roadblocks but should serve to provide caution signals and a challenge to use the best scientific methods available to collect facts and develop procedures which will help minimize these limitations and produce the means to objective evaluation.[2]

Approaches to Evaluation

There are several widely used approaches to evaluation: the survey approach, the experimental method, and the case study. The survey method clarifies the present program. Once clarification is accomplished, total service is improved. The experimental approach determines the amount of change which has taken place. In addition, value judgments are made relative to the change. Is it good? Is it better than no service? These and similar questions are typically asked during evaluation of the experimental type. The case study examines individual growth or movement toward goals. The object of a case study can be a pupil or a personnel worker.

---

[2] *Guidance Counseling and Testing*, U.S. Department of Health, Education, and Welfare (Washington, D.C.: U.S. Government Printing Office, 1961), p. 5.

The Survey Method

Peters and Shertzer suggest that the survey method "(1) uses predetermined criteria or standards for a guidance program, (2) collects evidence of the guidance services being offered, and (3) takes stock of how these existing services compare with the pre-determined standards."[3] Under this approach various survey forms are used to apply external criteria to the program being evaluated. Perhaps the best known of these instruments is the *Evaluative Criteria.*[4] The criteria are in checklist form utilizing a scale to determine the degree to which the service, facility, or activity are part of the program. One value, obtained under the Evaluative Criteria survey, deals with both in house and external observation. It is difficult to specify what follows the survey. Should schools accept every statement in the book and attempt to rate excellence? Is a good "high" rating meaningful? The survey method, utilizing either the Criteria or similar statements, is a popular method, because instruments are already prepared and previous studies satisfactorily completed.

Experimental Method

The second evaluative approach is the experimental method. Research methodology is applied to groups of pupils, and a determination is made as to the effect of the particular research process on the pupils. A project including group counseling or group guidance might be valuable in helping acting-out pupils better understand themselves and their behavior may be modified. These pupils and a closely matched control group are identified. At the end of a pre-determined period of group work,

---

[3] Herman J. Peters and Bruce Shertzer, *Guidance: Program Development and Management* (Columbus: Charles E. Merrill Books, Inc., 1963), p. 497.
[4] Evaluative Criteria, Section G, Guidance Services, in *National Study of Secondary School Evaluation* (Washington, D.C.: Cooperative Study of Secondary School Standards, 1960), pp. 273–288.

the behavior of both groups is assessed. If a difference exists for the counseled group, there is some basis for describing the group process as valuable. Rothney[5] and his associates are perhaps the best known exponents of this approach. It is used to evaluate specific, identifiable services.

The resistance of many persons to become involved in research efforts is its major limitation. Frequently counselors either do not find the time to develop the research effort, or they are frightened by the insistence of research specialists upon design, control, and clearcut objectives. Cory[6] proposes an alternative, action research, designed to study the problem with the hope of instituting change. Research, in this case, is less strict than the more sophisticated research efforts of professional researchers. The results are sometimes more meaningful.

Research efforts are limited by the fact that they are only parts of a total guidance picture. The relationship of counseling to change in acting-out behavior is studied, but it does not reveal the meaning or success of counseling in other situations.

Case Study

The case study method determines the current status of an individual or portion of the program. The counselor gathers a considerable amount of data on the individual, his goals, or growth toward goals. On the basis of the gathered data the assessor, along with the individual under study, thoroughly explore the situation. When applied proportionately to the program, the case study approach allows an in-depth examination of a particular aspect under observation. Thus, the counseling process, by means of the case study, describes several counseling situa-

[5] John W. M. Rothney, *Guidance Practices & Results* (New York: Harper & Row, Publishers, 1958).

[6] Stephen M. Corey, *Action Research to Improve School Practices* (New York: Bureau of Publications, Teachers College, Columbia University, 1953), 161 pp.

tions and explores general outcomes. Comparisons can determine counseling effectiveness over a number of cases.

The obvious limitation of the case study is time. The necessary amount of information and the subsequent analysis precludes large numbers of case studies. However, as the focus is upon individuals or specific processes it falls naturally under the rubric of guidance.

The approach used is partially determined by the objectives the counselor establishes for the evaluation. If the primary interest is counting or completing a checklist of external criteria, the survey approach is most reasonable. If this aspect is less important than a particular individual's progress in counseling, the survey method is less effective than the experimental or case study approaches. As with other aspects of guidance, the ultimate answer is eclectic, including parts of all the approaches.

Objectives in Evaluation

Evaluation objectives are cooperatively pre-developed by the school staff. Although general objectives can be evaluated, it is of greater value to precisely specify the program's objectives. Although the list of Cardinal Principles offers a basis for examining the guidance process, it is considerably more valuable to develop a comprehensive examination of guidance objectives. Since each program will be unique we will make no attempt to present such a list. However, the following illustrate some objectives:

1. The guidance program provides data to the pupil concerning his abilities, aptitudes, and interests.
2. The counselor provides individual assistance to a majority of the pupils in the school.
3. Pupils can describe, in general terms, the job of the counselor.

4. There are specific instances where teachers, counselors, and other pupil personnel workers assist the pupils.

These statements relate negatively and positively to the program. They tend to narrow the program by implying that the counselor fulfills only those specific, spelled-out objectives. On the other hand, the process of establishing objectives helps the counselor develop his role. So long as he remains flexible in his relation to the objectives, they are a meaningful aid to evaluation. As Hatch and Stefflre[7] note, it is impossible for the ship's captain to know if he is on course unless he knows his destination.

Criteria for Evaluation

Closely related to evaluation objectives is the criteria by which success is determined. Knowledge of one's self is valuable, but application to behavior is more important and is included in the final evaluation. This is stated prior to evaluation, so that the process can be as objective as possible. At the elementary level it is important to find out whether the pupil has the necessary knowledge about the transition from sixth to seventh grade. Examination of the pupil in the seventh grade indicates if he has applied the knowledge in behaving more maturely. If he has knowledge, but cannot apply it, the guidance process is falling short of its goal.

Measurement in Evaluation

When appropriate and available, the evaluator utilizes an objective measuring device. This assists him in making necessary judgments concerning the program's value. Of course, in many cases these devices are not readily available or they have been used on populations noticeably different from the one under observation. Examination of the pertinent literature helps the

---

[7] Hatch and Stefflre, *op. cit.,* p. 265.

counselor determine the available instruments and how they have been used. The final step in the process is the interpretation or action steps. Unless the evaluator interprets the meaning and introduces new behaviors into his activities, the evaluation is of little value. Evaluation is worthwhile when it indicates a desired goal, not when it points out past accomplishments.

Steps in Conducting an Evaluation Study

An evaluation study is conducted with a step-by-step procedure. Evaluation studies are described differently, but certain steps are basic to most approaches.

The following description presents skeletal information concerning the knowledge of various steps involved in an investigation.

Objectives of Study

Why is the study undertaken and what purposes does it serve? When objectives of the program are stated in terms of desired behavior, the evaluative results are determined more easily. Clear statement of objectives permits selection of appropriate techniques for the evaluation. After the objectives have been stated, criteria used as evidence relating to the objectives are established. Multiple criteria are advantageous. Whatever the criteria, they are stated in measurable terms.

Population for the Study

Appropriate subjects and materials are selected. After identifying the population, the counselor decides whether to collect data from the whole population or a representative sample of that population. Data can usually be obtained from every person of a small group. However, with a large group, it is often impossible or impracticable to reach each person. Therefore, in many studies data are collected from a carefully selected sample of the population. If this sample is truly representative of the total group, generalizations are applicable for the total population. Selecting a representative sample is no easy task and leads to difficulty in interpreting the findings.

Evaluation involves wide staff participation. If not enough members of the school staff participate in the study, the resulting interpretation of the data is personally toned and not as useful to the entire staff.

Collection of Data

The counselor employs various procedures in collecting the data used in evaluation studies. Approaches to evaluation are classified as survey, experimental, or case study. The survey evaluates existing procedures and techniques, determining the extent to which they achieve their objectives. This yields a description of the present services.

Experimental evaluation rigorously appraises a part of the program. Experimental evaluation uses either statistical control, the application of co-variance statistical methods to the data, or experimental control, the manipulation of independent variables in a deliberate and predetermined manner.

The case study approach evaluates an individual's change. The pupil formulates goals appropriate to himself; the counselor and other staff members help him achieve them. His progress toward the goals is determined by himself and external judges. Statements and descriptions concerning his behavior are gathered from persons dealing with the pupil.

Instruments are selected and constructed to fit the purposes of the local school. The counselor collects data by follow-up, client opinion, expert opinion, intra-group change, or extra-group change.

The counselor uses sociometric devices, checklists, questionnaires, interviews, and open-ended questions. Published evaluation forms are found in textbooks, state departments of education, or the U. S. Department of Health, Education, and Welfare.

Analysis and Interpretation of Data

After the data are gathered, analysis brings out significant likenesses, differences, or relationships. When necessary, appropriate statistical treatment is used to compare the data and the criteria. After the data and criteria are compared, interpretations are made to determine implications and draw conclusions. Recommendations to continue the effective aspects of the program can then be made. Modification is recommended, when improvement is indicated by the evaluation.

Presentation of Data

The facts about the state of affairs are made clear to laymen and school personnel before any changes result from the survey. The evaluation findings are reported in an intelligible, clear, convincing, and compelling manner. The essential findings of survey and experimental approaches, both favorable and unfavorable, are published in the local newspapers and formal publications. Graphs and tables assist in interpreting the report. There may be several reports, perhaps one for each major group of readers, but one recommended outline is suggested:

A. Present the purposes (or values) of the evaluation.
B. Report briefly the study outline.
C. Present the major conclusions.
D. Indicate cautions and limitations of conclusions.
E. State implications and recommendations which the data justify.

Implementation of Change

A counselor seeks more than bare description. He collects evidence on the basis of some hypothesis, carefully summarizes the data, and then thoroughly analyzes it, in an endeavor to draw meaningful generalizations. If the evaluation justifies its execution, the interpreted data help implement necessary change.

When the findings justify, data interpretation and evaluation lead to a planned development of modifications generally in the educational program and particularly in the guidance services. The effective school evaluation is followed up periodically to see whether or not recommendations are being carried out, and what results have followed from putting these suggestions into practice.

Hollis and Hollis[8] chart the three stages in evaluation: formation of an organizational structure, execution of the evaluation study, and implementation of recommendations. For adequate evaluation, several activities are performed. See Figure 9.[9]

Figure 9.

Stages and Activities in Operating

An Evaluation Service

Stage	*Activities to Perform*
1. Formation of an Organizational Structure	Define the purposes of the service.
	Designate a coordinator for the service.
	Specify personnel and their responsibilities.
	Determine the extent of readiness for change.
	Delimit scope of service.
	Determine evaluation schedule and priority list of future studies.
	Obtain support for the service and each study—money, time, and authority.
	Establish lines of communication within the service and for each study.
	Arrange for keeping records.

[8] Joseph William Hollis and Lucile Ussery Hollis, *Organizing for Effective Guidance* (Chicago: Science Research Associates, Inc., 1965), p. 416.

[9] From *Organizing for Effective Guidance* by Joseph William Hollis and Lucile Ussery Hollis. © 1965, Science Research Associates, Inc. Reprinted by permission of the publisher.

2. Execution of an Evaluation Study	Define the purposes of the study.
	Develop the design of the study, including selection of criteria and techniques.
	Determine evaluators and participants.
	Obtain data from research service.
	Collate data.
	Apply criteria to data and make interpretations.
	Draw conclusions and identify implications.
	Make recommendations.
	Disseminate findings.
3. Implementation of Recommendations	Outline the procedure for implementations.
	Obtain approval for implementing recommendations.
	Have coordinator serve in a consultative role for implementation.
	Have persons affected by changes assist in implementing recommendations.
	Establish the priority list and timetable for implementing recommendations.
	Identify changes necessary in postulates and action guidelines within the guidance program.
	Maintain continuity in guidance services and activities during implementation.
	Follow through to determine the effect of implemented recommendations.
	Prepare report on implementation.

Adequate Evaluation

Four questions examine the characteristics of an adequate evaluation program.

1. Is the design of the evaluation program comprehensive?
2. Are changes in an individual's behavior the basis for evaluating his growth and development?
3. Are the results of evaluation organized and integrated into a meaningful interpretation?
4. Is the evaluation program continuous and integrated within the curriculum?[10]

These considerations guide a counselor in examining his program. Evaluation is comprehensive, covering the entire guidance program. The counselor evaluates his methods, services, and their outcomes. Only by stating objectives in behavioral terms can the evaluation data be relevant to change. An evaluation results in organized findings that can be interpreted to the staff, pupils, and community. This aids in making judgments about the program and its relationship to the school. Decisions can be made as to the value of each aspect of the program and its relation to the local curriculum. Need for changes become based on local needs. National norms are important for comparisons, but concern is centered on the local situation.

Summary

Evaluation is an important part of an on-going school program. The opportunity to provide evaluation from the beginning of the elementary guidance program is unique. The counselor is in a most advantageous position to promote evaluative activities. There are numerous processes, instruments, and techniques used in evaluation. In general, there is a need to specify the objectives of the evaluation so that value judgments concerning the rele-

[10] J. Wayne Wrightstone, Joseph Justman, and Irving Robins, *Evaluation in Modern Education* (New York: American Book Company, 1956).

vance and degree of success can be made. This directs the choice of instruments and treatments. Evaluation is the beginning of a process designed to improve educational opportunities for elementary pupils.

SELECTED REFERENCES

Gilbert D. Moore, (ed.) *Research Guidelines for High School Counselors* (New York: College Entrance Examination Board, 1967).

Merle M. Ohlsen, *Guidance Services in the Modern School* (New York: Harcourt, Brace & World, Inc., 1964).

Franklin R. Zeran, & Anthony C. Riccio, *Organization and Administration of Guidance Services* (Chicago: Rand McNally, 1963).

BIBLIOGRAPHY

William Alexander, "Reporting to Parents—Why? What? How?," *National Education Association Journal,* 16 (1959).

Richard Anderson, "A Social Worker Looks at the Parent-Teacher Conferences," *Exceptional Children,* 28, 433, 434 (1962).

Dugald Arbuckle, "Occupational Information in the Elementary School," *Vocational Guidance Quarterly,* 12, 77–84 (1963).

Arthur A. Atwell and Robert R. Odon, "The Guv'nors Venture in Group Guidance," *Elementary School Journal,* 64, 124–130 (November, 1963).

D. Ausubel and P. Ausubel, "Ego Development Among Segregated Negro Children," in A. Passow, (editor), *Education in Depressed Areas* (New York: Columbia University Press, 1963).

Albert Bandura and Richard Walters, *Social Learning and Per-*

sonality Development (New York: Holt, Rinehart, and Winston, Inc., 1963).

Walter Barbe and Norman Chambers, "Career Requirements of Gifted Elementary Children and Their Parents," *Vocational Guidance Quarterly*, 11, 137–140 (1963).

Kenneth D. Benne and Paul Sheats, "Functional Roles of Group Members," *Journal of Social Issues*, 4, 42–47 (Spring, 1948).

Forest Bogan, "Employment of School Age Youth," Special Labor Force Report No. 68, Reprint No. 2493 (Washington, D.C.: U.S. Department of Labor, 1966), pp. 739–743.

Hubert Bonner, *Group Dynamics* (New York: The Ronald Press Company, 1959).

Henry Borow, "Development of Occupational Motives and Roles," in *Review of Child Development Research*, Lois Hoffman and Martin Hoffman, editors (New York: Russell Sage Foundation, 1966), p. 397.

Lawrence Brammer and Everett Shostrom, *Therapeutic Psychology* (Englewood Cliffs: Prentice-Hall, Inc., 1960).

D. W. Brison, "The Role of the Elementary Guidance Counselor," *National Elementary Principal*, 43, 41–44 (1964).

John Broedel, Merle Ohlsen, Fred Proff, and Charles Southard, "The Effects of Group Counseling on Gifted Underachieving Adolescents," *Journal of Counseling Psychology*, 7, 163–170 (Fall, 1960).

Edward Clark, "Influences of Sex and Social Class on Occupational Preference and Perception," *Personnel and Guidance Journal*, 45, 440–444 (1967).

Commission on the Reorganization of Secondary Education, "Cardinal Principles of Secondary Education," U.S. Office of Education Bulletin, 1918, No. 35 (Washington, D.C.: Government Printing Office, 1918).

Stephen M. Corey, *Action Research to Improve School Practices* (New York: Bureau of Publications, Teachers College, Columbia University, 1953).

Council of Chief State School Officers, "Responsibilities of State Departments of Education for Pupil Personnel Service" (Washington, D.C.: Council of Chief State School Officers, 1960).

Lee J. Cronbach, *Essentials of Psychological Testing*, 2nd Ed. (New York: Harper and Brothers, Publishers, 1960).

Richard Cutler and Elton McNeil, "Mental Health Consultation in the Schools," Unpublished Research Report (Ann Arbor: University of Michigan, 1963).

D. Davis, N. Hagen, and J. Strouf, "Occupational Choice of Twelve-Year-Olds," *Personnel and Guidance Journal*, **40**, 628, 629 (1962).

M. L. De Fleur, "Children's Knowledge of Occupational Roles and Prestige: Preliminary Report," *Psychological Reports*, **13**, 760 (1963).

Erwin Winfred Detjen and Mary Ford Detjen, *Elementary School Guidance*, 2nd Ed. (New York: McGraw-Hill Book Company, Inc., 1963).

Martin Deutsch, "Minority Group and Class Status as Related to Social and Personality Factors in Scholastic Achievement," *The Society for Applied Anthropology Monographs*, 1960.

Don Dinkmeyer, "Developmental Counseling in the Elementary School," *Personnel and Guidance Journal*, **45**, 262–266 (1966).

John Dollard and Neal Miller, *Personality and Psychotherapy* (New York: McGraw-Hill Book Company, Inc., 1950).

Karl Douglas, "Why Visit Homes?" *Parents and the Schools, Thirty-sixth Yearbook, The National Elementary Principal*, **37** (Washington, D.C.: National Education Association, 1957), pp. 239, 240.

Wilbur Dutton and John Hockett, *The Modern Elementary School Curriculum and Methods* (New York: Rinehart and Co., Inc., 1959).

Educational Policies Commission, *The Central Purpose of American Education* (Washington, D.C.: National Education Association, 1961).

Educational Policies Commission, *The Purposes of Education in American Democracy* (Washington, D.C.: National Education Association, 1938).

Erik H. Erikson, *Childhood and Society*, 2nd Ed. (New York: Morton Press, 1963).

Evaluative Criteria, Section G., Guidance Services, in *National Study of Secondary School Evaluation* (Washington, D.C.: Cooperative Study of Secondary School Standards, 1960), pp. 273–288.

Donald Ford and Hugh Urban, *Systems of Psychotherapy* (New York: John Wiley and Sons, Inc., 1963).

Clifford Froehlich and Kenneth Hoyt, *Guidance Testing* (Chicago: Science Research Associates, Inc., 1959).

Daniel Fullmer and Harold Bernard, *Counseling: Content and Process* (Chicago: Science Research Associates, Inc., 1964).

E. Galler, "Influence of Social Class on Children's Choices of Occupation," *Elementary School Journal,* **51,** 439–445 (1951).

Jack Gibb, "Defense Level and Influence Potential in Small Groups," in *Leadership and Interpersonal Behavior,* Luigi Petrullo and Bernard Bass, editors (New York: Holt, Rinehart & Winston, Inc., 1961), pp. 68–75.

Eli Ginzberg, *The Nation's Children,* Vol. 1, *The Family & Social Change* (New York: Columbia University Press, 1960), pp. 24–49.

Eli Ginzberg, Sol Ginsburg, Sidney Axelrod and John Herma, *Occupational Choice: An Approach to a General Theory* (New York: Columbia University Press, 1951).

Sheldon Glueck and Eleanor Glueck, *Predicting Delinquency and Crime* (Cambridge: Harvard University Press, 1959).

Golden Anniversary 1960 White House Conference on Children and Youth, "Recommendations," *Composite Report of Forum Findings* (Washington, D.C.: U.S. Government Printing Office, 1960).

Leo Goldman, "Group Guidance: Content and Process," *The Personnel and Guidance Journal,* **40,** 518–522 (February, 1962).

———, *Using Tests in Counseling* (New York: Appleton-Century-Crofts, Inc., 1961).

Armin Grams, *Facilitating Learning and Individual Development* (St. Paul: Minnesota Department of Education, 1966).

Lewis Grell, "How Much Occupational Information in the Elementary School?" *The Vocational Guidance Quarterly,* **9,** 52, 53 (1960).

Guidance Counseling and Testing, U.S. Department of Health, Education, and Welfare (Washington, D.C.: U. S. Government Printing Office, 1961).

Barbara Gunn, "Children's Conceptions of Occupational Prestige," *Personnel and Guidance Journal*, 42, 558–563 (1964).

Andrew Halpin, *Theory and Research in Administration* (New York: The Macmillan Company, 1966).

Robert Hanvey and Morton Teneberg, "University of Chicago Laboratory School Evaluates Team Teaching," *The Bulletin*, National Association of Secondary School Principals, 45, 189–197 (1961).

Raymond N. Hatch and Buford Stefflre, *Administration of Guidance Services*, 2nd Ed. (Englewood Cliffs: Prentice-Hall, Inc., 1965).

Robert Havighurst, *Human Development and Education* (New York: Longmans, Green, 1952).

Marion Heisey, "A Differential Approach to Elementary Guidance," *Elementary School Guidance and Counseling*, 1, 18–21 (1966).

George Hill, *Management and Improvement of Guidance* (New York: Appleton-Century-Crofts, 1965).

John Holland, "A Theory of Vocational Choice," *Journal of Counseling Psychology*, 6, 34–45 (1959).

Joseph William Hollis and Lucile Ussery Hollis, *Organizing for Effective Guidance* (Chicago: Science Research Associates, Inc., 1965).

Kenneth Hoyt, "Guidance: A Constellation of Services," *Personnel and Guidance Journal*, 40, 690–697 (1962).

Anthony Humphreys, Arthur Traxler, and Robert North, *Guidance Services* (Chicago: Science Research Associates, Inc., 1960).

Walter F. Johnson, Buford Stefflre, and Roy A. Edelfelt, *Pupil Personnel and Guidance Services* (New York: McGraw-Hill Book Company, Inc., 1961).

Goldie Kaback, "Automation, Work, and Leisure: Implications for Elementary Education," *Vocational Guidance Quarterly*, 13, 202–206 (1965).

Jerome Kagan and Howard Moss, *Birth to Maturity* (New York: John Wiley and Sons, Inc., 1962).

Gerald D. Kranzler, George Roy Mayer, Calvin O. Dyer, and Paul F. Munger, "Counseling with Elementary School Children: An Experimental Study," *The Personnel and Guidance Journal*, 44, 944–949 (May, 1966).

Leonard Krasner, "The Therapist as a Social Reinforcement Machine," in Hans Strupp and Lester Luborsky, editors, *Research in Psychotherapy* (Washington, D.C.: American Psychological Association, Inc., 1962), pp. 61–94.

John Krumboltz (Ed.), *Revolution in Counseling* (Boston: Houghton Mifflin Company, 1966).

John Krumboltz and Carl Thoresen, "The Effect of Behavioral Counseling in Group and Individual Settings on Information-Seeking Behavior," *Journal of Counseling Psychology*, 11, 324–333 (1964).

Sheldon Lochman, "Level of Aspiration: A Classroom Demonstration of Phenomena and Principle," *Journal of General Psychology*, 65, 357–363 (1961).

Kurt Lewin, Ronald Lippitt, and Ralph White, "Patterns of Aggressive Behavior in Experimentally Created 'social climates,'" *Journal of Social Psychology*, 10, 271–299 (1939).

Walter Lifton, "Vocational Guidance in the Elementary School," *Vocational Guidance Quarterly*, 8, 79–82 (1959).

Robert Mathewson, *Guidance Policy and Practice*, 3rd Ed. (New York: Harper and Row, Publishers, 1962).

Gaither McConnel, "What Do Parents Want to Know," *The Elementary School Journal*, 58, 84 (1957).

William McCreary and Gerald Miller, "Elementary School Counselors in California," *Personnel and Guidance Journal*, 44, 494–498 (1966).

Carroll Miller, *Foundations of Guidance*, (New York: Harper and Brothers, Publishers, 1961).

Gilbert D. Moore, editor, *Counselor Competencies in Occupational Information.* Mimeograph, (Washington, D.C.: U.S. Office of Education, 1966), pp. 1–50.

Donald G. Mortensen, Seymour P. Stein and Fred G. Rhodes, *Guidance Casebook and Study Materials* (New York: John Wiley and Sons, 1960).

Clark Moustakas, *Psychotherapy with Children: The Living Relationship* (New York: Harper and Brothers, 1959).

Richard Nelson, "Knowledge and Interests Concerning Sixteen Occupations Among Elementary and Secondary School Students," *Educational and Psychological Measurement,* **23,** 741–754 (1963).

————, "Physical Facilities for Elementary School Counseling," *Personnel and Guidance Journal,* **45,** 552–556 (1967).

Willa Norris, *Occupational Information in the Elementary School* (Chicago: Science Research Associates, Inc., 1963).

Robert O'Hara, "The Roots of Careers," *Elementary School Journal,* **62,** 277–280 (1962).

Merle M. Ohlsen, "Counseling Within a Group Setting," *Journal of the National Association of Women Deans and Counselors,* **23,** 104–109 (April, 1960).

Herman J. Peters and Gail F. Farwell, *Guidance: A Developmental Approach* 2nd Ed. (Chicago: Rand McNally and Company, 1967).

Herman J. Peters and Bruce Shertzer, *Guidance: Program Development and Management* (Columbus: Charles E. Merrill Books, Inc., 1963).

Herman J. Peters, Bruce Shertzer, and William Van Hoose, *Guidance in Elementary Schools* (Chicago: Rand McNally & Company, 1965).

Physical Facilities for Guidance Services, Office of Education Report OE-25013 (Washington, D.C.: U.S. Department of Health, Education, and Welfare).

Project on the Instructional Program of the Public Schools, *The Principals Look at the Schools* (Washington, D.C.: National Education Association, 1962), pp. 39, 40.

"Pupil Data Summary," State University College at Buffalo, Evaluation Service Center, 1963.

William Ragan, *Modern Elementary Curriculum* (New York: Holt, Rinehart, and Winston, Inc., 1966).

The Reports of the White House Conference on Education (Washington, D.C.: U.S. Government Printing Office, 1955), pp. 1, 2.

Anne Roe, "Early Determinants of Vocational Choice," *Journal of Counseling Psychology,* 4, 212–217 (1957).

Edward C. Roeber, Glenn F. Smith, and Clifford E. Erickson, *Organization and Administration of Guidance Services* (New York: McGraw-Hill Book Company, Inc., 1955).

Carl Rogers, "The Interpersonal Relationship: The Core of Guidance," *Harvard Educational Review,* 32, 416–429 (1962).

Francis Rosecrance and Velma Hayden, *School Guidance and Personnel Services* (Boston: Allyn and Bacon, Inc., 1960).

John W. M. Rothney, *Guidance Practices and Results* (New York: Harper & Row, Publishers, 1958).

Julian Rotter, *Social Learning and Clinical Psychology* (Englewood Cliffs: Prentice-Hall, Inc., 1954).

Warren Schmidt, "Executive Leadership," *The National Elementary Principal,* 41, 35–39 (1962).

Harold Shane, "Grouping in the Elementary School," *Phi Delta Kappan,* 41, 313–319 (1960).

Merville C. Shaw and Rosemary Wursten, "Research on Group Procedures in Schools: A Review of the Literature," *The Personnel and Guidance Journal,* 44, 27–34 (September, 1965).

Bruce Shertzer and Shelley Stone, *Foundations of Guidance* (Boston: Houghton Mifflin Company, 1966).

Dale Simmons, "Children's Rankings of Occupational Prestige," *Personnel and Guidance Journal,* 41, 332–335 (1962).

S. R. Slavson, *Child Psychology* (New York: Columbia University Press, 1952).

Ewart E. Smith, "The Effects of Clear & Unclear Role Expectations on Group Productivity & Defensiveness," *The Journal of Abnormal & Social Psychology,* 55, 213–217 (September, 1957).

Hyrum M. Smith and Louise Omwake Eckerson, "Guidance for Children in Elementary Schools," U.S. Department of Health, Education, & Welfare (Washington, D.C.: U.S. Government Printing Office, 1965), pp. 5, 6.

Julian C. Stanley, *Measurement in Today's Schools* 4th Ed. (Englewood Cliffs: Prentice-Hall, Inc., 1964).

Status of Elementary School Guidance Pilot Projects in New York State (Albany: The State Department Bureau of Guidance, 1966).

Lawrence Stewart, "Relationship of Socioeconomic Status to Children's Occupational Attitudes and Interests," *Journal of Genetic Psychology*, **95**, 111–136 (1959).

Lawrence H. Stewart and Charles F. Warnath, *The Counselor and Society A Cultural Approach* (Boston: Houghton Mifflin Company, 1965).

Ralph Stogdill, "Leadership, Membership, and Organization," *Psychological Bulletin*, **47**, 1–14 (1950).

Donald Super, "A Theory of Vocational Development," *American Psychologist*, **8**, 185–190 (May, 1953).

Donald Super and John O. Crites, *Appraising Vocational Fitness* 2nd Ed. (New York: Harper and Row Publishers, 1962).

"Teacher's Class Data Summary," State Universary College at Buffalo, Evaluation and Instructional Research Center.

Wesley Tennyson and Lawrence Monnens, "The World of Work Through Elementary Readers," *Vocational Guidance Quarterly*, **12**, 85–88 (1963).

David Tiedeman, "Decision and Vocational Development: A Paradigm and Its Implication," *Personnel and Guidance Journal*, **40**, 15–20 (1961).

Arthur E. Traxler and Robert D. North, *Techniques of Guidance* 3rd. Ed. (New York: Harper and Row, Publishers, 1966).

Charles Truax, "Some Implications of Behavior Therapy for Psychotherapy," *Journal of Counseling Psychology*, **13**, 160–170 (1966).

———, "Reinforcement and Nonreinforcement in Rogerian Psychotherapy," *Journal of Abnormal Psychology*, **71**, 1–9 (1966).

Leona Tyler, "The Antecedents of Two Varieties of Vocational Interests," *Genetic Psychological Monographs*, **70**, 177–227 (1964).

———, "The Relationship of Interests to Abilities and Reputation

Among First-Grade Children," *Educational and Psychological Measurement,* 11, 235–264 (1951).

Ralph W. Tyler, "Educational Objectives of American Democracy," in Eli Ginzberg, *The Nation's Children,* Vol. 2, *Development and Education,* White House Conference on Children and Youth (New York: Columbia University Press, 1960), p. 70.

Willis Vandiver, "Preparing Parents for the Conference," *Parents and the Schools,* Thirty-sixth Yearbook, The National Elementary Principal (Washington, D.C.: National Education Association, 1957), pp. 218, 219.

William Van Hoose, "The Emerging Role of the Elementary School Counselor," Paper read at American Personnel and Guidance Association Convention, Dallas, March, 1967.

Walter Waetjen, "Research from Educational Psychology that has Implications for Elementary School Guidance." Paper read at The Invitational Conference on Elementary School Guidance, Washington, D.C., March, 1965. Mimeograph.

John Wellington and Nan Olechowski, "Attitudes Toward the World of Work in Elementary School," *The Vocational Guidance Quarterly,* 14, 160–162 (1966).

Roy Willey and Melvin Strong, *Group Procedures in Guidance* (New York: Harper and Brothers, 1957).

Seymour L. Wolfbein, "The Transition from School to Work," *The Personnel and Guidance Journal,* 38, 98–105 (October, 1959).

W. H. Worth, "The Critical Years," *The Canadian Administrator,* 1965.

Gilbert Wrenn, *The Counselor in a Changing World* (Washington, D.C.: American Personnel and Guidance Association, 1962).

J. Wayne Wrightstone, Joseph Justman, and Irving Robins, *Evaluation in Modern Education,* New York: American Book Company, 1956).

Franklin Zeran and Anthony Riccio, *Organization and Administration of Guidance Services* (Chicago: Rand McNally & Company, 1962).

Earl Zwetschke and John Grenfell, "Family Group Consultation: A Description and a Rationale," *Personnel and Guidance Journal,* 43, 974–980 (1965).

INDEX OF NAMES

Alexander, W., 119, 275
Anderson, R., 113, 275
Arbuckle, D., 192, 275
Atwell, A., 173, 275
Ausubel, D., 197, 275
Ausubel, P., 197, 275
Axelrod, S., 180, 278

Bandura, A., 80, 96, 100, 275
Barbe, W., 194, 276
Bass, B., 33, 278
Benne, K., 168, 276
Bernard, H., 32, 278
Bogan, F., 179, 276
Bonham, S., 71
Bonner, H., 34, 276
Borow, H., 179, 192, 205, 276
Brammer, L., 97, 98, 276
Brison, D., 123, 276

Broedel, J., 173, 276

Cartwright, D., 34
Chambers, N., 194, 276
Clark, E., 195, 197, 276
Corey, S., 264, 276
Crites, J., 236, 283
Cronbach, L., 209, 234, 240, 246, 277
Cutler, R., 135, 277

Davis, D., 195, 277
DeFleur, M., 194, 196, 277
Detjen, E., 66, 277
Detjen, M., 66, 277
Deutsch, M., 196, 277
Dinkmeyer, D., 102, 127, 277
Dollard, J., 82, 277
Douglass, K., 117, 277

Durost, W., 234
Dutton, W., 132, 277
Dyer, C., 172, 280

Eckerson, L., 47, 282
Edelfelt, R., 58, 279
Erickson, C., 63, 282
Erickson, E., 15

Farwell, G., 119, 153, 219, 281
Ford, D., 77, 278
Froehlich, C., 109, 278
Fullmer, D., 32, 278

Galler, E., 195, 278
Gibb, J., 33, 278
Ginsburg, S., 180, 278
Ginzberg, E., 4, 135, 180, 181, 182, 190, 278
Glanz, E., 174
Glueck, E., 6, 69, 179, 278
Glueck, S., 6, 69, 179, 278
Goldman, L., 154, 155, 249, 254, 278
Grams, A., 105, 107, 128, 278
Grell, L., 176, 177, 278
Grenfell, J., 116, 284
Gunn, B., 194, 279

Hagen, N., 195, 277
Halpin, A., 39, 279
Hansen, J., 205
Hanvey, R., 144, 279
Hatch, R., 30, 41, 42, 43, 255, 256, 265, 279
Havighurst, R., 69, 279
Hayden, V., 115, 282
Hayes, R., 174
Heisey, M., 104, 279
Herma, J., 180, 278
Hill, G., 35, 279
Hillson, M., 152
Hockett, J., 132, 277
Hoffman, L., 179, 205, 276
Hoffman, M., 179, 205, 276
Holland, J., 187, 189, 190, 192, 279
Hollis, J., 43, 272, 279
Hollis, L., 43, 272, 279
Horrocks, J., 254

Hoyt, K., 109, 121, 278, 279
Hummel, D., 71
Humphreys, A., 26, 279

Johnson, W., 58, 279
Justman, J., 272, 284

Kaback, G., 178, 279
Kagan, J., 69, 133, 280
Kemp, G., 174
Kranzler, G., 172, 280
Krasner, L., 80, 280
Krumboltz, J., 80, 96, 100, 164, 170, 280

Lachman, S., 135, 280
Lewin, K., 34, 280
Lifton, W., 174, 198, 280
Lippitt, R., 34, 280
Luborsky, L., 80, 280

McConnel, G., 109, 280
McCreary, W., 75, 103, 123, 280
McNeil, E., 135, 276
Maslow, A., 185
Mathewson, R., 8, 9, 23, 62, 280
Mayer, G., 172, 280
Miller, C., 176, 197, 280
Miller, G., 75, 103, 123, 280
Miller, N., 82, 277
Monnens, L., 198, 283
Moore, G., 203, 273, 280
Mortensen, D., 249
Moser, L., 23, 71
Moser, R., 23, 71
Moss, H., 69, 133, 280
Moustakas, C., 133, 281
Munger, P., 172, 280

Nelson, R., 98, 196, 281
Noll, V., 234
Norris, W., 201, 202, 205, 281
North, R., 26, 223, 279, 283

Odum, R., 173, 275
O'Hara, R., 197, 281
Ohlsen, M., 173, 273, 276, 281
Olechowski, N., 177, 284

Parsons, F., 180
Peters, H., 9, 10, 23, 28, 43, 48, 71, 119, 153, 205, 219, 254, 263, 281
Petrullo, L., 33, 278
Prescott, G., 234
Proff, F., 173, 276

Ragan, W., 129, 131, 147, 152, 281
Rhodes, F., 249
Riccio, A., 41, 273, 284
Robins, I., 272, 284
Roe, A., 185, 190, 282
Roeber, E., 63, 282
Rogers, C., 91, 93, 94, 282
Rosecrance, F., 115, 282
Rothney, J., 264, 282
Rotter, J., 78, 80, 100, 101, 110, 128, 282

Sachs, B., 152
Schmidt, W., 35, 282
Shane, H., 130, 282
Shaw, M., 172, 282
Sheats, P., 168, 276
Sherrie, G., 51
Shertzer, B., 9, 10, 23, 28, 31, 43, 48, 71, 254, 263, 281, 282
Shostrom, E., 97, 98, 276
Slavson, S. R., 16, 17, 282
Simmons, D., 193, 282
Smith, E., 173, 282
Smith, G., 63, 282
Smith, H., 47, 282
Southard, C., 173, 276
Stanley, J., 208, 282
Stefflre, B., 30, 41, 42, 43, 58, 255, 256, 266, 279
Stein, S., 249

Stewart, L., 18, 196, 242, 283
Stodgill, R., 32, 283
Stone, S., 31, 282
Strong, M., 114, 284
Strouf, J., 195, 277
Strupp, H., 80, 280

Teneberg, M., 144, 279
Tennyson, W., 198, 283
Thoresen, C., 96, 164, 170, 280
Tiedeman, D., 183, 190, 283
Traxler, A., 26, 223, 279, 283
Truax, C., 91, 92, 93, 283
Tyler, L., 195, 197, 283
Tyler, R., 4, 284

Urban, H., 77, 278

Vandiver, W., 113, 284
Van Hoose, W., 9, 10, 23, 28, 48, 71, 112, 281, 284
Waetjen, W., 133, 284
Walters, R., 80, 96, 100, 275
Warnath, C. F., 18, 242, 283
Wellington, J., 177, 284
White, A., 34
White, R., 34, 280
Willey, R., 114, 284
Wolfbein, S., 6, 179, 284
Worth, W., 132, 284
Wrenn, G., 177, 178, 284
Wrightstone, W., 272, 284
Wursten, R., 172, 282

Zander, A., 34
Zeran, F., 41, 273, 284
Zwetschke, E., 116, 284

INDEX OF SUBJECTS

Abilities, 243
Ability tests, 228
Achievement tests, 228
Administrators, 62
Aims of education, 2
Anecdotal records, 218
Appraisal in guidance, 235ff
  limitations, 237
  of existing services, 28
  principles, 238
  problems, 235
  rationale, 240
  types, 242
Approaches to elementary guidance, 10
Aptitude tests, 228
Attendance officer, 60
Audio-visual aids, 202

Behavior, 79
  and learning, 78
  change, 91
  comparison of, 251
  maladaptive, 81
  modification of, 87
Behavioral approach to counseling, 18
Budget, 40

Case study, 124, 219ff
Central tendency, measures, 210
Child study, 11
Chi Square, 216
Commission of Reorganization of Secondary Education, 2
Communication
  letters, 119
  limitations in children, 15
  with parents, 118
  report card, 119

Communication (*cont.*)
  telephone, 120
Community relations, 21, 53
Comparison, measures of, 214ff
Conditioning, 85–86
Conferences, 112
  group, 114
  individual, 112
Consultation
  family group, 115
  guidelines, 110
  individual, 125
  methods of, 112, 124
  with parents, 19, 103, 105
  services, 122
  with teachers, 19, 50, 120
Correlation, 19, 74, 215
Counselee appraisal, 236
Counseling
  goals, 75
  and learning, 82
  techniques, 90
  theory, 76
Counselor, 47
  characteristics, 31
  competency in vocational guidance, 203
  as a leader, 32
  as a person, 31
  role in groups, 170
Counselor education, 170
Counselor training, 22
Counter-conditioning, 89
Critical years concept, 132
Cue, 83
Cumulative record, 217
Curriculum, 20, 200
  concept of, 130
  counselor role in, 139, 141, 145, 148
  factors affecting, 132
  grouping plans, 137ff
  homogenous groups, 140
  non-graded, 145
  self-contained, 137
  team teaching, 143
Curriculum goals, 149
  counselor role, 53, 149

Data gathering, 222

Department of labor, 178
Description of appraisal activities, 251
Developmental psychology, 15
Diagnosis, 223
Difference in secondary and elementary guidance, 14
Differential activities of counselor, 17
Discipline, 108
Discrimination of behavior patterns, 251
Drive, 83
Drop-outs, 6, 178, 179

Education and the community, 7
Educational Policies Commission, 2
Educational, vocational guidance, 20
Elementary and Secondary Education Act, 6
Elementary School Guidance Pilot Projects, 75
Emotional maladjustment, 106
Empathy, 91
Evaluation, 21
  adequacy of services, 258
  direction, 257
  foundations, 256
  limitations, 260
  personnel, 258
  purposes, 259
  scope, 257
Evaluation, approaches to, 262
  case study, 264
  experimental method, 263
  survey method, 263
Evaluation, objectives, 265
  adequacy, 272
  criteria, 266
Evaluative criteria, 263
Evaluative study, 265
  analysis of data, 268
  collection of data, 268
  objectives, 267
  population, 267
  presentation of, 268
Extinction, 88

Family consultation, 116
Follow up, 223

Foundation of guidance, 5

Genuineness, 92
Goals
  counseling, 75
  guidance, 8
Group counseling, 163
Group guidance
  behavioral approach, 160
  expectations, 161
  principles, 159
  purposes, 158
  specialist training, 163
Group leader tasks, 165
Groups, 137
  homogenous, 140
  initiating and continuing, 165
  outcomes, 172–174
  roles, 168–170
  rules, 167
  self-contained, 137
  size, 166
Group tasks, 161
Guidance
  committee, 35–36
  consultant, 47
  facilities, 40
  function, 30
  instruments, 216ff
  needs, 28
  program change and initiation, 29,
    39
  services, 30
  specialist, 13

Home visits, 117

Implementation of change, 271
Impressionistic techniques, 241
In-service education, 125
Interests, 244
Interpretation, 240
IRCOPPS, 102

Juvenile delinquency, 6, 69

Leadership, 31–33
Leadership, types of, 34
Learning
  cue, 83

  drive, 83
  reinforcement, 86
  response, 84
Learning and behavior, 78
Learning and counseling, 82
Letters to parents, 119
Life style, 189, 245
Line and staff relationships, 37–38

Mean, 210
Median, 210
Mental health, 11
Mode, 211
Modeling, 160, 196
Model reinforcement, 96

National Defense Education Act, 4,
  6
Nomothetic assessment, 253
Normal curve, 212
Normative role, 249

Objective data, 249
Objectives of education, 3–5
Obervation in vocational develop-
  ment, 200
Observation, teacher, 67
Occupational development, 197ff
  school influences, 198
  sex differences, 197
Occupational information, 177, 204
Occupational knowledge, 193
Odiographic assessment, 253
Organizational climate, 39–40
Organizational plan, 37
Organization Climate Description
  Questionnaire (OCDQ), 39
Organizing the guidance program,
  36
Orientation activities, 115, 161

Parents
  consultation with, 53, 103
  contributions, 105
  guidelines for working with, 110
  want to know, 108
Personality measures, 229
Planning a guidance program, 27
Play media, 97
  free, 98
  controlled, 99

Positive regard, 91
Prediction, 250, 252
Preventative guidance strategy, 18
Principal, 64
Profile comparison, 249
Prognosis, 223, 237
Progressive education, 7
Promotional guidance strategy, 18
Psychologist, 55
Psychometric techniques, 240
Public relations, 260
Pupil conferences, 68
Pupil Data Summary, 51
Pupil personnel services, 46, 60
Pupil personnel specialists, 55ff
  interrelationships, 61

Range of scores, 211
Rating scale, 219
Readiness tests, 228
Reading, 202
Reinforcement, 86
  model, 96
  verbal, 94
Reliability, 248
Remedial guidance strategy, 18
Report cards, 119
Response, 84
Resources, 202
Role
  counselor, 17, 33, 54
  teachers, 64, 121ff

School nurse teacher, 60
Score discrimination, 249
Self-concept, 170, 190
Self-report, 243
Significance of difference, 215
Social environment, 102
Social learning principles, 110ff
Social worker, 57, 117
Socio-economic status, 109, 195
Sociogram, 224ff
Space requirements, 41
Speech and hearing therapist, 61
Staff functions, 35
Staff involvement, 31
Staffing, 31

Standard deviation, 212
Standard error, 213
Standardized tests, 227ff
Standard score, 213
Statistics, 210ff
Strategies of guidance, 18
Structuring, 93
Subjective data, 250

Teachers, 12, 64
  involvement in groups, 171
Teacher's Class Data Summary, 52
Team approach to consulting, 126
Test evaluation, 23
Testing program, 208
  continuity, 232
  initiation, 230
  organizing, 229
  principles, 232
  responsibility for, 231
Testing, purposes of, 208
Time, concept of, 16
Training for group, 170

Unemployment, 179

Validity, 246
  concurrent, 247
  construct, 247
  content, 247
  predictive, 246
Values, 107
Variability of scores, 211
Vocational development, 179
Vocational guidance, counselor competency, 203
Vocational information, 199
Vocational theory, 180
  Ginzberg, 180
  Holland, 187
  Roe, 185
  Super, 181
  Tiedeman, 183

White House Conference, 3, 134, 176
Work, 177
  attitudes toward, 177
  changing status of, 177